T0328833

Supply chain integration, quality management and firm performance in the pork processing industry in China

Supply chain integration, quality management and firm performance in the pork processing industry in China

Jiqin Han

International chains and network series – Volume 7

Wageningen Academic
P u b l i s h e r s

ISBN 978-90-8686-110-1
ISSN 1874-7663

First published, 2009

© Wageningen Academic Publishers
The Netherlands, 2009

Dedicated to my husband Dongyi and to my daughter Ruohan

Acknowledgements

The long journey of six and a half years of PhD studies marks the fulfillment of my dream and the beginning of another experience. First and foremost, I would like to thank Willem Brinckman, Arnold van Wulfften Palthe and Hendrik Kupper for the years of good cooperation and stimulating my academic interest in agri-food supply chain management. Through you, I met Prof. Onno Omta and Dr. Jacques Trienekens in Wageningen in 2001 and started dreaming about my PhD studies. At the end, you as a team helped me with my Dutch summary.

I would like to thank Wageningen University for offering me one year scholarships and supporting the publication of this book. I greatly acknowledge the LEB Foundation for contributing to my participation in the international conference.

I am greatly indebted to my advisors, Onno Omta and Jacques Trienekens for their continuous support and encouragement. Onno, you taught me the skills of conducting scientific research. Every time I returned to the group, I asked myself to make as few mistakes as possible, as I didn't want to make you astonished. Jacques, your constructive comments and many fruitful discussions helped me find a path toward finishing my PhD. You improved my language and patiently guided me to the end. Only when the deadline for submitting my thesis to the reading committee was nearly due, I received an e-mail from you with 8 exclamation marks! Ron Kemp, your knowledge of methodology and analysis was essential for me to have good models. Nowhere else, have I so anxiously looked forward to Wednesdays as this is the only day of the week you work in the group.

I would like to thank the entire Management Studies Group at Wageningen University for their friendship and support. Douwe-Frits, Jack, Jos, Harry, Emiel, Geoffrey and Willem, thank you all for your fruitful suggestions in our discussions or knowledge you gave me in course delivery. I would like to thank Leonie, Ina and Janna for your willingness to help me during all these years. My sincere gratitude also goes to my fellow PhD colleagues for their discussions as well as the laughs we had. They are Anna, Derk-Jan, Frances, Guangqian, Hualiang, Jaime, Joanna, Lilly, Maarten, Mark, Mersiha, Rannia, Wijnand, Xia and Zhen. Frances, Lilly, Leonie and Ina, it was great having time to discuss with you about our daughters. The encouragement you gave me can never be forgotten. A great word of thanks goes to my paranymphs: Huaidong and Maarten.

This study would never have come true if it were not for the support from the meat processing companies and meat associations in the survey areas. Numerous managers and practitioners have been involved. I thank you all for your contributions. A special word of appreciation goes to Mr. Lizhong Meng, Deputy general-manager of Jiangsu Food, Mr. Ning Zhao, assistant to the General Manager of Jiangsu Yurun, Mr. Yuhai Lin, technical manager of Shanghai Hormel and Mr. Qiankun Zheng, R&D manager of Shangdong Delisi. Your knowledge and insight into the meat processing industry and your kind support rendered to me in the empirical studies were most helpful to understand the Chinese meat industry. I would like to express my heartfelt thanks to the research group led by Professors Guanghong Zhou who helped me in the pilot studies and introduced me to the meat industries. Dr. Tao Tan and Dr. Hualiang Lu, thank you very much for your help in introducing the technique and operation of data analysis by using AMOS and PLS. Jundi Liu and Feng Zhang, both of you helped me greatly in looking for literature. I greatly appreciate your assistance.

I also would like to thank my colleagues at NAU for their great support. During my absence, they took my work and gave me encouragement, which helped me to walk this long way. My gratitude also goes to my NAU friends for helping me in various ways and for the enjoyable gatherings we had during our stay in Wageningen. They are Shuyi Feng, Qi Jing, Huashu Wang, Wen Yao, Xiaoping Shi, Zhongxing Guo, Weixin Ou, Qun Wu and Xianlei Ma. There are many others who have helped me greatly in the process of PhD studies. You won't be forgotten by me.

My special appreciation goes to the Willem, Arnold, Hendrik, Xiaoyong and Zhenghong families. Your friendship and hospitality made me feel very warm during lonely times.

Dreaming about my PhD studies and realizing this dream could not have been possible without the valuable assistance and help of my family. Papa and Mama, I thank you for giving me the same perseverance, diligence, and optimistic attitude as you, which have benefited my entire life. Parents-in-laws, thank you for your support and taking care of Ruohan during my PhD period. Ruohan, when I began my PhD studies, you were only ten years old. During the process of your growing up, I sometimes was unable to be with you when you needed me. But I am very happy to see that you have become an independent and enthusiastic big girl. I have one word for you: never say can't until you try your best. My most special thanks go to my husband, Dongyi Zhang, who shared all the frustrations and the happiness during the course of my PhD research. Your continuous support and encouragement accompanied me along the way. Your willingness and dedication to take care of Ruohan made it possible for me to concentrate on my research in Wageningen. Thank you for your love, support, patience and understanding!

Jiqin Han

Wageningen, May 2009

Table of contents

Chapter 1. Introduction

You are not obliged to manage quality. You can also choose to go out of business.

W.E. Deming, 1986

Quality management and supply chain management issues have dominated the discussion in management research and have been on the agenda of most manufacturing and service organizations in the last few decades (Tan, 2001; Tan *et al.*, 2002; Robinson and Malhotra, 2005). The core propositions underlying these two areas of research is that the application of quality management (QM) and supply chain management (SCM) practices lead to competitive advantage and superior performance (e.g. Armistead and Mapes, 1993; Narasimhan and Carter, 1998; Tan *et al.*, 1999; Kim, 2006; Kaynak, 2003). Although scholars and practitioners generally agree about the importance of QM and SCM, the factors that underlie the process of achieving good practices in QM and SCM are much less explored, especially in developing countries. The main objective of this book is to identify the critical success factors of QM and SCM that contribute to higher performance of pork processing firms in China. It thereby aims to provide an integrated perspective of the impact of these two research areas on firm performance in the fast emerging pork sector in China.

The chapter starts with the introduction of the research background regarding China's pork supply chain. Section 1.2 addresses the problem statement and the research questions we are going to deal with in this study. Then, Section 1.3 discusses the theoretical outlines and research design. The chapter ends with an outline of the book in Section 1.4.

1.1 Research background

Until about the early 1980s, diets with daily consumption of milk and meat were the privilege of OECD country citizens and a small wealthy class elsewhere. For most people in Africa and Asia, meat, milk and eggs were an unaffordable luxury, consumed only on rare occasions. However, in the 1990s China overtook the United States and the entire European Union of then 15 countries in terms of animal production (Livestock report, 2006). At the same time consumption has increased accordingly. Huge developments have also taken place in the pork sector since the government removed state procurement quotas and price controls in 1985. Since 1990, China has become the largest pork production and consumption country in the world. The total pork production reached nearly 52 million tonnes in 2006, accounting for more than 50% of pork production in the world (China Statistical Yearbook, 2007). The second largest pork production country in that year was the USA (USDA, 2007), accounting for more than 10% of total pork production in the world (Reddington, 2008). China is also the largest pork consumption country in the world. In 2006, pork consumption in China accounted for half of the world pork consumption, with an average of 39.6kg[1] per capita (Deng, 2007). Although among the main meat varieties pork, beef and mutton, and poultry, the proportion of pork consumption decreased from 85% in 1985 to 64% in 2006 (Deng, 2007), pork consumption increased in absolute terms and it is still the most popular meat in China. A detailed description for the pork sector in China is available in Chapter 2 of this book (chapter on research domain). This part focuses on the most important characteristics of the sector.

The features mentioned by Ruben *et al.* (2007) with regard to transactions between companies in developing countries also prevail in the pork sector in China:

1. Uncertainty: Business transactions are subject to uncertainty regarding quantity, quality, delivery conditions, and price. These uncertainties are caused by poor physical infrastructures (storage/cooling facilities, roads, telecommunication, etc.), weak institutional infrastructures and unbalanced trade relationships.
2. Poor information exchange: Transactions need to be supported by information on characteristics of the product/service, production, and delivery conditions, etc. At present, information exchange in pork supply chains in China is still hampered by large information asymmetries between chain partners due to inadequate communication infrastructures, especially in the upstream pork chain.
3. Opportunism: Uncertainties about supply and demand may easily force members at different stages in the chain to adopt opportunistic behaviour so as to be able to sell their products.
4. Limited investment: Modern retail driven food chains require investment in cooling facilities, transportation means and information & communication technology. In China, the investment in this sector is still very limited, especially in small companies.

Figure 1.1 presents the pork supply chain in China. In addition to the above-mentioned features, several other characteristics of the chain can be distinguished.

Firstly, the fragmentation of the sector induces high transaction cost. Contrary to the USA, the Netherlands and other developed countries, China's leading position in pork production is accomplished by a large number of small farmers. Many backyard-households raise 1 to 5 hogs in simple housing facilities. Although commercial operations and specialised households are growing, they provide only about 20% of all hogs in China. The remaining 80% of the hogs are provided by backyard farms (Pan and Kinsey, 2002), implying production arrangements inducing high transaction costs. Slaughtering plants or processors depend on traders to collect hogs from small farm households to acquire a certain lot size. Figure 1.1 shows the important

---

[1] The data for average per capita possession (total national production divided by national population) is used due to problematic statistics for pork consumption in China. The per capita consumption of pork products was 20.15 kg for urban households and 15.62kg for rural households in 2005. However the average per capita possession of pork products was 38.3 kg. Export of pork products only accounted for 385,967 metric tonnes that year (China Statistical Yearbook, 2006; Bean and Zhang, 2007).

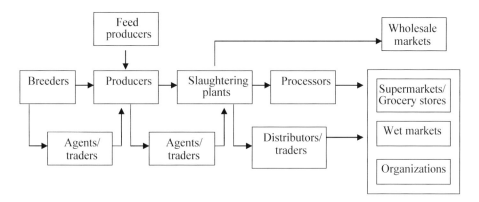

Figure 1.1 China's pork supply chain (adapted from Pan and Kinsey, 2002).

role of the traders/agents in bridging buyer-supplier relationship. Fragmentation also exists in the pork slaughtering stage. In 2004, there were altogether about 30,000 designated meat slaughterhouses in China. Of those, only 7% are regarded as 'scale companies'[2] (Deng, 2005). As pork production and consumption is still the main source of animal protein for Chinese consumers, pork slaughtering and processing firms[3] accounted for 80% of the 30,000 designated meat slaughterhouses. In the last few years, there has been a consolidation process in the meat sector in China. The number of slaughterhouses decreased to 25,000 in 2006. Some municipal governments provided subsidies to support the merger or closing down of slaughterhouses. Though the consolidation is strongly promoted by the various levels of authorities, the small slaughterhouse will still prevail for the next decade in China[4].

Secondly, governance arrangements in Chinese pork supply chains are diversifying. Previous empirical research has indicated that traditional spot market transactions are still the most popular market channel for farmers in China to sell their hogs. However, leading meat-processors like Shineway and Yurun Co. Ltd. have established closer vertical coordination with their retailers in recent years through franchise and long-term contracts (Zhou and Dai, 2005). They have invested heavily in developing cold chains and providing consumers with brand products.

Finally, Chinese consumers are becoming more aware of quality and safety. Studies show that it has become one of the most important concerns of consumers in purchasing pork products

---

[2] The classification of the meat companies is not well developed in China at the moment. 'Scale Companies' is usually used to refer to those companies with annual sales of more than RMB 5 million Yuan (approximately 500,000 €).

[3] As pork slaughtering is the first stage of processing (Boal, 2006), we refer pork slaughterhouses and processors as 'pork processors' or 'pork processing firms' in our study, under conditions that no necessity in the differentiation of the two terms is needed.

[4] Expert interview in Nanjing Designated Pork Slaughtering Administrative Office in October 2007.

(e.g. Wu, 2006). Therefore, pork quality and safety has become the major constraint on the further development of the sector and on competitiveness in the international market (Dong and Hou, 2005; Wu, 2006). In this regard, the above-mentioned sector fragmentation is one of the most important sources of quality and safety problems. Due to scattered backyard production, it is very difficult for processors to monitor the hog production processes. Lack of monitoring could be one of the factors explaining the high drug residues and the existence of illegal slaughterhouses in China (Pan and Kinsey, 2002; Pan, 2004). Barriers also exist in the application of modern technology in hog production due to the limited education of most of the producers (Han et al., 2006). Another important reason is animal disease. The outbreak of the Porcine Reproductive and Respiratory Syndrome (PRRS) disease, also known as Blue Ear Disease, resulted in a substantial reduction in pork production in China in 2006.

Small-scale backyard farming operations are declining but remain dominant. This type of production model presents problems, including non standardised hog sizes and disease control difficulties. How successful China will be in establishing stringent disease and food safety controls remains to be seen (Boal, 2006). To solve the problems of the Chinese pork sector and improve the competitiveness of the pork processing firms, the integration between production and marketing may provide a possible solution. Nowadays final consumer goods have gone through many hands and crossed many borders. Quality problems in one stage may cause problems for the whole industry. The 2008 Chinese milk scandal is just one example. The scandal has affected countries on all continents[5].

1.2 Problem statement and research questions

Across the pork sector, particularly in developed countries, the pork industry is being forced to operate with increasingly stringent requirements regarding food quality and within a stricter regulatory environment. The numerous food scandals relating to the pork supply chain in recent years call for better management and coordination among the stakeholders of the chain, for example, the 'Jinhua Ham Incident'[6] in November 2003 in Zhejiang province,

---

[5] http://en.wikipedia.org/wiki/2008_baby_milk_scandal.

[6] The 'Jinhua Ham Incident' was caused by several small producers of Jinhua hams. They produced out of season hams during warmer months and treated their hams with pesticides to prevent spoilage and insect infestation. The hams were soaked in the pesticide Dichlorvos, which is a volatile organophosphate insecticide used for fumigation. The incident was first reported by the media. It strongly affected the legitimate makers of the ham and caused a sharp drop-off in the market demand for this famous pork product with more than 1000 years of history (http://en.wikipedia.org/Jinhua_ham, accessed on Jan. 30, 2009; Chen et al., 2007).

outbreak of *Streptococcus suis*[7] in swine and humans in June 2005 in Sichuan province and the outbreak of Clenbuterol food poisoning in November 2008 in Zhejiang province[8]. The Chinese government has responded to these incidents with food quality and safety laws and regulations and by reinforcing the awareness of chain participants' social responsibility. Great efforts have also been made in the development of agricultural industrialization. Although the Chinese government has done much to stimulate firms to implement quality management and improve product quality, there has not been satisfactory progress.

Being the largest country in economic transition, China will still be dominated by large numbers of backyard hog producers, small slaughterhouses and processors suffering from poor facilities and low-grade technology, and the traditional outlets of wet market and wholesale markets. Though supermarkets and specialised stores established by pork processors are playing a more important role and becoming more attractive to the Chinese consumers, the market share for pork products in these outlets is still limited (Dai *et al.*, 2006).

To deal with the challenges facing the Chinese pork sector, the stakeholders need a new mindset for managing buyer-supplier relationships in the pork supply chain in order to improve QM and firm performance of the pork processing sector. Efforts by the legislative institutions as well as the researchers and practitioners should be directed at:
- identifying the key QM practices and how they contribute to firm performance;
- identifying the critical factors in SCM and how they contribute to firm performance;
- aligning appropriate governance mechanisms with QM practices;
- making strategy choices that strengthen QM and firm performance.

1.2.1 Efforts to identify the key QM practices contributing to higher firm performance

Many companies have adopted quality programs as a reaction to a changing and challenging competitive environment (Lee and Fawcett, 2002). There are as many different approaches to quality management as there are businesses (Evans and Dean Jr., 2000). Both the popular

---

[7] The outbreak of *Streptococcus suis* began in late June 2005. In the first week of August, there were 641 cases in pigs with 219 deaths, and 206 cases in humans with 38 deaths. *Streptococcus suis* is a zoonotic disease caused by a gram positive bacteria which is endemic in most pig rearing countries of the world. Human infections with *Streptococcus suis* can result in meningitis, septicemia, permanent hearing loss (in 50% of cases), pneumonia, endocarditis, arthritis, and toxic shock syndrome. Transmission among swine occurs through the air and through direct contact with secretions and blood of infected pigs. Piglets can be infected during birth. Transmission to humans occurs when skin wounds, or possibly mucous membranes, are contaminated by the blood or secretions of infected pigs (http://www.aphis.usda.gov/vs/ceah/cei/taf/emergingdiseasenotice_files/strep_suis_china.htm, accessed on Jan. 30, 2009).

[8] Since November 10, 2008, 70 employees of the Zhongmao Plastics Products Company in Zhejiang province, China, have been diagnosed with the poisoning of clenbuterol. According to the data available, there have been 18 clenbuterol food poisoning cases in China since 1998. More than 1,700 people have been poisoned, with one confirmed death (The PigSite News Desk, 2008, http://www.thepigsite.com/swinenews/19698/outbreak-of-clenbuterol-food-poisoning).

press and academic journals have published a plethora of articles describing both successful and unsuccessful efforts at implementing QM in the past decade (Kaynak, 2003). Most studies have analysed the relationship between QM practices and their effects on firm performance, elements that affect QM implementation, and the major barriers to quality program success (e.g. Das *et al.*, 2000; Lee *et al.*, 2002; Kaynak, 2003; Mehra *et al.*, 2001; Soltani, 2005). The QM practices focused on these studies generally include: management leadership, role of the quality department, training, employee relations, quality data and reporting, supplier quality management, product/service design and process management (Kaynak, 2003). In these studies there is a consensus that total quality management (TQM) is a way of managing an organization to improve its overall effectiveness and performance. However, how specific QM practices contribute to various performance levels has not yet been investigated.

1.2.2 Efforts to identify critical factors in SCM contributing to higher firm performance

In Europe, competitive pressures, together with regulatory and industry responses to food safety and quality issues already in the 1990s had impacted on the development of coordinated supply chains between retailers, processors and farmers (Fearne, 1998). This kind of chain-wide integration of quality management systems is regarded as the best strategy to deal with complex quality demands because no individual firm is able to handle quality on its own (Omta *et al.*, 2002). Therefore, more and more companies are using the SCM philosophy to operate inter-organizationally and merge both strategic initiatives and upstream and downstream processes in the chain to achieve business excellence (Robinson and Malhotra, 2005).

The characteristics of perishable product supply chains imply that transaction and product quality attributes are strongly dependent on supply chain coordination, while at the same time organizational adjustment mechanisms should be used to call upon an endogenous process of supply chain integration (SCI) and optimization (Ruben *et al.*, 2007). The integration of supply chains has been described by Clancy as: '... attempt to elevate the linkages within each component of the chain, (to facilitate) better decision making [and] to get all the pieces of the chain to interact in a more efficient way [and thus]...create supply chain visibility [and] identify bottlenecks' (Clancy, cited in (Putzger, 1998)).

The benefits of SCI for the profit and competitive position of the companies has been empirically tested by some scholars. For example, Zailani and Rajagopal (2005) conducted a large survey in US and East Asian companies and found out that a successful SCI helps bring the organization to a higher level of growth and market share. Johnson (1999) shows, via a survey of industrial equipment distributors, that strategic integration results in enhanced economic reward for the firm.

Firms are at the centre of a network of suppliers and buyers. To improve supply chain efficiency and performance, firms are required to answer important questions such as what key suppliers and buyers to coordinate and what key supply chain processes to integrate. For example, the ultimate goal of SCM is accurate information and a smooth, continual high-quality product flow between partners to maximise buyer satisfaction (Van der Vorst, 2000). Once a firm decides to invest in information technology and logistics management, managers will face important questions: such as whether these investment initiatives will contribute to QM and firm performance? Will information technology contribute positively to logistics management? Previous research on the application of information technology and integrated logistics management has emphasised their relationships with firm performance (Stank *et al.*, 2001; Wang *et al.*, 2006).

1.2.3 Efforts to align governance mechanisms and QM

For analysing economic organization between firms Transaction Cost Economics (TCE) has been arguably the dominant theory (Rindfleisch and Heide, 1997; Leiblein, 2003). TCE focuses on governance structures, in which the term 'governance' is broadly defined as 'mode of organization' (Williamson, 1991). Governance is viewed in terms of particular mechanisms supporting an economic transaction where there is an exchange of property rights. Three assumptions that underlie decisions on a given governance mechanism are important in TCE, bounded rationality, opportunistic behaviour and information asymmetry (Rindfleisch and Heide, 1997). TCE has conceptualised three general types of governance forms: markets, vertical integration and hybrid or intermediate mechanisms. A popular way for firms to safeguard against opportunism and information asymmetry is to integrate with their suppliers. Moreover, integrated collaboration can reduce coordination costs and increase control over investments (Williamson, 1991; Buvik and Reve, 2001).

TCE has especially emphasised the importance of investments in choosing the right governance form, which makes it a very useful theory in this study. To assure the quality of products, firms have made transaction-specific human and physical investments (Ahire and Dreyfus, 2000; Van Plaggenhoef, 2007), for example advanced production equipment and technology as well as training employees to use the equipment and technology. In addition, employees are trained to handle the buyer's quality requirements (Claro *et al.*, 2003).

Quality and certification schemes in the supply chain lead to increased control and more integrated governance, such as long-term contracts. Mechanisms like output quality control and residual claimancy[9] are common in any food chains. Since the 1990s, Western retailers have defined various standards for the production and processing of food, such as British Retail Consortium (BRC), EUREP-GAP, and SQF. These standards are now applied by supermarkets and importers to coordinate supply chain activities and control food quality and safety (Ruben *et al.*, 2007). This implies that more integrated governance mechanisms are

---

[9] Moral hazard is a problem typical of information asymmetry. Closer coordination in the buyer-supplier relationship is increasingly important for reducing moral hazard. Both sides can therefore claim mutual benefit resulting from better quality products.

in general accompanied by integrated quality systems. Transaction cost economics offers one perspective on the relationship between governance arrangements and product quality. One class of transaction costs are measurement or information costs (Hobbs, 1996), which include the cost of searching for information about buyers or sellers in the market, quality inspection and price negotiation. When quality attributes are difficult to measure, information asymmetry may occur and producers may engage in opportunistic behaviour. This is expected to lead to contracts with added security features to mitigate the hazard (Martinez and Zering, 2004).

Given the importance of contractual governance mechanisms in quality management, some researchers argue that in practice, a 'complete' contract is very difficult to make (e.g. Poppo and Zenger, 2002), especially in developing countries with poorly developed institutional structures. Many companies tend to prefer relational contracts implying interpersonal relationships and trust (Ruben *et al.*, 2007). An ongoing relationship generally fosters trust and enables trading partners to adopt more flexible models of cooperation and create value together (Yu *et al.*, 2006) This is the major view of relational exchange theory (MacNeil, 1978, 1980). Relational governance is therefore included in this study in addition to the other two dominant governance mechanisms in China's pork supply chains, spot market and formal contractual governance.

1.2.4 Efforts to make strategic choices that strengthen QM and firm performance

The strategy of a firm provides its overall direction by specifying the firm's objectives, developing policies and plans to achieve these objectives and allocating resources to implement these policies and plans (Johnson and Scholes, 1999). The strategy literature makes an assumption that the appropriateness of a firm's strategy can be defined in terms of the alignment – that is the fit, match, coalignment or congruence – of its strategy with both its external and its internal contingencies (Lawrence and Lorsch, 1967; Miles and Snow, 1994; Verdú Jover *et al.*, 2005). Where internal fit requires that a chosen strategy is in compliance with the firm's internal structures and processes, external fit demands that a firm matches its strategy with the opportunities and threats provided by the external environment (Lawrence and Lorsch, 1967). It is thus important for companies to find the right balance between the relevant contingencies in the business environment (external fit) and the firm's internal resources, competencies and capabilities (internal fit). For agribusiness companies, good QM practices are critical resources and competencies for them to make competitive advantage in the (inter)national marketplace. Though some of the studies have empirically supported the proposition that QM practices are contingent on a firm's manufacturing strategy context (e.g. Reed *et al.*, 1996; Sousa and Voss, 2001), the question of whether positive QM practices-firm performance is monotonic across different strategies has not been fully investigated (Matsuno and Mentzer, 2000). Allen and Helmes (2006) also reveal that prior studies have not linked specific strategic practices with each strategy type and exploration of the association between the specific practices and overall organization performance are limited. We would thus like to investigate the potential moderating role of strategy in the relationship between firm's QM practices and firm performance. In addition to this, attention is also given to the external fit of the companies.

Public institutions are heavily involved in food safety and quality management. Several studies have clearly indicated the role of government legislation on more strict QM practices applied by the chain members. For example, the evolution of partnerships in British beef supply chains owed much to the 1990 Food Safety Act (Fearne, 1998). Proactive support of the technological infrastructure by the government and the conduciveness of the industrial and national technology climate is a catalyst for firms to achieve the full technological potential and improve firm performance (Sharif, 1994). In the present era of deregulation, privatization and increasing global market competition, most industries in developing countries have realised that better technology is needed for the survival of their enterprises. They acknowledge that technological considerations must be properly incorporated into overall business strategies (Sharif, 1994). We then ask ourselves such questions: what is the impact of government support on firm performance? Will the choice for a certain strategy strengthen the impact of government support on firm performance?

Despite the great importance and significance of agri-food SCM in cost reduction and maximizing market opportunities, it is still a new concept for the agribusiness sector in China. The earliest research on agri-food supply chain issues appeared in 1999. Moreover, the existing research is limited to qualitative analysis of the problems in the supply chains. There is a shortage of reliable and validated constructs and models for agri-food SCM based on quantitative research (Liu *et al.*, 2008). To the best of our knowledge, none of the theoretical models and quantitative studies covers the interactions among integrated SCM, QM practices, governance structure and firm performance of the pork processing industries in China. Therefore, the objective of this study is to identify the critical success factors of SCM and QM practices on firm performance of the pork processing firms in China. We investigate the current situation of Chinese pork chains and the mechanism of supply chain governance and quality management in the chain. By identifying the critical elements in SCM and QM practices, we aim to contribute to successful quality management of the pork supply chain in China. To fulfil this objective, the present study addresses the following central research question:

> *What are the key factors in supply chain management and quality management that affect the performance of pork processing firms in China and how do governance mechanisms align with quality management processes in pork processing firms?*

To answer this central research question, we attempt to deconstruct the above-mentioned four key research elements: supply chain integration, quality management practices, governance structure and firm performance, and examine their interactions through empirical studies. Understanding the interaction of these four major factors may contribute to a better theoretical and empirical understanding of the critical success factors for firm performance. In the following we will formulate the five sub-questions of our research.

The relationships between supply chain management and quality management and the lack of research into combining the two perspectives were already mentioned in Section 1.2 of this chapter. We therefore propose the first research question:

> *RQ1: What is the joint impact of supply chain integration and quality management practices on firm performance in the pork sector in China?*

In the last decade, the application of integrated information technology (IIT) and integrated logistics management (ILM) has drastically changed the way companies operate their production and distribution systems (Chiu, 1995). IIT and ILM form the structural and infrastructural processes relating to the transformation of materials into value-added products, and the delivery of finished products through appropriate channels to customers and markets so as to maximise customer value and satisfaction (Narasimhan and Kim, 2001). Quality of food is strongly dependent on logistics systems in food chains. These systems concern exchange of planning data (harvesting, storage, and transportation), post-harvest storage and transportation (cooling, type of vehicle depending on type of products and distances in time), order-delivery cycle (frequency, demands), use of information and (tele) communication technologies (internet, cell-phones, etc.). Quality and logistics systems are in many cases enabled and supported by information and communication technologies (Ruben *et al.*, 2007). In China, the investment in information technology and logistics management is still limited in pork processing firms. Only large and medium-size firms are willing to develop information enablers (such as enterprise resource planning system) and cold chains to meet the increasing quality requirements of the supermarkets. Therefore it is a challenge to explore the interactions between integrated information technology, logistics management and firm performance. We thus propose the second research question:

> *RQ2: How do information technology and logistics management interact with quality management practices and how do they influence the performance of pork processing firms in China?*

Existing empirical studies have supported the positive relationships between the degree of vertical integration and the degree of transaction specific investment and uncertainty in China's pork sector (Dai and Zhou, 2005; Han *et al.*, 2006). These studies are in line with past studies in industrial organization theory which have focused on the relationship between transaction attributes and the selection of different organizational arrangements (Hobbs, 1996; Martinez and Zerring, 2004). Relatively little research has been done on the relationships between different organizational arrangements and quality management practices. We thus formulate the following research question:

RQ3: What is the relationship between governance mechanisms and quality management practices in China's pork processing sector?

The management of supply chains and quality is not an independent stand-alone concept but is embedded in a specific business environment. The business environment in China has a strong transitional character and at the same time is applying international QM practices to the firm's operation. One would expect that government support still plays an important role in business operations due to the impact of a long history of centralised management systems. It is thus interesting to explore the effect of government support on firm performance of pork processors.

As Clark (2006) put it, it is not the lack of a strategy that causes a business to fail but rather the organization's inability to act upon a chosen strategy. To understand strategic fit, we need to investigate which factors determine the alignment of China's pork processing firms' strategy with its external environment as well as its internal resources and competencies. In our study, we pay particular attention to the 'prospector strategy'. According to Miles and Snow (1978), the prospectors' prime capacity is that of finding and exploiting new product and market opportunities. They seek competitive advantage by distinguishing themselves from their competitors through a wide range of products and sound company image (Miller, 1988; Slater and Olson, 2000). To explore the QMP-strategy-performance and government support-strategy-performance paradigms, we thus propose the following two research questions:

RQ4: What are the relationships between specific quality management practices and firm performance and what is the role of firm strategy to moderate this relationship?

RQ5: What is the impact of government support on firm performance and what is the role of firm strategy to moderate this relationship?

In our study, firm performance includes not only financial indicators (e.g. profitability), but also factors which have an impact on the long-term continuity of a firm, such as market share, strategic position, and consumer satisfaction.

1.3 Theoretical components and research design

The research questions in Section 1.2 will be dealt with by integrating five theories. Supply Chain Management describes how business transactions are conducted in supply chains (Lambert and Cooper, 2000). For the management of quality, the study focuses on Total Quality Management and creates an interlinking with Supply Chain Management. To study appropriate governance forms in the supply chain, Transaction Cost Economics (Rindfleisch and Heide, 1997), Relational Exchange Theory (MacNeil, 1978, 1980) and Contingency Theory (Lawrence and Lorsch, 1967) provide important theoretical insights. In addition, Contingency Theory also helps to explain the strategic alignment between firms' internal structure and processes and their external environment. The next part only focuses on the rationale of applying these theories to our study since each of them will be introduced when specific research questions are dealt with in the following chapters of this book.

SCM is an important theory for managing business relationships. However, it has been criticised due to its lack of a robust conceptual framework for the development of the theory (Croom *et al.*, 2000; Lamming *et al.*, 2000). This study will contribute to the development of SCM theory by combining it with Total Quality Management (TQM) on the one hand. And on the other hand, in the evolution of quality management the application of TQM is increasingly studied in a supply chain perspective (Robinson and Malhotra, 2005, Foster Jr., 2008; Kaynak and Hartley, 2008). Here it supports the suggestion of Robinson and Malhotra (2005) that research into quality practices have to change from a firm-based perspective to an inter-organizational supply chain perspective involving suppliers and buyers (Van Plaggenhoef, 2007).

As mentioned in Section 1.2, TCE has been criticised as having neglected the implications of the affective and other features of trust in buyer-supplier relationships (Rindfleisch and Heide, 1997; Barney and Hesterly, 1999). In fact many forms of organizational interactions are based on the gradual development of trust, helping firms to lower transaction costs and to safeguard against opportunism (Anderson and Narus, 1990). Several studies have confirmed the role of relational governance in business relationships. We thus complement TCE with RET, by including relational governance mechanism in studying the alignment of governance structure with transaction attributes and with quality management practices of the pork processing firms.

The other limitation of TCE is that transactions are considered a phenomenon isolated from their business environment. TCE focuses on a single transaction as the unit of analysis, while ignoring other relationships that surround the focal transactions (Cook and Emerson, 1978). To achieve a fit between a firm's external environment and its processes is the starting point of Contingency Theory (Lawrence and Lorsch, 1967). Therefore Contingency Theory also plays a complementary role for TCE.

In summary, each of these theories offers its own focus, assumptions and framework for studying buyer-supplier relationships. Nevertheless, they do provide complementary explanations for buyer-supplier relationships and thus are important elements in our study.

Having illustrated the complementary nature of the theories used in this study, we will present the research design. Three steps are followed in developing the measures and conducting empirical studies. The first step starts with grounded theory research and afterwards pilot studies in pork processing firms and academic institutions. As few studies have been done to explore the impact of supply chain integration and QM practices on firm performance of the pork processing firms in China, insight from researchers and practitioners was very important for the reliability and validity of the scales to be used in the survey. In the second step, a large-scale survey was conducted in the pork processing sector in two Eastern China provinces, namely Jiangsu province, Shandong province and the municipality of Shanghai[10]. Data collection was conducted with personal interviews in more than 250 pork slaughterhouses and processors. A total of 229 samples are valid. This stage serves as hypotheses testing. In the third step, the findings from the quantitative part of the research were verified using 5 in-depth case studies of pork processing firms in the survey area. The objective of this step was to gain feedback on the results and to get more practical insight into how the relationships found in the second step work in practice (Van Plaggenhoef, 2007). The in-depth case studies will not produce an independent chapter, but provide a better insight into the final chapter of discussion and conclusions.

1.4 Outline of the thesis

This book consists of 7 chapters and is divided into three parts, as illustrated in Figure 1.2. The three parts include introduction, theoretical and empirical research and finally the discussion and conclusions.

The first part introduces the research background and presents the rationale for this research, including the development of the central research questions. Chapter 2 analyses the structure of the pork supply chain in China. The major stages of the chain, production and supply, slaughtering and processing, distribution and marketing, and consumption are introduced. In addition, QM systems and the region in China where the empirical study has been performed are also described in this chapter.

The second part comprises four main chapters based on quantitative analysis of data collected in 2005 in the pork processing sector in east China. We start in Chapter 3 with an examination of the joint impact of supply chain integration and QM practices on the performance of pork processing firms both from an upstream and downstream perspective. In Chapter 4, the focus is on the interrelationships between integrated information technology, integrated logistics management, QM practices and firm performance of the pork processing industry. Chapter 5 investigates the impact of pork chain arrangements (governance forms) on QM practices. Focus is on the relationship between asset specificity and uncertainty in the chain and chain governance mechanisms and what is the impact of these governance mechanisms on QM practices. Three major governance mechanisms are studied, spot market, contractual governance and relational governance. Next in Chapter 6, we extend our theoretical framework to include competitive strategy as a potential moderator and government support as an independent variable in our analysis. Specifically the behaviour of firms with a 'prospector strategy' is investigated. The rationale behind this is to see (1) whether prospector strategy moderates the relationships between QM practices and firm performance on the one hand and between government support and firm performance on the other hand. Government support

---

[10] The rationale of conducting empirical studies in this region is presented in 2.6 of Chapter 2 Research domain.

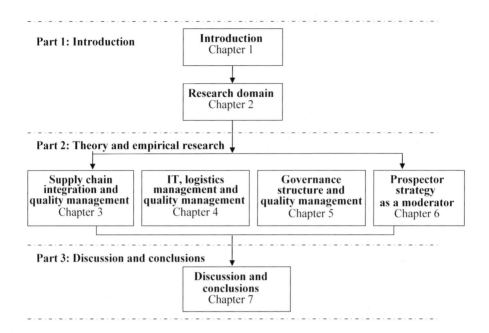

Figure 1.2. Outline of the book.

is specified in financial and technological support provided by the central and provincial government authorities to the slaughterhouses and processors.

The third part, Chapter 7 provides a synthesis of the findings derived from each of the specific analyses and presents some promising pathways to improve supply chain coordination and QM practices in the pork processing sector of China. Elaboration on the answers to our research questions is also addressed in this part. The chapter concludes with a discussion of the theoretical contributions of this study and managerial implications as well as directions for future research.

Chapter 2. Research domain[11]

Population growth, urbanization, and income growth in developing countries are fuelling a massive global increase in demand for food of animal origin (Delgado *et al.*, 1999). As China becomes more and more integrated in the global economy and has become a key player in global agro-food markets, interest in China's livestock production and consumption has increased noticeably over the last decade. Foreign investors are keen to step into China's fast-growing meat market. The country is expected to become the second-biggest consumer market by 2014, according to economists at Credit Suisse Group[12]. While the domestic meat processors are trying to increase their profit, various government departments try to increase the food quality and safety and improve people's livelihood. This chapter provides an overview of pork production and marketing in China in general and then specifically in the selected survey area in the east of China. Section 2.1 looks at the pork supply from the perspectives of pork production, production region, and supply uncertainty. Whereas pork slaughtering and processing is presented in Section 2.2, Section 2.3 introduces the structure of pork distribution and marketing in China. Emphasis is placed on the three development periods of distribution, the main marketing outlets and their characteristics. Section 2.4 introduces pork consumption. As food safety has become a very import issue all over the world, Section 2.5 describes the institutional involvement in pork quality and the safety standards in China. The subsequent Section 2.6 provides a general introduction of pork production and marketing in the survey areas, namely Jiangsu province, Shandong province and Shanghai municipality in the eastern China. This chapter ends with some concluding remarks in Section 2.7.

2.1 Pork production and supply: undergoing rapid change

Like the other agro-sectors in China, the pork sector also experienced the transition from a highly planned system to a market-driven system. In this part, we will review the development of pork production and supply in a global and a domestic context. It will focus on types of hog producers, production regions and supply uncertainty.

2.1.1 Development of pork production

The conditions required for the development of the pork industry only began to emerge with the economic reforms after 1978 in China. In the agricultural sector, two major policy changes (reforms) in particular were important. The first was the dismantling of the communes after

---

[11] Part of the chapter was published as 'The Chinese pork sector' in the European Pork Chains edited by J. Trienekens, B. Petersen, N. Wognum and D. Brinkmann, 2009, Wageningen Academic Publishers, the Netherlands, pp. 213-231.

[12] Foreign investors fighting for Chinese meat processor in www.ap-foodtechnology.com/news/, accessed on July 12, 2007.

1978 and the introduction of the Household Responsibility Systems (HRS)[13]. Under the HRS, individual households were able to lease allocated plots of land, take ownership of livestock and receive returns based on output. The introduction of the HRS greatly stimulated the agricultural sector. The increased production and demand for agricultural commodities by the introduction of the system spawned a proliferation of rural markets in which households and state companies could trade 'surplus' agricultural commodities. By 1985, with the exception of pork-price stabilization measures, the market for livestock and meat products (along with fruit and vegetables) was decontrolled. This move to free markets for most agricultural products was the second major reform that paved the way for the rapid development of livestock production (Longworth *et al.*, 2001). Since 1990, China has become the largest pork production and consumption country in the world. The total output of pork production reached 51. 97 million tonnes in 2006 (Chinese Statistical Yearbook, 2007), accounting for more than 50% of the total production in the world. The absolute and relative growth of the Chinese pork sector is reflected in Table 2.1. which lists the output of main pork production countries of the world in selected years.

Despite the strong growth in poultry and beef, with their share gradually increasing in total output of livestock products, pork still dominates the meat scene in China. Though the share of pork in total meat production declined from nearly 86% in 1985 to 65% in 2005 (calculated according to the China Statistics Yearbook, 1986 and 2006), in absolute terms, pork production still increased more than any of the other meats. In proportionate terms, both beef output and its share of total meat production grew the fastest of the major meat products (Longworth *et al.*, 2001). The Chinese cattle herd continues to expand bolstered by genetics and feed improvement, as well as government supported production practices (Bean and Zhang, 2007). Pork production is grain-intensive, therefore shifting to beef production is strongly promoted by the Chinese government. The changing composition of the meat sector and its expansion in the last 20 years from 1985 is depicted in Table 2.2.

---

[13] The Household Responsibility System (HRS) was first adopted in agriculture in 1981 and later extended to other sectors of the economy. In agriculture, farmland was distributed equally to farm households based on labor availability. A certain quantum of production had to be delivered to the state, the remaining yield could be sold by the farmers on the free market at unregulated prices. This system partially supplanted the egalitarian distribution method, whereby the state assumed all profits and losses. The HRS has stimulated the farmers' agricultural production and enhanced agricultural productivity and food security in China (Lu, 2007; http://en.wikipedia.org/responsibility_system).

Table 2.1. Comparison of pork output by country (1000 tonnes) of 10 main pork production countries in the world (FAO, 2007).

	2005		2000		1995		1990	
Country	**Output**	**%**	**Output**	**%**	**Output**	**%**	**Output**	**%**
World total	104,333	100	90,086	100	80,091	100	60,872	100
China	50,106	48.02	41,406	45.96	36,484	45.55	24,016	39.45
The USA	9,390	9.00	8,597	9.54	8,097	10.11	6,964	11.44
Germany	4,498	4.31	3,918	4.35	3,602	4.50	4,458	7.32
Brazil	2,710	2.60	2,556	2.84	2,800	3.50	1,050	1.72
Spain	3,164	3.03	2,916	3.24	2,175	2.72	1,789	2.94
Canada	1,914	1.83	1,640	1.82	1,417	1.77	1,192	1.96
Viet Nam	2,201	2.11	1,409	1.56	1,012	1.26	729	1.20
France	2,274	2.18	1,900	2.10	2,144	2.68	1,727	2.84
Denmark	1,793	1.72	1,624	1.80	1,516	1.89	1,209	1.99
Poland	1,926	1.85	1,923	2.13	1,963	2.45	1,855	3.05

Table 2.2. The output of major meats in selected years in China (10,000 tonnes) (China Statistical Yearbook, 1986, 1996, 2006).

	1985		1995		2005	
	Output	**%**	**Output**	**%**	**Output**	**%**
Pork	1,655	85.9	3,648	69.4	5,010	64.7
Poultry	160	8.3	935	17.8	1,464	18.9
Beef	47	2.4	416	7.9	712	9.2
Goat and mutton	59	3.1	202	3.8	436	5.6
Other meat	6	0.3	60	1.1	122	1.6
Total meat output	1,927	100.0	5,260	100	7,743	100.0

2.1.2 Types of hog producers

There are three types of hog producers in China: unspecialised households, specialised households and commercial farms. The proportion of the hog supply from these three sources is as follows: about 62% of China's pork output comes from small individual unspecialised backyard hog producers with less than 50 heads per year, whereas nearly 35% comes from specialised households with more than 50 head to 9,999 heads and merely 3% from large commercial farms with more than 10,000 heads per year (China Statistical Yearbook of Animal Husbandry, 2005). Table 2.3 shows hog production scale and the total number of hogs produced in 2004.

Unspecialised households: Most backyard hog producers keep 1 to 5 hogs. This type of producer can be found in most areas of China. However, their number is decreasing due to migration to the fast developing cities in East and Southeast China for job opportunities. Hog production costs for unspecialised households are rather low due to three reasons. The first is low labour costs. The second is low investment in animal housing since most pigsties are semi-open with mud walls. The third is the low cost of feed. Pig feed mostly come from vegetables, table scraps, green fodder and unprocessed grains and oilseeds. Manufactured compound feed or concentrated feed is used as a supplement (Poon, 2006).

Specialised households and commercial farms: Although small-size pig farms still account for a major share of hog production, several studies have noticed a decrease in backyard production while medium- and large-scale production has been slowly expanding (Hu *et al.*, 2007). Specialised household and commercial farms use more advanced management practices, better swine breeds and animal feed. Whereas hogs raised by backyard farms tend to have higher fat ratios, hogs from the commercial farms are of the lean type (Pan and Kinsey, 2002). Moreover, as the Chinese government pays great attention to meat quality and safety, medium and large-scale hog production is strongly encouraged. Several programs were launched to promote lean meat, and local government authorities established medium- and large-scale farms around big cities to guarantee meat supply in urban areas. Consumers' preference for lean pork will continue to stimulate the development of specialised and commercial hog production. However, the dominant position of unspecialised hog production will not change in the foreseeable future, taking into account China's large rural population (Poon, 2006).

Table 2.3. Hog production scale for 2004 in China (China Statistical Yearbook of Animal Husbandry, 2005).

Number of hogs/year	Number of hogs at the end of the year (10,000 heads)	Percentage of the total hogs
Below 50	38,406.61	62.14
50 ~ 499	14,884.38	24.08
500 ~ 2,999	4,542.57	7.35
3,000 ~ 9,999	2,061.53	3.34
10,000 ~ 49,999	1,567.32	2.54
More than 50,000	338.29	0.55
Total	61,800.70	100

Commercial farms: Government has been paying great attention to large-scale pork production. The proportion of producers with more than 500 pigs increased from less than 1% in 2003 (Table 2.3) to 7.35% in 2004 (Hu *et al.*, 2007). Further development is partly constrained by the availability of skillful workers and higher risks for these production farms (e.g. outbreak of diseases).

2.1.3 Main hog production regions

Hog production is scattered all over China. With the rapid development of swine production, grain shortage has increasingly become a major constraint. The Yangtze River and Northern China regions are the key swine production and internal exporting zones in China. Northeastern China used to be short of pork due to the colder climate, but this region is becoming self sufficient and is starting to export to other regions due to cheap regional corn supply and the high costs of grain transportation in other areas (Wang, 2006). Table 2.4 shows the regional distribution of hog production in 2005 in China.

The important position the Yangtze River Region has played in hog production and supply is worth mentioning. Its output was always around 50% of the national pork output until the end of the 1990s. Table 2.5 compares the output of hog production in the top 10 provinces for 1995 and 2005.

From Table 2.5, we can see that the main swine production areas haven't changed much during the last decade. Only Guangxi province and Jiangxi province were replaced in the production ranking by Yunnan province and Anhui province. According to experts, the major reason for the rapid increase of swine production in Yunnan province was the major investment from both the central and local governments. In 2007 investment by these two levels of authorities

Table 2.4. Regional distribution of major hog production areas in 2005 in China (China Statistical Yearbook, 2006).

Region	Provinces	(%) Share of the national hog output
The Yangtze River Region	Sichuan, Chongqing, Guizhou, Hunan, Jiangxi, Zhejiang, Jiangsu and Anhui	34.9
Northern China	Hebei, Shandong and Henan	22.9
Southeastern and Southwestern China	Fujian, Guangzhou, Yunnan and Hainan	13.4
Northeast China	Liaoning, Jilin and Heilongjiang	8.0
Percentage of these areas among the total hog production		79.2

Table 2.5. Top 10 pork production provinces in 1995 and 2005 (10,000 tonnes) (China Statistical Yearbook 1996 and 2006).

Province	1995 (National total: 3,648.4)			Province	2005 (National total: 5,010.6)		
	Output	%	Accumulated percentage		Output	%	Accumulated percentage
Sichuan	526.3	14.43	14.43	Sichuan	513,7	10.25	10.25
Hunan	310.1	8.50	22.93	Henan	440,8	8.80	19.05
Shandong	267.7	7.34	30.27	Hunan	437,0	8.72	27.77
Hubei	239.6	6.57	36.84	Shandong	367,1	7.33	35.10
Henan	210.4	5.77	42.61	Hebei	337,4	6.73	41.83
Jiangsu	195.9	5.37	47.98	Hubei	256,3	5.12	46.95
Guangxi	195.7	5.36	53.34	Guangdong	256,3	5.12	52.07
Guangdong	188.8	5.17	58.51	*Yunnan*	244,2	4.87	56.94
Jiangxi	188.5	5.17	63.68	Jiangsu	218,5	4.36	61.30
Hebei	187.4	5.14	68.82	*Anhui*	215,6	4,30	65,60

Note: the provinces in **bold italics** show the difference of main swine production in the last decade.

accounted for € 60 million. Under this support scheme, hog producers received € 5 per sow added to the stock. There are also subsidies for vaccination and hog reproduction. In the Anhui province, besides government financial support, other explanations for the rapid development of swine production were the rich grain production and low labour cost. To get a better idea of the geographical location of swine production areas in China, see Figure 2.1.

2.2 Pork slaughtering and processing: fragmentation and integration coexist

Approximately 660 million hogs were slaughtered in China in 2006. An overview of the pork slaughtering and processing sector and the industry structure will be given in this section. The description will show that fragmentation and integration coexist in this sector.

2.2.1 Evolution of pork slaughtering and processing industry

Before 1985, the slaughtering sector was under state monopoly. Slaughtering operations and distribution outlets were organised by the General Food Companies (GFC) set up under the previous Ministry of Foreign Trade and Economic Cooperation (renamed Ministry of Commerce when some responsibilities of the State Planning Commission and the State Economic and Trade Commission were merged in March 2003). Reforms in meat marketing

Figure 2.1. Major swine production areas in China.

from 1985 created the opportunity and incentive for other, primarily state-owned, agencies to become involved with pork processing and marketing. In addition, throughout the second half of the 1980s and into the early 1990s, many county governments established slaughtering and processing plants to generate their own sources of fiscal revenues and development funds. Various smaller slaughterhouses were therefore established at the township and village level (Longworth *et al.*, 2001). Meanwhile, private butchers also developed rapidly because of their easy access for backyard farms and low-cost operations. However, illegal slaughtering also caused potential quality and safety problems. This had become a major concern of the Chinese government. Therefore, at the end of 1997, the Designated Hog Slaughtering Act was issued by the government. The Act regulated that all hogs were to be slaughtered at designated slaughterhouses. In 2003 there were already about 40,000 designated slaughterhouses all over the country, many of which were small-scale and moderately equipped at best (Pan, 2003). If the late 1980s and 1990s were the periods of rapid increase in slaughter capacity, then the last few years have been all about consolidating and restructuring. Many of the designated slaughterhouses established during the late 1990s operated well below capacity, and, in many cases, have survived by charging service fees from private slaughterhouses or butchers. The private slaughterhouses or butchers pay the designated slaughterhouses an agreed price for each hog they slaughter. Due to the importance of pork industry in the livelihood, the local governments currently actively promote economic reform to the sector and seek external sources of finance including private investment. However, because of consolidation, the number of slaughterhouses is decreasing. In 2006, there were 25,000 meat slaughterhouses left in China (Deng, 2007a).

2.2.2 Structure

Pork slaughtering and processing enterprises in China are far from a homogeneous group. Operations vary according to size, ownership, location, source of hogs and the markets they service (Figure 2.2). The sources and production locations of hogs have been described in section 2.1.2 and 2.1.3 respectively. The following section will introduce the size, ownership and the markets the pork slaughterhouses and processors serve.

Size

Slaughtering and processing companies can be divided into three categories: small-scale, medium-size and large-scale companies. By Western standards, pork slaughtering and processing in China is really small-scale. The Chinese Ministry of Commerce classified a company into 'scale company' if its annual sales reached RMB 5 million Yuan (approximately € 500,000). According to the statistics of the China Meat Association (2008), there were 2,847 scale companies in meat slaughtering and processing in 2007 with total sales of approximately €34 billion, of which pork and poultry slaughterhouses and processors accounted for 1672 and 1175 respectively. In addition, there were 96 companies in canned meat production business. A survey by the Association showed that these meat companies achieved a total profit of about € 1.35 billion in 2007, 28.7% more than in 2006. Only 373 companies suffered losses.

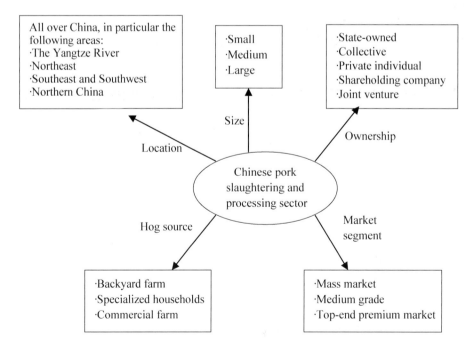

Figure 2.2. Dimensions of Chinese pork slaughtering sector (adapted from Longworth et al., 2001).

In general, the designated pork slaughterhouses at village level are rather small in scale, slaughtering only several dozens of hogs per day. Only when there are important festivals, do they slaughter more than usual. The hogs are slaughtered into half/quarter carcasses for local sale. The medium-size slaughterhouses kill around a million hogs per year. The largest processor slaughters about 13.1 million hogs per year. The percentage of hogs slaughtered by the three leading meat processors was less than 5% in 2007 (Li, 2008). Usually, large slaughterhouses are vertically integrated with further processing. In addition to the difference in the number of hogs slaughtered, a major difference between the medium-size and the large-scale companies is that the latter operate better cold storage facilities. Hogs killed by small and medium-size slaughterhouses are normally sold immediately in nearby rural or urban markets as fresh meat, to avoid the need for cold storage facilities. The medium-size and large-scale slaughterhouses and processors account for about 20% of total production. The top 10 pork slaughterhouses and processors and their turnover are listed in Table 2.6.

The concept of 'Dragon head enterprises' in Chinese agriculture is worth mentioning. In the mid-1990s, Chinese government strongly promoted the idea of 'dragon head' enterprises and provided incentives for their establishment and development. The purpose was to strengthen the link between farmers and processing and marketing companies and raise farmers' income. Leading companies were selected by local government authorities to contract with hundreds of individual farmers in their region, and procure, process and market agricultural products from the farmers. Under the contract, farmers provide labour and land, while the dragon head enterprises provide seed, operating loans, fertiliser, and technical expertise. Within this system, farmers have less control over the marketing process, but they are also less vulnerable to market risk as compared to conducting business through traditional open markets (Poon, 2006).

Table 2.6. Top ten pork slaughtering and processing companies in China in 2004 (China Meat Association, 2006).

Name	Turnover (million RMB)
Henan Shineway Group (Shuanghui)	16,020
People's Food Holding Ltd	10,047
China Yurun Food Industry Group Co. Ltd.	7,921
Henan Zhiyuan (Sunway) Food	4,860
Delisi Group	3,625
Chengdu Hope Food	1,823
Henan Zhongpin	1,784
Sichuan Gaojin	1,710
Beijing Shunxin	1,583

As previously mentioned the Chinese meat industry is experiencing a consolidation and restructuring period. In this regard, Prof. Guanghong Zhou, chairman of the Chinese Society of Animal Products Processing, expects that large and medium-size meat processors will have 70% of the market by 2020 supplying mainly large supermarkets (Zhou, 2006).

Ownership

Economic reform and market imperatives have placed great pressure on state-owned slaughterhouses to restructure. The different scope, timing and nature of this restructuring process have resulted in a variety of ownership structures and management practices (Longworth *et al.*, 2001). For example, many of the General Food Companies previously owned by township governments or village collectives are now run by small groups of private shareholders. Medium-scale state-owned slaughterhouses have also been under great pressure to restructure and seek external funding and acquire the necessary management skills to survive. Even the large, modern agro-industrial abattoirs have a wide range of ownership structure. Once very popular, the state-owned plants 'Meat Alliance' were reformed to private ownership in large numbers. These companies source hogs from all over the country. Though they sell some of their products through wet markets, they mostly cater for supermarkets, hotels, restaurants, and other institutional buyers (Fabiosa *et al.*, 2005). With regard to foreign investment, some international players have already started operation in China. So far, the 100% foreign-owned companies in the sector are very few due to uncertain profit margins, but joint ventures do exist. The American Hormel Foods operate two joint ventures in Shanghai and Beijing, with a retail market share of 0.6% in 2005 (Euromonitor International, 2006).

In 2006, China Association of Food Industry investigated the ownership of the meat processors in China. There were 1067 members, generally large and medium-size companies. Table 2.7 shows the ownership of the companies and some main economic indicators.

From the table, we can see that share-holding companies played a very important role in the meat processing sector. There were 638 companies with total assets of more than € 2.9 billion, accounting for 46.6% of the sector. The sales volume of these share-holding companies stood at 51.5% of the sector. With total assets of nearly € 2.9 billion, the foreign joint ventures had a sales volume of € 4 billion, contributing up to 40% to the sector. Thus far, the share-holding companies and foreign joint ventures have been the main players in the meat processing industry. Their total asset, sales volume, and profit accounted for more than 90% in the sector.

Market segment

Pork slaughtering and processing operations can be classified into three broad groups according to the type of market they service. The first group comprises the private individual butchers and county/town level slaughterhouses. They usually provide non-grading fresh pork meat to mass markets in urban and rural areas. This category of slaughterhouse accounts for

Table 2.7 Ownership of meat processing companies in China and main economic indicators during Jan. and Sept. 2006 (€ 10 million) (Statistics and Information Department, China Association of Food Industry, Dec. 2006).

	No. of companies	Total asset	Sales turnover	Total profit	No. of employees (10,000)
Meat processors and by-product processing companies	1,067	630.5	1,031.5	46.4	27.2
Among which					
State owned	52	19.3	16.1	0.4	1.1
Collective	34	5.0	13.4	0.5	0.3
Share-holding	638	294.1	531.6	25.2	13.6
Foreign joint venture	171	285.9	407.0	17.2	10.4
Other type	172	26.2	63.4	3.1	1.8

the overwhelming proportion of hogs slaughtered in China. The second group consists of medium-grade slaughterhouses that service the middle-class premium market, although much of their product also ends up on the mass market in urban and rural areas. Some of the better managed county and township level slaughterhouses also fit into this category. The third group of slaughterhouses supplies part of the carcass to the top end of the premium market, with the remaining cuts sold to the middle class and mass market. Slaughterhouses in this category include the modern and relatively large works often constructed as part of agro-industrial or meat industry development projects. Another group of slaughterhouses in this category are the joint ventures. To meet the requirements of the premium market, these slaughterhouses need to source better quality hogs. In many cases, they contract farmers or suppliers with specific requirements on feeding, management and physical criteria.

2.3 Pork distribution and marketing

There were over 600 million head of hogs slaughtered in China in 2006, almost all designated for the internal market. How these pork products (including the offal) reach the final consumers varies from the very simplest distribution systems to rather complex channels akin to those common in Western countries (Longworth et al., 2001). Current pork markets in China consist of wholesale markets, retail markets (mainly wet markets and supermarkets) and international markets. The role of international markets for pork can almost be ignored as pork export in China only accounts for about 1%. The great bulk of the meat is distributed through wet markets and travels along very short (in terms of time and space) local marketing chains. Figure 2.3 depicts the marketing channels of pork products.

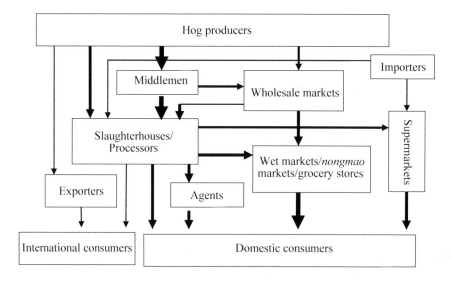

→ Arrows indicate product flows.
The size of the arrows indicates the relative importance of the channel.

Figure 2.3. Pork market structure in China (adapted from Lu, 2007). Arrows indicate product flows.

2.3.1 The development of the Chinese pork distribution and marketing

According to Tan and Xin (2001), pork distribution and marketing has experienced three periods of development since the founding of the People's Republic of China:

The first period (from 1949 to 1954): To restore the national economy and meet the societal needs after the People's Republic of China was founded in October 1949, the central government encouraged private operation of pork and poultry business. The percentage of hogs produced by state-owned companies was only 12.73% in 1953. In terms of supply to consumers, consumption quota was applied to cities with a population of more than 100,000. During this period, both state-owned and private business entities were involved in pork distribution and marketing on the basis of free market competition, with 46% of pork supply from state owned companies.

The second period (from 1955 to 1984): during this period the State planning system for both hog slaughtering and pork marketing was applied, state-owned slaughtering companies became dominant. Hog procurement quota was applied in the main hog production areas meaning that the collectives and farmers had to sell quota at fixed prices to the State. Only over-quota pork was supposed to be sold freely in the market. However, at times when there was plenty of hog supply, prices were also fixed for the surplus production. The state controlled planning system played an important role at that particular time. However, there were several shortcomings. The main one was that the state monopoly not only resulted in rigid marketing channels, but also hindered competition. The pork prices set up by the State did not reflect market demand. Therefore, it was imperative to reform the system.

The third period (since 1985): In 1985, the national government issued 'Ten policies on further vitalizing rural economy'. The government started to liberalise pork production and marketing. With the elimination of the quota production system, pork production and marketing started to perform based on market mechanism. The policies included free access to markets, free transactions, market-driven and quality-oriented price setting. Thus, 1985 represents the watershed in the development of the modern pork distribution system in China (Longworth *et al.*, 2001). The state monopoly ended. Many non-traditional operators became involved in pork slaughtering and marketing. Many state, collective and private business entities started to compete at all levels in the pork distribution and marketing chain. And a large number of pork wholesale and retail markets were set up during this period. The marketing channels were therefore diversified. Farmers were allowed to sell their products to urban areas directly. And traders began to play an important role in bridging hog producers and markets. Larger traders became wholesalers in wholesale markets. In addition to these two forms of marketing, integrated production and marketing also appeared. The reform provided farmers with great incentives and enlivened the market. However, the early stages of free market operations also posed challenges to the functioning of the market mechanism. The un-established market mechanism made it possible for opportunistic brokers and butchers to make money by doing illegal business. For example, the brokers can inject water into hogs to make more profit. The butchers sometimes slaughter hogs caught with disease and sell the pork meat to consumers. Eventually there was coexistence of different kinds of pork processors, e.g. modern enterprises, illegal slaughterhouses and private butchers.

2.3.2 The main marketing outlets and their characteristics

Pork products reach final consumers via many different channels. This part will describe the main channels for both fresh and processed pork products.

Wholesale market

As in other centrally planned economies, wholesale markets did not exist in China before the reforms started. Under the reforms, wholesale markets expanded from 892 in 1986 to 4387 in 2000 and the transaction value increased from € 280 million to €33.5 billion (Xu and Liu, 2003).

Until the mid-1990s, wholesale markets were usually owned by municipal governments or state-owned enterprises (SOEs) as a reflection of the government's perceived responsibility to provide urban citizens with stable, low-priced food. Moreover, these entities had the best access to finance while private agents still faced constraints in legally establishing their business. Since then the situation has changed and there has been a massive entry of private companies (Hu *et al.*, 2004). The government was focused on the establishment of standardised management procedures and market registration and monitoring systems (OECD, 2006).

Wet market

A wet market can be defined as a place where local farmers and traders supply agri-food products to the consumers. Nowadays, many wet markets in cities are being closed or consolidated since local authorities in most cities view the wet markets as unsanitary. The outbreak of SARS in 2003 has been reckoned as an important factor in accelerating this process. In addition, tax revenues from wet markets are small compared to other better regulated market. In some areas, local authorities have decided to transform the wet markets into supermarket-style venues where multiple vendors can operate in a cleaner and better regulated environment (Bean, 2003; Poon, 2006). If supermarket-type markets could not be established, the local authorities moved the open markets indoors. These indoor markets are usually called *nongmao* (agricultural produce) markets. They are the most popular and preferred avenue outlets for consumers in most cities to purchase fresh meat. In rural areas and small towns, wet markets remain the most popular retail outlets. In the markets, butchers sell fresh pork products on wooden tables. Facilities are rather simple.

Nongmao markets have developed a wide portfolio in recent years. With a population of about 6 million people in Nanjing, a medium-size city in China, there were nearly 300 *Nongmao* markets in 2005[14]. They vary from very large markets with hundreds of separate stalls located in specially constructed, sometimes multi-storied buildings, to open air markets with a large number of stalls, to small, simple markets consisting of a few stalls. They are open all day and most stall operators are full-time traders. The operations are licensed and inspected by the local branch of the Industry and Commerce Administration Bureau (ICAB) (Longworth *et al.*, 2001). In *nongmao* markets, most stallholders sell fresh pork products. However, there are also some stallholders selling cooked and other processed pork products, such as sausages and ham. In some of the more sophisticated and highly developed *nongmao* markets, several major Chinese meat companies have installed what could be described as Western-style butchers' shops. These shops/stalls have freezing facilities and display products in glass cabinets. This may be in sharp contrast to the open-air display of pork on wooden tables in other stalls in the same *nongmao* markets.

Supermarkets/hypermarkets

More than a decade ago, supermarkets emerged in Chinese cities. Studies have shown that supermarkets, hypermarkets and convenience stores are spreading rapidly in the top 60 cities of China and they have become a major force in retailing since the late 1990s. In addition

---

[14] provided by Nanjing Vegetable Company.

to the major coastal cities, supermarkets are now also gaining a foothold in the second and third tier cities all over China (Reardon *et al.*, 2003; Bean, 2003). Until the 1990s, the fresh produce section of the supermarkets only had a limited range of fruit and vegetables. However, there is a concerted move by the supermarkets to be involved in the marketing of fresh foods including fresh meat. Traditional offerings had been cooked meat, frozen meat or processed meat products sold over what, in Western supermarkets, would be called delicatessen counters. Since the late 1990s, two important innovations have been introduced by the supermarkets. First, there were offers of a wide range of vacuum-packed and branded cooked pork and pork offal products from open-fronted chiller cabinets. Second, shoppers were offered purchasing opportunities that more closely resemble the traditional *nongmao* market situation (Longworth et. al., 2001). However, generally speaking, the quality of the produce in the supermarkets and the way it is presented to the shoppers is significantly better than in most of the stalls in the *nongmao* markets. This also means, however, that prices are higher.

Compared with domestic supermarket chains, the foreign hypermarkets have a better managed cold chain for meat products. The popular foreign hypermarkets include Carrefour, Makro, Metro and Wal-Mart. These hypermarkets, together with the large Chinese supermarket chains, usually have a limited number of suppliers of meat products. These carefully selected suppliers are mostly integrated commercial-type producers that can assure both product quality and consistency in supply (Fabiosa *et al.*, 2005). As local government authorities have been aggressive in relocating, merging and shutting down wet markets in urban areas, supermarkets are growing rapidly. Experts predict that the market share of meat sales through supermarkets will increase from 15% to 40% in the next decade (Zhou, 2006).

2.4 Pork consumption

Due to macro-economic developments such as rising incomes, increasing urbanization of the population, greater availability of ruminant meat (beef, goat meat and mutton) and the rapid development of the poultry industry in the last decade, the share of pork consumption among all meat has decreased substantially. However, pork still remains the most popular meat in China. Annual per capita consumption stood at 39.6 kg in 2006 (Deng, 2007a). The following will describe key pork consumption areas in China; the main characteristics of pork consumption and future consumption.

2.4.1 The key pork consumption areas

The amount of pork consumption varies across regions in China due to the impact of habit, production structure and religion. In north-eastern areas of China, the proportion of beef and veal consumption is bigger than the other areas, while pork consumption is lower. Among the regions where pork is consumed least, Beijing was in the 5th place with an annual average per capita pork consumption of 17.2 kg (46% of the consumed meat) (Table 2.8). Two possible reasons may explain this. Firstly, there is more outside dining in Beijing due to its

Table 2.8. Areas with the least pork consumption in China in 2006 (in kg) (National Bureau of Statistics of China, 2007).

Area	Xinjiang	Ningxia	Tibet	Qinghai	Inner Mongolia	Beijing
Monthly average per capita consumption	0.51	0.67	0.88	0.98	0.94	1.43
Percentage in livestock and poultry (%)	20.3	31.4	27.98	35.12	43.06	46.10

Note: there is a difference between the per capita pork availability and per capita pork consumption in the statistics of the National Bureau of Statistics of China. For example, the per capita pork availability was 39.97 kg in 2006. However, the National Bureau of Statistics of China indicated that the urban household consumed 20 kg of pork per person while the per capita rural household consumed 15.46 kg of pork that year (National Bureau of Statistics of China, 2007). The major reason was that the proportion of pork products dining out was excluded from the consumption as the amount is difficult to be calculated in the official statistics.

position as the capital and political and cultural centre of China. Secondly, people in Beijing enjoy a higher income than most areas of China and are therefore more inclined to eat beef, poultry, and veal. The main pork consumption area is in the south of the Yangtze River area (traditionally this has been the main pork consumption region) and the southeast coast (the economically developed area). Guizhou province consumed the highest amount of pork in 2006 in China (Table 2.9). Figure 2.4 shows the major pork consumption areas and the least pork consumption areas in 2006 in China.

China is among several countries with relatively large pork consumption. Table 2.10 shows the per capita pork consumption in selected countries.

Table 2.9 Areas with most pork consumption in China in 2006 (in kg) (National Bureau of Statistics of China, 2007).

Area	Guizhou	Jiangxi	Hubei	Yunnan	Fujian	Sichuan	Hunan
Monthly average per capita consumption	2.11	2.01	1.67	1.90	2.29	2.24	2.02
Percentage in livestock and poultry (%)	67.19	67.44	65.61	64.00	61.78	61.90	62.73

Note: the same as in Table 2.8.

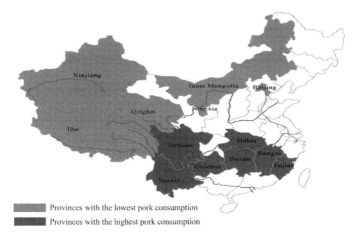

Provinces with the lowest pork consumption
Provinces with the highest pork consumption

Figure 2.4. Provinces of major pork consumption and provinces with the least pork consumption.

Table 2.10. Per capita pork consumption in selected countries and regions (Kilograms per person).

	2002	2003	2004	2005	2006[2]	2007[3]
Australia	19.2	20.8	20.8	21.4	21.0	20.6
Brazil	11.0	10.8	10.7	10.5	11.6	12.0
Canada	33.6	31.2	32.8	29.5	28.5	26.5
Chile	18.9	18.2	17.1	17.7	19.0	19.4
China, P. R.	33.6	34.9	35.9	38.0	39.4	40.8
EU[1]	43.4	44.0	43.3	43.3	43.7	43.6
Hong Kong	62.4	65.6	71.9	65.7	65.7	65.3
Japan	18.7	18.7	20.1	19.7	19.2	19.7
Korea, South	25.0	26.8	27.5	26.8	28.7	29.6
Mexico	13.2	13.7	14.8	14.7	14.7	14.5
Philippines	13.7	13.8	13.6	13.6	13.9	14.0
Russia Federation	16.9	16.7	16.2	17.3	18.5	19.9
Taiwan	43.1	41.9	42.2	41.5	41.8	40.8
Ukraine	12.5	13.1	12.8	11.6	11.3	12.4
United States	30.2	30.4	30.1	29.3	29.0	28.9
Vietnam	14.9	15.4	16.9	19.2	20.3	21.5

Sources: USDA-FAS attaché reports, official statistics, and results of office research. Population statistics from U.S. Census Bureau, Population Division, International Programs Center, April 10 2007
Note: The per capita pork consumption for the Chinese consumers refers to the per capita pork availability.
[1] EU data includes 25 member states for all years.
[2] Preliminary.
[3] Forecast.

As regards the type of pork products consumed, three kinds of raw meat can be found in the market, namely: fresh, frozen and chilled meat. Fresh pork meat has been the most popular meat in China until now. In recent years, economic development has provided rural residents with higher income. This factor, together with the growing number of supermarkets in towns and rural areas, has made the frozen products also affordable and available in these areas. Sales of frozen processed food in China reached RMB 32,738 million and 1,503 million tonnes, representing a value and volume growth of 6% and 7% respectively in 2005 (Euromonitor International, 2006; Poon, 2006). With regard to chilled products, sales of chilled processed food reached RMB 11,849 million and 365,000 tonnes (Euromonitor International, 2006). Increased importance of food combined with rising living standards and the hectic urban lifestyle, are believed to result in a rise in the demand for chilled processed food, particularly in developed regions. Figure 2.5 gives a picture of the variety of chilled processed meat products in China.

2.4.2 Features and trends of pork consumption in China

In the past decade, pork consumption shows the following features. Firstly, the increase in pork consumption is positively correlated with income. Higher income families consume more pork than those with lower income. In this regard, the south eastern coastal area enjoys higher pork consumption than other areas of China because of the much faster economic development. Secondly, the main consumption areas are also the main hog production areas. This can be concluded from Figure 2.6. Thirdly, the difference in pork consumption between urban and rural areas is becoming smaller. Urban residents consumed 2.2 times the amount

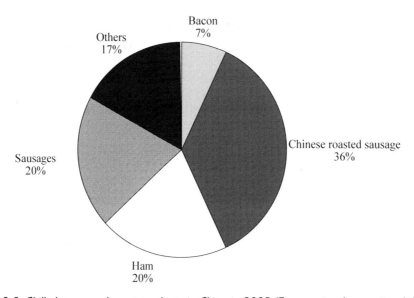

Figure 2.5. Chilled processed meat products in China in 2005 (Euromonitor International, 2006).

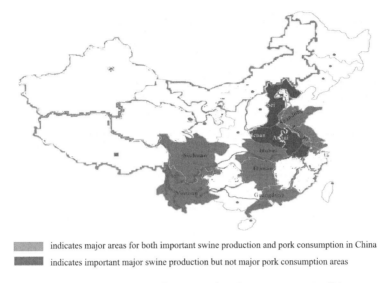

indicates major areas for both important swine production and pork consumption in China

indicates important major swine production but not major pork consumption areas

Figure 2.6. Major areas for both swine production and pork consumption in China.

of pork consumed by rural residents in 1981. Whereas, in 2001, the difference was 1.4 times and in 2006 only 1.3 times the consumption of rural residents.[15] In Figure 2.7 we can see the steady increase in pork consumption in rural areas since 1995.

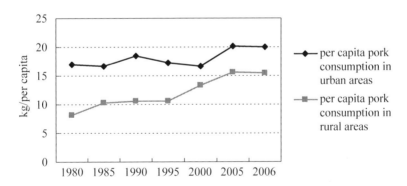

Figure 2.7. Per capita pork consumption in selected years in China (China Statistical Yearbook, various issues).

---

[15] Calculated according to data in China Statistical Yearbook, 2007.

Though pork consumption has steadily increased in the past decade, the recent economic crisis has had some impact on pork consumption. According to the managers of the three leading pork processors in China, the impact is reflected by the following indicators. First, the time taken for pork consumption to recover after the traditional high consumption peak in the Spring Festival of 2009 was delayed. Compared with the past three years, the time lag was about one week. Second, the amount of pork consumption in 2009 has decreased about 10%~30% compared with the same time period in 2008. In terms of sales income, it was about 20%~30% less than the same period of the previous year. However, the innate volatility of grain feed and hog supply also contributed to the low price of pork products in 2009. After the high price period from the beginning of 2007 to the first half of 2008, the pork price has shown a decreasing trend since the second half of 2008. Figure 2.8 indicates the fluctuation of pork price. From the perspective of hog supply, the pork processors also have opportunities. The economic crisis influenced job creation in cities. The number of immigrants from the rural areas to cities is decreasing. Hog production has been one of the income generation sources for the rural residents. The increase in hog production will result in a decrease in hog prices. From a longer term perspective, the continuing economic development and increasing income will inevitably cause an increase in pork consumption in the next few decades. According to some experts in the field, the future development in pork consumption will have the following trends:

- The proportion of pork consumption in dining out will increase.
- Urban residents will consume more beef and poultry products. Pork consumption will decrease in relative terms. However, pork consumption will still continue to increase, especially in the large rural areas.
- With the faster pace of life for the working middle-class and rising incomes, convenient and smaller retail packs will continue to gain consumer popularity. Ready-to-eat meat packages offer convenience to consumers and therefore market growth potential for processors.
- Consumers are increasingly concerned about food safety and quality. This will drive companies to invest more in quality management. Technology investments will focus on safety, hygiene, convenience, cost effectiveness and environmentally friendliness.
- Companies will be more brand-oriented. Large firms like Yurun and Shineway are investing more in promotions, such as TV commercials, sample trials in shops and price discounts to win customer loyalty to their brands.
- Supermarkets are becoming the major channel for urban consumers, especially for the younger generation.
- Specialty shops will become more important channels for large and medium pork processing companies.
- Demands for convenience food, functional food and leisure pork products will increase: (1) small packages and chilled cuts in cities; (2) low temperature western style meat products among middle-class urban households; (3) frozen meat in rural areas due to the availability of refrigerators; (4) high-temperature ham sausages in rural markets.
- More foreign investment can be foreseen in meat sector in China.

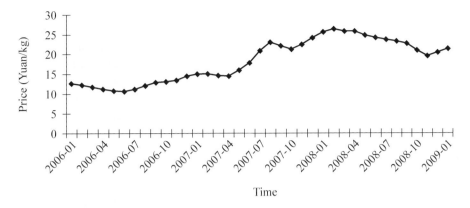

Figure 2.8. Change in pork prices from Jan. 2006 to Jan. 2009 (Feng, 2009).

2.5 Quality management and regulation

Food quality and safety is becoming increasingly important all over the world. This section will discuss the following points: legal systems and institutes involved in pork quality and safety management, quality management schemes, and factors affecting pork quality and safety in China.

Several studies have already shown that pork quality and safety is the main constraint for pork export from China (Dong and Hou, 2005). It has also become the main concern of Chinese consumers in purchasing pork products. A consumer survey carried out by Wu (2006) among 608 consumers in Sichuan province in the summer of 2005 clearly indicated both the importance of pork quality and safety for consumers and the source of their worries. About 77% of the respondents indicated 'greatly worried' or 'worried' about pork quality and safety while only 3.6% indicated 'not worried'. Table 2.11 shows the major factors affecting pork quality and safety according to the respondents.

Table 2.11. Factors influencing pork quality and safety (n=608) (Wu, 2006).

Factors (selecting the most important three)	Frequency	%
Water injection	351	19.3
Drug residue (e.g. antibiotics)	407	22.3
Heavy metal residues	278	15.2
Chemical pollution (e.g. Clenbuterol)	134	7.3
Biological pollution	407	22.3
Others	204	11.2
Total	1,824	100.0

2.5.1 Legal systems and regulations for pork quality and safety management

In China, the National People's Congress (NPC) – which is equivalent to the legislature in Western countries – is at the top of the pyramid of the legal system. The NPC is the institution that makes laws/acts. Under the NPC is the State Council, which has jurisdiction over individual ministries and commissions. The State Council makes regulations at the central level. Individual ministries introduce the related administrative measures. In addition to these central level legal institutions, there are corresponding institutions at local levels from provincial level down to city, county and township levels. The corresponding institutions at provincial/local levels have the same functions as the institutions at the central level. But basically the lower level institutions are mainly responsible for supervising and enforcing the laws and regulations introduced by the central and provincial legal institutions, rather than for enacting by-laws and sub-regulations themselves (Liu *et al.*, 2004).

Due to food safety incidents in recent years, the Chinese government has attached special attention to the establishment of legal systems and related administrative systems for food quality and safety. Table 2.12 shows the main laws/regulations issued with relevance to pork production, distribution and marketing.

Amongst these regulations, the law with relevance to animal welfare has quite a limited impact. According to some experts interviewed, awareness about animal welfare is not as strong in China as in developed countries. In China, we have the 'Law on Wild Animal Protection',

Table 2.12. Laws and regulations relevant to pork supply chains issued in the recent decade.

Laws/Regulations	Time launched	Issuing by	Enforced by
Quarantine Inspection Act on Plant-Animal Import and Export	June 4, 1982	State Council	AQSIQ
Food Hygiene Act	Oct. 30, 1995	NPC	MOH, AQSIQ
Pesticide Administration Regulation	May 8, 1997	State Council	MOA, SEPA, MOH and AQSIQ
Designated Hog Slaughtering Act	Dec. 29, 1997	State Council	MOA, MOC
The Action Plan for Pollution-free Agricultural Products (APPAP)	2001	State Council	MOA, SEPA
Veterinary Drug Management Regulation	2004	MOA	SEPA, MOA
Animal Husbandry Law	Dec. 29, 2005	NPC	
Law on Agri Product Quality and Safety	April 29, 2006	NPC	SEPA, AQSIQ, MOA

Source: searched and prepared by the author (http://www.gov.cn).
Note: The name of the various ministries is indicated under Figure 2.9.

the 'Law on Animal Quarantine' and the 'Animal Husbandry Law'. Only the latter has clear indications on animal welfare in its general clauses, regarding production, transaction and transportation. In transportation, measures should be taken to protect the safety and comfort of the animals, such as providing enough space and water. The international communication on animal welfare has also been strengthened in the last two years. For example, in 2005, the first international forum on animal welfare and meat safety was held in Beijing. According to the experts interviewed great improvements may be made in China as soon as things attract the attention of the central government.

To reinforce the effort to improve food safety and quality management and decentralise power, the central government assigned responsibilities to wide-ranging institutions to manage safety aspects of agri-food production, processing and marketing. Figure 2.9 shows the institutions directly involved in the administration of pork safety and quality. It also clearly indicates the overlapping functions between the administrative departments in managing pork safety and quality. In addition, each department is responsible for several stages of the chain. The State Food and Drug Administration (SFDA) was established in 2002 to coordinate and deal with food quality and safety problems on behalf of the nine departments. However, as it has a strong expertise in the area of drug administration, it cannot replace the other departments in fulfilling the functions of food safety monitoring and supervision. The power of administration still lies in the hands of the MOA, MOH and AQSIQ. Moreover, the SFDA hasn't been authorised by the Chinese government to operate with the right of law enforcement. The current responsibility of SFDA is only to deal with serious food safety scandals. This situation will be improved by June 1 2009, with a National Food Safety Committee established and with only MOH, AQSIQ, SAIC and SFDA involved in the administration network.

Since 1999, the Chinese government has invested €3 million every year for setting up or improving standards for agricultural products. In 2003, there were more than 1,000 national and sector standards with relevance to animal husbandry and veterinary medicines. Among them, there were 351 standards with direct relevance to livestock safety accounting for 34.8% of the total standards. The Chinese government has developed three types of quality standards, namely 'Pollution-free food', 'Green food' and 'Organic food'. Green food has two different levels: Green A and Green AA, with the later equal to Organic food standards (Lu, 2007). Among the three standards, the quality standards for Pollution Free Agricultural Products (PFAP) are compulsory for all agricultural production in China. It was launched by the MOA in 2001. In 2004, a total of 359 operators had their hogs or pork products certified with PFAP. In 2005, the number of certified operators was reduced to 145. As the certification of PFAP only started in 2003, it will take time for consumers to become aware of this quality standard. These operators were mainly located in south China, i.e. Sichuan province, Guangdong province, Tianjin municipality, Fujian province, Guangxi province and Hubei province.

The green food and organic food standards are voluntary standards. The formulation and certification of green food standard started in 1992. The Green Food Development Center

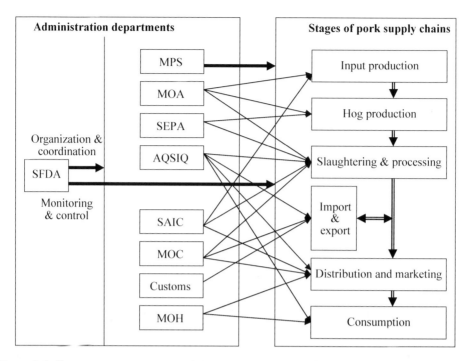

Figure 2.9. Government institutions and their administered stages of the pork chain (before June 1, 2009).

Note: SFDA refers to State Food and Drug Administration, www.sda.gov.cn; MPS refers to Ministry of Public Security (www.mps.gov.cn); MOA refers to Ministry of Agriculture (www.agri.gov.cn); SEPA refers to State Environmental Protection Administration (www.zhb.gov.cn); AQSIQ refers to the General Administration of Quality Supervision, Inspection and Quarantine (www.aqsiq.gov.cn); SAIC refers to State Administration for Industry and Commerce (www.saic.gov.cn); MOC refers to Ministry of Commerce (www.mofcom.gov.cn); Customs refers to the General Customs of China (www.customs. gov.cn); MOH refers to Ministry of Health (www.moh.gov.cn).

The thick arrows referring to the stages of pork supply chains mean that SFDA and MPS are coordinating quality and safety activities along the pork supply chains. In addition, the SFDA also plays a coordinating role among the nine government agencies responsible for food safety and quality management.

(GFDC) was responsible for this work on behalf of the MOA. The objective of the green food quality standard is to protect the ecological environment, upgrade agri-food quality and increase export of agricultural products (Lu, 2007). The development of green food industry has been very rapid since the early 1990s. In 2004, a total of 6496 products produced by 2836 companies obtained the right to use the Green Food label. With an annual turnover of more than $10 billion, the export value reached $1.25 billion. Statistics show that most of the certified green food products are from the primary plantation sector, accounting for 61.4%. Animal products accounted for 17.2%, fishery 4.1% and the other products 17.3%

(Wu, 2006). Up to 7 November 2005, the number of certified green food products reached 7117. Among them, there were only 48 certified pork products produced by 10 companies.

To promote the development of organic food, the Certification and Accreditation Administration of China (CAAC) was established in August 2001, assuming this responsibility from the State Environmental and Protection Agency (SEPA). Up to the end of 2004, there were a total of 588 certified organic food products produced by 148 companies. Among these products, export products accounted for 35%. Meanwhile, the CAAC certified 461 green AA products produced by 181 companies. Looking at the product category, livestock products only accounted for 5.27% (Wu, 2006).

A special note should be made with regard to the Q-S standard which refers to Quality Safety. As a standard for market accession, it was initiated at the end of 2002 in five food sectors, namely rice, edible plant oil, wheat powder, soy sauce and vinegar. Implementation of the Q-S standard has been compulsory in these sectors since 1 January 2004. The standard includes the following three important requirements:
- Production enterprises must obtain a business license (they must pass an audit on basic production conditions).
- Products must meet the requirements of relevant national standards and regulations and must be checked and approved before they are allowed to be sold in the market.
- Products must be labelled with 'Q-S'.

The accreditation process for the second batch of food products started at the end of 2003. Meat products were among the 10 categories of the second batch of food products, for which it has been compulsory to have Q-S standard certification since 1 July, 2005.

Compared with PFAP, Green and Organic products, Q-S products have the following similarities and differences:
- Similarities
  - They all hold 'food quality and safety' as objective.
  - Relevant requirements are levied on production environment, technological standards, quality standards, packaging, labelling, transportation and storage.
  - Certification by authentic organizations and use of labels.
- Differences
  - 'Q-S' standard is compulsory for products listed whilst the other three are voluntary.
  - PFAP focuses on primary edible agricultural products; Green food standard focuses more on processed agricultural products; Organic food standard focuses on both primary unprocessed and processed products while the Q-S standard focuses on a series of food products. For example, the Q-S standard for meat products includes five products: cured meats, smoked and roasted meats, sauced meats, smoked sausages and fermented meat products.

2.6 Selected areas for the empirical study

Jiangsu province, Shandong province and Shanghai municipality, located in the east of China (Figure 2.10), constitute an economically well-developed area in China. Jiangsu province and Shandong province have a long hog production history. They have been amongst the 10 top hog production provinces for several decades. Table 2.13 indicates the pork output of the three areas and their percentages among the total pork output in China.

Table 2.13 indicates that both Jiangsu province and Shandong province play a very important role in China's hog production. As a major consumption metropolitan, Shanghai's role in hog

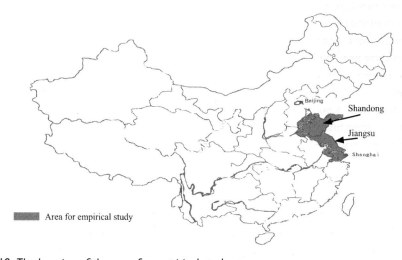

Figure 2.10. The location of the area for empirical study.

Table 2.13 Output of pork products in the surveyed area (10,000 tonnes) (China Statistical Yearbook, various issues).

Year	Total pork output in China	Jiangsu		Shandong		Shanghai	
		Output of pork	% of total pork	Output of pork	% of total pork	Output of pork	% of total pork
1995	3,648.4	195.9	5.4	267.7	7.3	23.9	0.7
2000	4,031.4	205.7	5.1	285.9	7.1	25.9	0.6
2004	4,701.6	219.8	4.7	461.0	9.8	5.8	0.1
2005	5,010.6	218.5	4.4	367.1	7.3	18.0	0.4
2006	5,197.2	218.7	4.2	380.7	7.3	16.3	0.3

production is very minor, accounting for less than 1% of the national pork output. Due to potential environmental problems related to hog production, procurement from other areas of China is greatly encouraged by the municipal government.

In terms of slaughtering and processing, the surveyed areas have more large pork processing firms than the other areas, especially in Shandong province. Among the 50 top meat processing firms, Shandong province had the most (China Meat Association, 2008). With 17 firms of the 50 top meat processing firms, the province has 13 firms focusing on pork slaughtering and processing. Among the important pork processors, Linyi Jinluo Meat Co. Ltd. deserves to be mentioned here. Established in 1994, the company is a conglomerate mainly engaged in meat production, with production bases in Shandong, Heilongjiang, Jilin, Inner Mongolian, Hunan, Sichuan and Henan provinces. It became a listed company firstly in Singapore in 2001 and then in Hong Kong one year later. The company has total assets of about €400 million and 30,000 employees. As the second largest meat processing company in China next to Shineway of Henan province, the company has an annual slaughtering capacity of 15 million pigs and 45 million chickens and an annual processing capacity of about 2 million tonnes of meat and meat products. The company's sales network covers the whole of China, comprising 42 sales offices, more than 3,300 franchise shops, and over 9,000 authorised dealers. The company has set up business branches or representative offices in Hong Kong, Singapore, and Japan for exporting meat products.

Jiangsu province has only 3 pork processors in the list of top 50 meat processing companies. Among the three, China Yurun Food Group Ltd. is one of the largest meat processing companies. Established in 1993, this company has developed into a large food complex, with pork processing as its core business. It was listed on the Stock Exchange of Hong Kong on October 3, 2005. At the end of 2007, the group company had more than 30 slaughterhouses and more than 20 processors scattering over 28 provinces, autonomous regions and cities of China. Among these 50 firms, the slaughtering and processing integrated ones accounted for 12. The annual number of pigs slaughtered by the company was 12 million. It has a processing capacity of 186,000 tonnes, producing more than 1,000 kinds of meat products. The company sold approximately 444,000 tonnes of chilled and frozen pork and 105,000 tonnes of processed meat products. Its pork products were exported to Russia, Southeast Asian countries and Hong Kong. The company has been recognised as a 'National Technology Center' and 'Enterprise with AAAA Standardised Good Practices'.

In terms of sales revenue, profit and total assets of the meat processing industry, Shandong province is well ahead of the other provinces and regions. While Jiangsu province ranks the fourth in sales revenue and profit, it is in the third place as regards total assets (Figures 2.11, 2.12 and 2.13).

Unlike the other two surveyed areas, Shanghai is a major consumer city with a population of 16 million. In the three areas of study, Shanghai households consume the most pork products.

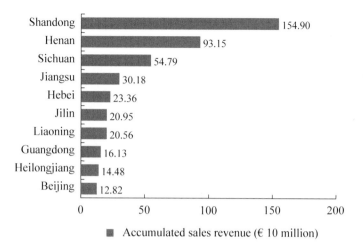

Figure 2.11. Ranking of major provinces in sales of pork products (Beijing Huajing Economic Consultancy Center, data of 2004 as baseline).

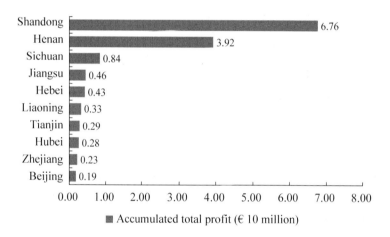

Figure 2.12. Ranking of major provinces in pork sector profits (Beijing Huajing Economic Consultancy Center, data of 2004 as baseline).

Per capita consumption of major meat products in the three regions are presented in Table 2.14. The annual consumption of pork in Shanghai reached about 550,000 tonnes, which is equivalent to 9 million hogs slaughtered. However, local hog supply is only about 6 million.

Three interesting examples of meat companies in Shanghai can be given. The first one is the joint venture between the Ng Fung Hong Limited and Shanghai Jinjiang International Trading Co. Ltd. With 51% of the investment, Ng Fung Hong Limited is the largest and leading supplier of fresh, live and frozen foodstuff in Hong Kong. With production technology that

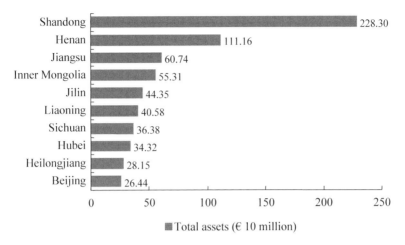

Figure 2.13. Total assets of meat processing firms in major provinces (Beijing Huajing Economic Consultancy Center, data of 2004 as baseline).

Table 2.14. Per capita consumption of major meat products in the surveyed areas in 2006 (kg)

Region	Urban (Pork, beef, veal, poultry and processed products)[1]	Compared with the national average (%)[2]	Rural (Pork, beef, veal, poultry and processed products)[1]	Compared with the national average (%)[2]
Shanghai	33.2	+3.4	35.9	+61.0
Jiangsu	34.1	+6.2	23.0	+3.1
Shandong	22.0	-31.5	14.8	-33.6
National average	32.1		22.3	

[1] China Statistical Yearbook, 2007.
[2] Calculated by the author.

matches the safety standards of the EU and the USA and is comparable to most advanced equipment in the EU, the company has an annual capacity to slaughter 3 million hogs and produce 15,000 tonnes of meat products. An integrated supply chain of hog production, slaughtering, processing and distribution is the aim of this company. In addition to this company, the traditional Chinese style meat producer Jiangsu Yurun Food Group Ltd. started their operations in Shanghai in March 2005. The Group will set up a marketing network of 500 shops in the form of franchises. In May 2006, Linyi Jinluo Meat Co. Ltd. in Shandong province started cooperation with the Shanghai Agri-food Wholesale Market. 'Jinluo' will be one of the most important meat brands in the Shanghai market.

2.7 Concluding remarks

In this chapter, the major stages of the pork supply chain in China have been described. Although its relative importance among the meat varieties is declining, pork is still one of the most important sectors in Chinese agriculture and a potentially attractive market for foreign investors. In addition to the description of characteristics and developments related to hog production, pork processing, marketing and consumption, special focus has been given to quality and safety management systems in China.

Although China enjoys a long history in hog production and pork will continue to be the dominant meat for Chinese consumers, a number of weaknesses are deemed very important for the stakeholders to tackle if the industry is expected to achieve sustainable development. For example, the fragmentation in major stages of the pork chain, especially in production and slaughtering stages, the mass product oriented production without a sound grading system, poor logistics management and traceability system. In addition, the technology contribution to the sector development is limited. However, the Chinese government is increasingly aware of the great importance of pork quality and safety. Greater investment is made into hog production and disease control. Large and medium-size companies are striving to develop integrated chain management in pork supply chains. In the remaining chapters of this study we will carry out more in-depth research into how to achieve better quality management and chain performance.

Chapter 3. The joint impact of supply chain integration and quality management on firm performance[16]

3.1 Introduction

Supply chain management (SCM) and total quality management (TQM) are two important tools that manufacturing companies use to achieve competitive advantage (Sila *et al.*, 2006). These two concepts are discussed extensively in both theoretical and empirical contexts. Since competition is no longer between individual firms, but between supply chains, the understanding and practising of SCM has become an essential prerequisite for staying competitive in the global competition and for enhancing profitability (Power *et al.*, 2001). The enhancement of organizational performance should be attained through closely integrating the internal functions within a company and effectively linking them with the external operations of suppliers, customers and other channel members (Kim, 2006).

Much like the recent emergence of SCM initiatives, the topic of quality management and the contribution of quality management practices (QMP) to firm performance have dominated most manufacturing and service organizations. Some recent efforts have been made in studying quality management at the chain level. For example, Van Plaggenhoef (2007) investigated the integration of quality management in poultry meat, fruit and vegetables and the potted plant chains. In this study, significant positive relations have been found between the integration of quality management systems and the performance of the three chains in the Netherlands. Han *et al.* (2007) studied the joint impact of supply chain integration on firm performance of pork processors in the upstream pork supply chain. However, the number of studies interlinking SCM and quality management are still limited (Robinson and Malhotra, 2005). In the struggle for marketplace advantage, businesses need to move from the traditional firm and product-based mindset to an inter-organizational supply chain orientation involving customers, suppliers and other partners (Robinson and Malhotra, 2005). Traditional quality programs focus on quality management schemes like TQM, HACCP, and ISO 9001 (international quality management system standards). Nowadays, more and more companies apply a SCM philosophy to achieve quality improvement gains critical to customer satisfaction. In addition to addressing the relationship between QMP and firm performance, and between SCM and firm performance, this study will also examine the interaction between integrated SCM and QMP.

---

[16] The joint impact of supply chain integration and quality management on the performance of pork processing firms between the dyadic relations of supplier and processors in China was published in International Food and Agribusiness Management Review Vol. 10 Issue 2, 2007, pp. 67-98. The paper was written by J. Han, S.W.F. (Onno) Omta and J. H. Trienekens. It won the Best Paper Award for the theme 'the application of a business theory to agri and food business management' in the 17th Annual World Food and Agribusiness Forum and Symposium held in June in Parma, Italy.

The study domain of this research is the pork processing industry in China. Since the government removed state procurement quotas and price control in 1985, fundamental changes have taken place in the pork sector. It has become the largest pork production and consumption country in the world since the early 1990s. China produced nearly 52 million tonnes of pork in 2006, accounting for half of the total pork production in the world (Deng, 2007). The Chinese people also consume about half of the total amount of pork products in the world. Although pork consumption has had the tendency to fall in the last two decades, it is still the most popular meat in China, accounting for about 64.6% of the major meat products in 2006 (China Statistics Yearbook, 2007). Based on current pork consumption at various income levels, it is estimated that pork consumption will grow more than 7% in Chinese cities and 1.5% in the countryside over the next ten years. This generates an additional consumption of 12 million pounds of pork by 2011 (Pan and Kinsey, 2002). With increasing incomes and changing life-styles generated by rapid economic and social development, the pork industry will be driven to emphasise safety, quality and convenience. However, the current pork industry is characterised by the dominant position of more than 80% of small household hog producers (USDA FAS China Gain Report, 2006) and a large number of small slaughterhouses. Traditional spot market transactions are still the most popular market channel that farmers use in selling their hogs (Zhou and Dai, 2005). The current organization of the pork processing industry induces potential quality and safety problems in tracking and tracing pork from 'field to table'.

In recent years, some leading meat processing companies like Shineway and Yurun Co. Ltd. have established closer vertical coordination mechanism with their suppliers and retailers and invested heavily in developing cold chains to provide consumers with brand products. Will this kind of inter-organizational supply chain orientation and quality management improve firm performance? Will the level of supply chain integration facilitate the implementation of quality management in these companies? Which supply chain integrations and QMP lead to the greater performance improvements? These are the main questions that this chapter will address in order to identify critical success factors for the competitiveness of pork processing firms in China. To the best of our knowledge, there has been limited empirical research on this issue in the pork processing sector in China. This paper attempts to shed more light on the relationship between supply chain integration, QMP and firm performance in pork SCM in China. As companies may have many suppliers and customers, we only focus on the relations between the focal firms (pork slaughterhouses and processors in our study) and their most important upstream suppliers and downstream customers. Therefore two models have been developed and tested using empirical data collected in the focal firms.

In Section 3.2 we present the literature review on SCM, QMP and firm performance and describe a theoretical model that relates these constructs. Thereafter, the three constructs and the hypotheses are discussed. In Section 3.3 we present the instrument development and a description of the study sample. The methods to assess construct validity and reliability are also discussed in this part. Once an acceptable measurement model is obtained, the hypothesised structural model will be tested using structural equation modelling (SEM) techniques in Section 3.4. In Section 3.5 our findings in the pork processing industry will be evaluated in the light of earlier studies, and the conclusions will be drawn. Finally, in Section 3.6, suggestions for further research and the implications for pork SCM are presented.

3.2 Theory and research hypotheses

This part will present theory on SCM and quality management. The presentation will include the literature review on the relationships among supply chain integration (SCI), QMP and firm performance. Hypotheses will be developed on the basis of theoretical background. We propose the following research framework (Figure 3.1) for our subsequent discussions.

3.2.1 Supply chain integration and firm performance

Supply chain management (SCM) was first used in the logistics literature as an inventory management approach in the 1980s (Van der Vorst, 2000; Trienekens and Beulens, 2001). During that time suppliers started experimenting with strategic partnerships with their most important suppliers (Tan, 2001). Since then, it has received a lot of attention by managers and academics. Research shows that the most successful supply chains are those which have integrated their internal processes with their suppliers and buyers (Frohlich and Westbrook, 2001).

Integration in a supply chain context is defined as a process of integration and collaboration in which companies in the supply chain work together in a cooperative manner to arrive at mutually acceptable outcomes (Pagell, 2004). Most supply chain literature considers supply chain integration as the collaborative effort in linking functions and supply chain networks in terms of process, information and physical flow (Frohlich and Westbrook, 2001).

Coordination is the central lever of SCM (Ballou *et al.*, 2000). Supply chains are complex with many activities spread over multiple functions or organizations. A better collaborative supply chain helps two or more independent companies work jointly to plan and execute

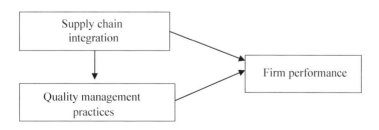

Figure 3.1. Research framework.

supply chain operations with greater success than when acting in isolation (Simatupang and Sridharan, 2002). Stank *et al.* (1999) studied inter-firm coordination processes characterised by effective communication, information exchange, partnering and performance monitoring. The movement towards long-term cooperation and partnering is based on the premise that a co-operative philosophy leading to more integration of processes and systems with firms in the supply chain creates greater network-wide efficiencies (Lambert and Cooper, 2000).

Global competition demands for a linkage among suppliers, internal processes, and customers to facilitate information flow and inbound and outbound flow of goods/services. Due to the complexity of buyer-supplier relationships, information sharing within business units and with suppliers and other strategic alliances is essential. This information sharing can be accomplished by the continuous automation and standardization of each internal logistics function. Porter and Miller (1985) asserted that the utilization of information technology has a significant influence on the relationships among value chain activities as well as the physical aspects of individual value chain activities. Information technology helps to create and maintain the competitiveness of a company. The extent to which information is shared can create opportunities for firms to work collaboratively to remove supply chain inefficiencies, and thus has a significant direct impact on the relationship between buyer and the supplier (Hsu *et al.*, 2008). Therefore the integration of information technology and logistics are the other two perspectives in SCI.

Integration has been studied at two different levels of analysis. External integration examines integration that occurs between organizations. Much of the buyer-supplier literature falls into this category (Pagell, 2004). Internal integration examines integration across various parts of a single organization. By summarizing relevant literature on SCI and in order to consider all different types of integration, this research has included the following dimensions of SCI: internal integration, external integration, supplier-buyer relationship coordination, integrated information technology and integrated logistics management.

Despite the SCI advancing closer working and some documented cases of success, in most industries it has proved extremely difficult to achieve genuine integration between firms operating in the chain. Fawcett and Magnan (2002) have illustrated that even in the US market where supply chain techniques are more widely understood, the extent of integration between firms is limited. Furthermore, the SCI level of Chinese firms has been lagging behind compared with the Western firms (Chen and Luo, 2003). Su *et al.* (2008) examine the status of SCM in 206 companies (manufacturing industry, logistics industry and others) and find that Chinese firms have already recognised the strategic importance of the SCM, but they have not paid enough attention to the logistics performance and the applications of information technology. SCM level in the logistics industry is significantly behind that of manufacturing and other industries.

Nevertheless, SCI should engender superior performance (e.g. Tan *et al.*, 1998; Frohlich and Westbrook, 2001). Vickery *et al.* (2003) also mentioned a growing body of literature that has suggested a positive relationship between the degree of integration across the supply chain and firm performance (e.g. Stevens, 1989, Lee *et al.*, 1997; Frohlich and Westbrook, 2001). Wood (1997) also indicated that integration of the supply chain could improve both profit potential and competitive position. Shen (2005) did a very comprehensive investigation into the factors that are critical to the success of future supply chains. Among them, SCI is one of the factors showing the most obvious link to firm performance, with the strongest link to financial and operational metrics. Based on these empirical findings, we thus hypothesise the following relationship:

> *H1: There is a positive relationship between SCI and performance of pork processing firms in China.*

3.2.2 Quality management practices and firm performance

Great interest has been aroused in the academic circle and business world to investigate the adoption and implementation of total quality management (TQM) approaches over the last decades (Soltani, 2005). Quality gurus have identified key process improvement practices that affect quality, including top management support and quality policy, employee training, employee relations, product and process design management, supplier quality management, management of processes and operating procedures, the role of the quality department, and the collection and usage of data on quality shortfalls (Saraph *et al.*, 1989). Recent research on TQM has examined the relationships between the practices of quality management and various levels of organizational performance (Kaynak, 2003). For example, Saraph *et al.* (1989) reported that eight critical factors could be used for quality management assessment, namely the role of the quality department, training, quality design, supplier quality management, process management, quality data and reporting, and employee involvement. Madu *et al.* (1995) studied QMP in Taiwan's manufacturing firms. They found a significant causal relationship between quality dimensions (i.e. customer satisfaction, employment satisfaction, and employee service quality) and organizational performances. In their research on QMP in the largest US firms, Mohrman *et al.* (1995) found that 83% of the surveyed companies had a 'positive or very positive' experience with quality management, and 79% planned to 'increase or greatly increase' quality management initiatives in their companies in the next 3 years. Most of the studies have supported the hypothesis that QMP is related to performance improvement, e.g. productivity, quality of products, customer service, profitability and competitiveness. A comprehensive summary of studies on the relationship between quality management and firms' performance can be found in Kaynak (2003). However, some studies also produced sobering results. D. Little survey of 500 executives in US manufacturing and service firms indicated that only one-third believe that quality management made them more competitive (Mathews and Katel, 1992). Dooyoung *et al.* (1998) also reported estimates of quality management failure rates as high as 60-67%. These mixed findings put forward the necessity to study the QMP-performance link in companies of various sizes and in different countries. In addition to this, the necessity to study the link is due to the shift of the quality-based paradigm from the traditional company-centered setting to complete supply chain systems (Kuei and Madu, 2001). Robinson and Malhotra (2005) find that much attention has been paid to SCM and quality management separately, but that the combination of these concepts in research has been rare. They conclude that quality management should further develop from traditional firm-centered and product-based approaches to inter-organizational supply chain approaches in which all customers and suppliers are involved. The successful evolution of this mindset in business operation enables organizations to meet the demand for superior products and services.

The importance of quality management and its associated benefits, such as improvements in customer satisfaction and firm performance, have been well acknowledged (e.g. Hendricks and Singhal, 1997). The objective of quality management efforts should be focused on achieving customer satisfaction. Performance outcomes are driven by quality management practices (QMP), which in turn lead to customer satisfaction (Choi and Eboch, 1998). To identify the impact of QMP on firm performance, we thus propose:

> H2: There is a positive relationship between QMP and performance of pork processing firms in China.

Before we develop steps for hypothesis testing, it is important to clarify the concept of 'quality management' since many definitions of 'quality' and frameworks of TQM have been proposed in the literature, but a consensus definition does not exist (e.g. Ahire et al., 1996; Flynn et al., 1995; Rungtusanatham et al., 2005). Within the important dimensions of QM, we employ a process definition, emphasizing inputs (management practices) rather than output (quality performance) in our analysis. Therefore, QM is defined as an approach to achieving and sustaining high quality output (Flynn et al., 1994). By summarizing the literature review and in accordance with the suggestions of the managers in the pilot studies in the pork processing companies, we will use the following dimensions to measure quality management practices: management leadership, supplier/customer quality management, quality design and process management. Further introduction of the operationalisation will be presented in construct measures in 3.3.1.

3.2.3 Supply chain integration and quality management practices

Organizations world-wide recognise the need to improve product quality to succeed in the competitive international market place. They also realise that the involvement of suppliers and customers is critical to improve quality and to meet customer specifications (Wong et al., 1999). Therefore it is imperative to study the dynamics of quality management in a supply chain context (e.g. Ellram, 1991; Bamford, 1994).

The integration of the supply chain in the meat industry is particularly important since the outbreaks of animal diseases such as Foot and Mouth disease and BSE. Previous research (Fearne, 1998, 2000; Palmer, 1996) has highlighted the importance of greater vertical coordination within meat supply chains in order to reduce risk and uncertainty, improve quality and foster value creation (Taylor, 2006). However, the industry is dogged by adversarial relationships and a commodity culture that makes it hard for companies to reach a position of sustainable profitability (Simons et al., 2003). In various meat sector studies, a stress on the relationship between close chain coordination and product quality has also been noticed. For example, Klein et al. (1996) asserted that one of the two primary steps that were regarded as essential to ensure better Canadian pork quality was excellent communication and teamwork among all sector participants through the formation of strategic alliances or vertical integration. In the study of Hobbs et al. (1998), a coordinated approach to production, processing and marketing was regarded as the driving force behind the fact that the Danish pork industry remains one of the most successful industries in the world. This approach was built on a thorough understanding of the requirements of different markets, a dedication to quality which includes the ability to provide a consistent and reliable supply of high quality products tailored to the needs of different markets. Co-operation between players at different stages of the supply chain enables information to be disseminated effectively and efficiently throughout the supply chain. In a study of 38 UK firms, Armistead and Mapes (1993) indicate that the level of SCI improves quality and operating performance. Thus, we formulate the following hypothesis:

> H3: The level of SCI is positively related to quality management practices in pork processing firms in China.

3.2.4 Firm performance indicators

In literature much attention has been devoted to three main aspects of performance: financial, organizational and strategic performance. Organizational theory offers three approaches to measure organizational effectiveness or performance (Murphy, Trailer and Hill, 1996), namely the goal-based, systems and multiple constituency approach. After comparing different measures of performance, they suggest that multiple dimensions of performance should be considered where possible, including both financial and non-financial measures. Accounting-based indicators, efficiency, sales growth rate and profitability (e.g. return on sales or investments) are the financial indicators most commonly used (Murphy, Trailer and Hill, 1996). In addition, operational (non-financial) performance measures, such as product quality, customer satisfaction and market shares are often examined. Our research uses both financial and non-financial indicators to measure performance. The indicators we use to measure performance of pork processing firms are: growth rate, market share, profitability and perceived customer satisfaction. The operationalisation of these indicators is shown in Table 3.1.

Table 3.1. Operationalisation of constructs, source and measures (detailed questions are presented in

Constructs	Operational definition
Supply chain integration (second order construct)	
Internal integration	Horizontally aligning operations across processes within the focal firms, e.g. good integration of purchasing, production and distribution activities of the focal firms.
External integration	Linking external processes to external suppliers and customers through involving them in the development of strategic plans and production processes.
Supplier-buyer relationship coordination	A mutual ongoing relationship between the focal firms and their suppliers and customers that involves a high level of trust, commitment over time, long-term cooperation, joint conflict resolution, and sharing of risks and rewards.
Integrated information technology	Integrating information technologies (such as computerised production systems, electronic data interchange) to facilitate the collection of vital information concerning key business processes and the sharing of such information across functional areas and across firm boundaries.
Integrated logistics management	Increased logistics-related communication, greater coordination of the focal firms' logistics activities within the firms and those of their suppliers and customers.
Quality management practices (second order construct)	
Management leadership	The involvement in and constant commitment of the company management in all its functions to quality improvement.
Supplier/customer quality management	The involvement of key suppliers and customers in quality planning and improvement process, e.g. selection of key suppliers/customers on the basis of quality and evaluation.
Quality design	Designing manufacturable products and designing quality into the products by including customers' requirements in new product/service design review prior to production.
Process management	Tools are used to ensure the machinery and the various production processes are under control and meet quality specifications.
Firm performance	
Sales growth	The extent to which the sales of the firm grow slower or faster when compared to its main competitors in last three years.
Market share	The extent to which the market coverage of the firm's pork products grows faster or slower compared to its main competitors in last three years.
Profitability	The extent to which the profit of the firm grows faster or slower compared to its main competitors in last three years.
Perceived customer satisfaction	The degree to which a firm's customers continuously perceive that the firm's quality needs are being met by the firm's products and/or services.

Appendix A).

Source	Measures
Vickery *et al.* (2003), Frohlick and Westbrook (2001), Narasimhan and Kim (2002)	Integ1-3
Vickery *et al.* (2003), Frohlick and Westbrook (2001), Rosenzweg *et al.* (2003)	Exintup1-4; Exintds1-4
Vickery *et al.* (2003), Carr and Pearson (1999), Clark (1989), Han *et al.*(1993)	Coordup1-4; Coordds1-4
Vickery *et al.* (2003), Frohlick and Westbrook (2001), Chen and Paulraj (2004)	Infoup; Infods1-3
Chen and Paulraj (2004), Frohlick and Westbrook (2001), Vickery *et al.* (2003), Stock *et al.* (2000)	Logis1; Logisup 1-2; Logisds1-2
Forza and Filippini (1998), Saraph *et al.* (1989), Ahire *et al.* (1996), Garvin (1986), Kaynak (2003)	QMP1-8
Forza and Filippini (1998), Tracey and Tan (2001), Ahire *et al.* (1996), Chen and Paulraj (2004), Kaynak (2003)	SQM1-4; CQM1-3
Saraph *et al.* (1989), Ahire *et al.* (1996), Forker *et al.* (1996), Flynn *et al.* (1995), Forza and Filippini (1998), Kaynak (2003)	Design1-2
Flynn *et al.* (1994), Forza and Filippini (1998), Kaynak (2003)	PM1-3
Tan *et al.* (1998), Tracey and Tan (2001), Narasimhan and Kim (2002), Claro (2004)	FP1
Frohlick and Westbrook (2001), Vickery *et al.* (1999), Tracey and Tan (2001)	FP2
Kaynak (2002), Narasimhan and Kim (2002), Claro (2004)	FP3
Frohlick and Westbrook (2001), Tracey and Tan (2001), Chen and Paulraj (2004), Rungtusanatham *et al.* (2005)	FP4

3.3 Research methodology

Supply chain integration and quality management initiatives and their relationships form the core of this research. The focus of the research is on the pork slaughtering and processing firms[17] and their most important suppliers and customers. The approach of surveying the firms' top purchasing and supply management executives to study buyer-supplier relationships has been widely practised in the field of operations management (Carr and Pearson, 1999, Shin *et al.*, 2000). Therefore this survey methodology was employed to set up the quantitative part of empirical research and to collect data to test the hypotheses developed in this research. Structural equation Modelling (SEM) was used to test the measurement model and the structural model of this research. SEM is one of the most applied and consolidated means of testing relations and causality in the field of buyer-supplier relationships (Malhorta *et al.*, 1999). The advantage of SEM over standard regression analysis (i.e. OLS) is its explicit consideration of the measurement error in the indicators and simultaneously estimation of a system of structural equations.

Moreover, SEM is a powerful method for testing causal models, because it enables the simultaneous evaluation of the individual paths constituting the model, total effects and the complete model's goodness-of-fit (Hair *et al.* 1998). In the next part, we will describe the process of scale development and determination of the validity and reliability of the research constructs. Afterwards, the results of measurement model and structural model will be described.

3.3.1 Construct measures

Figure 3.2 illustrates the analytical steps for scale development which incorporates aspects of both theoretical and statistical modelling to achieve construct validity and reliability as well as hypotheses testing. This framework is an amalgamation of similar frameworks of Segars (1997), Chen and Paulraj (2004), and Lu *et al.* (2007). A valid and reliable construct is very critical for research. Multiple scale items for each of the factors in the constructs are developed. As noted by Churchill (1979), many variables of interest are inherently complex in nature; therefore, they cannot be accurately measured with a single scale. Single measures typically contain considerable uniqueness and subsequently low correlation with the attribute being measured.

Additionally, single items tend to frame concepts narrowly resulting in considerable measurement error. Multiple measures can overcome these difficulties. The specificity of individual items can be averaged out and more robust conceptualizations of complex variables can be developed thereby reducing measurement error (Segars, 1997). The scale development for the construct SCI was adapted from Chen and Paulraj (2004), Claro (2004), Vickery

---

[17] Pork slaughtering and processing firms will be referred to as focal firms in the study.

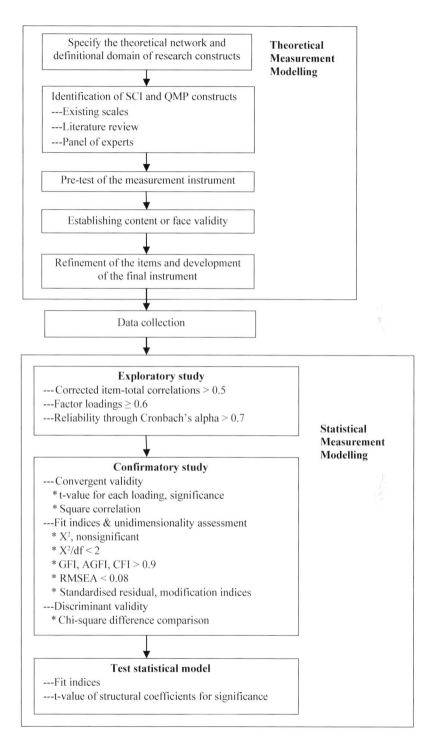

Figure 3.2. An analytical paradigm for construct development and data analysis (adapted from Segars, 1997; Chen and Paulraj, 2004; Lu et al., 2007).

et al. (2003), Narasimhan and Kim (2002), Frohlick and Westbrook (2001) and Carr and Pearson (1999). It has five sub-constructs: internal integration, external integration, supplier-buyer relationship coordination, integrated information technology and integrated logistics management. Items on QMP were mainly derived from Saraph *et al.* (1989), Garvin (1986), Flynn *et al.* (1994), Ahire *et al.*, (1996) and Kaynak (2003). We initially identified four sub-measurements to measure QMP: management leadership, supplier/customer quality management, quality design and process management. Items on firm performance were mainly from Tan *et al.* (1998), Tracey and Tan (2001), Vickery *et al.* (1999), Frohlick and Westbrook (2001) and Claro (2004). Based on their studies and through interviews with practitioners, the items for the sub-measurements of the constructs were developed. Where appropriate, additional items were created to cover the domain of the constructs. As our analysis deals with how the focal firms work with their most important suppliers and customers in supply chain integration and quality management, we develop two models to test the hypotheses using the empirical data collected. The upstream model tests the relationships between the focal firms and their most important suppliers in application of SCI and QMP and their impact on firm performance. The downstream model tests the relationships between the focal firms and their most important customers in the application of SCI and QMP and their impact on firm performance. The company specific questions are used for both upstream and downstream modes. We initially developed four company specific questions for sub-dimensions of SCI constructs and 14 for dimensions of QMP construct. In addition, another 19 item questions were generated to measure the dimensions of the upstream pork SCI and QMP constructs and 20 for the downstream two constructs. Firm performance was measured by 4 items. A seven-point Likert scale was used where 1=not agree at all, 4=neutral and 7=totally agree. The scale was evaluated by practitioners and academicians in a formal pre-test study in order to establish both content and construct validity. These were general managers from meat processing industries and professors from economics and management, food science and technology at Nanjing Agricultural University in China. In addition, the scales were pilot tested in 10 pork processing companies through structured interviews. Based on suggestions by the managers and academics, items were added, changed, or deleted to form a revised instrument which contained 32 items for dimensions of the upstream SCI and QMP constructs and 33 items for downstream model. The 4 performance indicators were kept. The operational concepts, their sources and the measures used are listed in Table 3.1. Appendix A presents the items used in the questionnaire.

As SCI and QMP are second order reflective constructs[18], their dimensions were computed as the observed variables for subsequent SEM analysis, which means that we use computation of the scores derived from the multiple-item scales by unweighted average (Hair *et al.*, 1998). There are three reasons for equally weighting the items instead of using another method (e.g. with factor score as weighted). Firstly, we have no theoretical argumentation why one item should be weighted more heavily than another. In formulating the items, we expected them to measure the construct to the same degree. Secondly, factor analysis is used to check the convergence of the measurement scale, not to determine the scale. Thirdly, a weight based on a factor score is as arbitrary as any other kind of weight, and thus an unweighted average is the least arbitrary in giving them more importance over the others. Moreover, there might be sampling variation in the factor analysis, which could result in considerable changes in the weights if the analyses were to be repeated on another random sample (Claro, 2004).

3.3.2 Data collection

During the pre-test period, it turned out that it was difficult to get questionnaires back from the meat processing companies by post. The companies in China are still not used to answering mail questionnaires. Therefore the survey was carried out by students from Nanjing Agricultural University majoring in marketing, management and animal sciences, during the winter and summer vacations in 2005. As China is a big country, our research only focused on the pork slaughtering and processing companies in the eastern two provinces (Jiangsu province and Shandong province) and one direct jurisdiction district of the central government of China (Shanghai). Four training sessions were organised for the students who were willing to do the survey. Each lasted for two hours. The students were divided into small groups to improve the effectiveness of the training. A written guideline on how to do the survey was distributed to the students. After explaining the research background and the questions to be asked, students were asked to work in pairs to practice the roles as respondent and interviewer.

A stratified sampling technique was deemed appropriate to collect the data after consultation with experts and professionals in the pretest. They provided valuable information on the distribution of the focal firms in the sampling areas. Cities include pork slaughtering and processing companies of various sizes, in the villages small scale slaughterhouses prevail. Eighty-eight cities were selected. A list of pork slaughtering and processing firms was provided by the meat associations of Jiangsu and Shandong provinces. As the members of the meat association are usually large and medium-size companies, students were also asked to pay attention to

---

[18] Indicators or items (i.e. observed variables) composing a scale that underlines a construct (i.e. operationalized concept) can generally be distinguished as reflective or formative (Diamantopoulos and Winklhofer, 2001). Reflective (effect) indicator constructs depend on the latent variable. The latent variable is the operationlization of a construct in structural equation modelling. A latent variable cannot be measured directly but can be computed by one or more indicators. The reflective indicator models assume that a latent variable is the common cause of its indicators. They are interchangeable, which means that the removal of one item does not change the essential nature of the underlying construct. This is quite different from formative indicators (Claro, 2004).

the small firms in the sector. The list of pork slaughterhouses, including small companies, could be obtained from the Designated Pork Slaughtering Administration Office in each city. Students were taught to use the method of systematic sampling techniques for selection of slaughterhouses. To minimise response bias, we targeted the top management team as the informant within each focal firm in terms of acquaintance with buyer-supplier relationships and quality management. They could be general (deputy-general) managers and managers of quality departments. Two rounds of telephone contacts were conducted during the surveys in order to trace the progress of the survey and answer the questions of the students. The first two rounds produced 202 questionnaires. Among these, twenty were not completed by the companies and therefore were useless. In the second round, another 56 questionnaires were returned. Among these, nine were useless. Therefore, the sample base for the empirical research was 229 questionnaires, 102 for Jiangsu province, 112 for Shandong province and 15 for Shanghai municipality.

A comparison of the early and the late respondents was carried out to test for the non-response bias (Armstrong and Overton, 1977). T-tests were performed on the responses of the early and late respondents. At the 5% confidence level, there were no significant differences between the responses of these groups. This suggests that non-response was not a major problem in our sample.

The profiles of the respondents and their company characteristics are displayed in Table 3.2. The results show that 40.6% of the participants in the survey were general and deputy general managers, indicating a good quality of the respondents, who should have a clear understanding of what practices their firms use with regard to their relationships with their most important suppliers and customers. As for the status of the organizations, private industry is developing very fast in China. Our survey also proved this, with 65.5% of the firms being privately owned or private share-holding companies. The survey on the business scope of the firms showed that 41% of the firms were slaughterhouses and 32.2% were integrated slaughtering and processing companies. Processors only accounted for 26.4% of the sample. The respondents were also asked to provide information on the number of employees and the level of turnover which indicate the scales of these companies. The results in Table 3.2 indicate that 40.6% of the companies had 101 to 500 employees. In China, the company is called a 'scale-company' if its annual turnover is more than RMB 5 million Yuan (approximately € 500,000). The number of companies with a turnover ranging from more than € 500,000 to € 30 million was 71.6%. In our sample, 7.9% of the companies had a yearly turnover of more than €30 million.

3.3.3 Data analysis

Based on studies by Koufteros (1999), the following section will discuss statistical analysis used to determine the validity and reliability of each construct. The methods employed for the development of exploratory evaluation of the measurement scales for the two latent variables of SCI and QMP in this study is shown in Appendix C1 (the upstream model) and Appendix

Table 3.2. Profile of the respondent companies (n=229).

Characteristics of the respondents	Number	Percentage
Job title (n=229)		
General or deputy general managers	93	40.6
Quality control managers	49	21.4
Sales managers	39	17.0
Head of the office and others	48	21.0
Organizational status (n=229)		
State-owned	32	14.0
Collective	31	13.5
Private	70	30.6
Joint venture	16	7.0
Private and share holding	80	34.9
Main business (n=227)		
Slaughterhouses	94	41.4
Further processing	60	26.4
Slaughtering/processing	73	32.2
Employees (n=229)		
Below 50	48	21.0
51-100	48	21.0
101-500	93	40.6
More than 500	40	17.4
Level of turnover (€ 1000) (n=229)		
Below 500	47	20.5
501-3,000	82	35.8
3,001-30,000	82	35.8
Greater than 30,000	18	7.9

C2 (the downstream model). They included corrected item-total correlations, exploratory factor analysis and reliability estimation using Cronbach's alpha. The description of these methods will be given in combination with the data analysis of this research.

Exploratory factor analysis

As our constructs SCI and QMP were based on previous research to enhance validity, we first conducted a principal component analysis with oblique rotation for these constructs to see whether the items fell under the defined constructs. The results for the upstream model and downstream model are explained separately. With regard to the upstream model, the exploratory factor analysis for SCI construct turned out to be four factors for SCI integration with integrated information technology and integrated logistics management into one factor. By looking at the questions, we found an interrelationship between these two sub-measurements. The result for QMP was also different. There were five factors instead of the originally defined four factors. It was more appropriate to rename the first dimension as 'in-company quality management' (coded as QMP1, QMP6 and QMP8) and the new factor into 'employee involvement in quality management' (coded as QMP3, QMP4, QMP5 and PM2). When looking carefully at the measurement items, these four items actually reflected the contents of this new factor. It reconfirms the validity and reliability of previous studies on this dimension in QMP construct (e.g. Saraph *et al.*, 1989; Kaynak, 2003). The remaining items in the three scales loaded on their factors, with QMP2 and QMP7 adding to the factor 'quality design'. With regard to the downstream model, Integ1 and Integ2 were suppressed due to lower factor loadings than 0.4. All the other items loaded on the five factors of SCI construct, indicating sound construct validity. For QMP construct, the exploratory factor analysis turned out to be the same as the upstream model with only three items for *customer quality management* replacing the four dimensions of *supplier quality management*. The results of the factor analysis for the two models are presented in Appendix C1 and C2. We then checked the item-total correlation which refers to a correlation of an item or indicator with the composite score of all the items forming the same set (Koufteros, 1999). The results of the analysis for the scales of SCI and QMP are also shown in Appendix C1 and C2. Each scale was purified by eliminating items if their corrected item-total correlation was less than 0.50 (Koufteros, 1999; Lu *et al.*, 2007). As a result, Coordup4, QMP2, QMP4, SQM3 were deleted from the upstream model while Exintds1, Coordds4, QMP2 and QMP4 were deleted from the downstream model.

In the next step, we did another exploratory factor analysis to assess the dimensionality of the remaining items using principal component analysis with oblique rotation. A factor loading can be used as an indicator in interpreting the role each item plays in defining each factor. Factor loadings are in essence the correlation of each item to their underlying construct (Lu *et al.* 2007). Absolute values less than 0.40 are suppressed in exploratory factor analysis. Items that are not pure (e.g. items with cross loadings) are eliminated and it is desired that the factor loading is above 0.6 (Hair *et al.*, 1998). We didn't find any cross-loading factors. However, the factor loading of Exintup4 was below 0.60, and was subsequently eliminated. The percentage of variance explained by the factors for SCI and QMP constructs of the upstream model accounted for 69.4% and 65.7% respectively. For the downstream model, the explained variances for SCI and QMP constructs were 71.8% and 71.74% respectively. This may indicate that our two constructs have a good unidimensionality for both models.

Cronbach's alpha has several disadvantages, including the fact that it is inflated when a scale has a large number of items, and it assumes that all of the measured items have equal reliability (Gerbing and Anderson, 1988). Despite these shortcomings, it is still one of the most widely used measures for evaluating reliability (Hair *et al.*, 1998; Koufteros, 1999). Appendix C1 and Appendix C2 show the Cronbach's alpha value for each factor of the upstream model and the downstream model respectively. Except for the factor 'buyer-supplier relationship coordination' for the upstream model which has a reliability value of 0.658, the reliability value for all the other factors was above 0.70, which is considered satisfactory (Hair *et al.*, 1998).

According to Gerbing and Anderson (1988) and Segars and Grover (1993), exploratory factor analysis does not provide an explicit test of unidimensionality as each factor from an exploratory analysis is defined as a weighted sum of all observed variables in the analysis. In addition, O'Leary-Kelly and Vokurka (1998) point out that exploratory factor models do not provide any explicit test statistic for assessing convergent and discriminant validity. Therefore, we will discuss in the next part the assessment of unidimensionality and other properties related to construct validity and reliability through confirmatory factor analysis (CFA).

Results for the measurement model

CFA involves the specification and estimation of one or more hypothesised models of factor structure, each of which proposes a set of latent variables (factors) to account for covariances among a set of observed variables (Koufteros, 1999). The path diagram for the SCM construct with four latent variables of the upstream model is presented in Figure 3.3. A similar path diagram can be drawn for the QMP construct. To save space, this is not illustrated here.

According to the convention of AMOS analysis (Arbuckle, 1997), observed variables are represented by squares and latent variables by circles and labelled with the Greek letter ξ. The Greek letter δ is seen as error in manifest or observed variables. A straight arrow pointing from a latent variable to an observed variable indicates the causal effect of the latent variable on the observed variable (Lu *et al.*, 2007). It is worth mentioning that on the estimation of the measurement model of constructs with more than one item (actually preferable in structural equation modelling), one of the loadings in each construct can be set to a fixed value of 1.0 in order to make the constructs comparable (Jöreskog and Sörbom, 1996).

Convergent validity and item reliability

Convergent validity measures the similarity or convergence between the individual items measuring the same construct. It can be assessed by using EFA and CFA. In the exploratory factor analysis both constructs have achieved convergent validity. In CFA, convergent validity can be assessed by examining the loadings and their statistical significance through t-values (Dunn *et al.*, 1994). In the AMOS text output file, the t-value is the critical ratio (C.R.), which represents the parameter estimates divided by its standard error. A t-value greater than 1.96 or smaller than -1.96 implies statistical significance (Byrne, 2001).

On the first-order level of measurement models, the proportion of variance (R^2) in the observed variables that is accounted for by the latent variables influencing them can be used to estimate the reliability of a particular observed variable (term). R^2 values above 0.50 provide

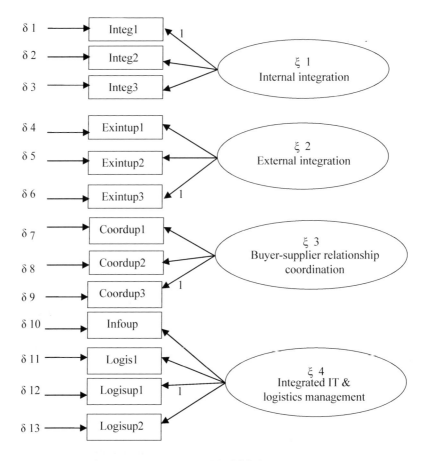

Figure 3.3. Path diagram of the measurement model of SCI for the upstream model.

evidence of acceptable reliability (Bollen, 1989). If any items exhibit R^2 less than this value, these can be dropped from the respective scale and parameter values can be re-estimated. Table 3.3 and Table 3.4 show the result of parameter estimates, error terms, t-values and R^2 for the two main constructs of the upstream and downstream model respectively. An examination of the results of the upstream model reveals that 4 items (i.e. Coordup1, Coordup2, Coordup3 and QMP5) of the upstream model did not meet the 0.50 criterion of the R^2. As previous studies considered R^2 above 0.30 acceptable (e.g. Carr and Pearson, 1999) and also due to the fact that most of the above-mentioned items reflected the coordination between the supplier and the buyers which was an important dimension in our study, they were kept for the forthcoming assessment of fit indices. The downstream model reveals that the scores of R^2 for the factor 'buyer-supplier relationship coordination' in SCI construct was not satisfactory. Due to its importance in the scales, they were kept for structural equation modelling. This analysis exhibited marginally acceptable R^2 and the critical ratios were all higher than 1.96, indicating a good convergent validity.

Table 3.3. Parameter estimates, error terms, t-values, and R^2 for the model (upstream model).

Latent variable	Item	Unstandardised factor loading	Standardised factor loading	Error term	t-values	R^2 (item reliability)
SCI Construct						
ξ1	Integ1	1.00	0.76			0.76
	Integ2	1.08	0.78	0.10	10.61	0.60
	Integ3	1.28	0.73	0.13	10.12	0.54
ξ2	Exintup1	1.11	0.58	0.14	7.86	0.51
	Exintup2	1.14	0.72	0.13	9.17	0.52
	Exintup3	1.00				0.75
ξ3	Coordup1	0.93	0.645	0.14	6.82	0.42
	Coordup2	0.81	0.692	0.12	6.99	0.48
	Coordup3	1.00	0.640			0.41
ξ4	Infoup	0.73	0.809	0.05	13.61	0.65
	Logis	0.90	0.809	0.07	13.61	0.66
	Logisup1	1.00	0.845			0.72
	Logisup2	0.71	0.66	0.07	10.43	0.50
QMP Construct						
ξ1	QMP1	1.00	0.70			0.78
	QMP6	1.43	0.89	0.11	12.73	0.78
	QMP8	1.11	0.87	0.09	12.44	0.80
ξ2	SQM1	1.46	0.86	0.14	11.15	0.68
	SQM2	0.91	0.64	0.10	8.80	0.57
	SQM4	1.00	0.69			0.53
ξ3	QMP3	1.17	0.82	0.14	8.60	0.58
	QMP5	1.00	0.72			0.36
	PM2	1.05	0.61	0.13	7.79	0.67
ξ4	QMP7	1.26	0.61	0.18	6.88	0.50
	Design1	1.67	0.82	0.22	7.49	0.51
	Design2	1.00	0.60			0.51
ξ5	PM1	1.13	0.88	0.09	12.85	0.51
	PM3	1.00	0.79			0.52

Fit indices for SCI construct: χ^2=105.148 (P=0.00), df=59, χ^2/df=1.782, GFI=0.936, AGFI=0.901, NFI=0.913, TLI=0.946, CFI=0.959, RMSEA=0.059.
Fit indices for QMP construct: χ^2=132.887 (P=0.00), df=66, χ^2/df=2.013, GFI=0.926, AGFI=0.882, NFI=0.924, TLI=0.944, CFI=0.96, RMSEA=0.067.

Table 3.4. Parameter estimates, error terms, t-values, and R^2 for the model (downstream model).

Latent Variable	Item	Unstandardised factor loading	Standardised factor loading	Error term	t-values	R^2 (item reliability)
SCI Construct						
ξ1	Integ3	1.00				
ξ2	Exintds2	1.00				0.69
	Exintds3	0.914	0.83	0.09	10.44	0.52
	Exintds4	0.70	0.62	0.08	8.98	0.38
ξ3	Coordds1	0.71	0.49	0.11	6.54	0.24
	Coordds2	1.00	0.95			0.91
	Coordds3	0.75	0.53	0.11	6.97	0.28
ξ4	Infods1	0.93	0.68	0.09	10.74	0.50
	Infods2	0.84	0.68	0.06	13.54	0.68
	Infods3	1.00	0.85			0.73
ξ5	Logis	0.95	0.80	0.09	10.47	0.60
	Logisds1	1.00	0.77			0.72
	Logisds2	0.74	0.69	0.08	9.48	0.50
QMP Construct						
ξ1	QMP1	0.71	0.72	0.05	13.08	0.52
	QMP6	1.00	0.90			0.80
	QMP8	0.78	0.87	0.04	18.22	0.76
ξ2	CQM1	0.70	0.73	0.06	11.38	0.53
	CQM2	1.00	0.86			0.74
	CQM3	0.97	0.82	0.08	8.88	0.66
ξ3	QMP3	1.00	0.81			0.66
	QMP5	0.86	0.72	0.10	8.90	0.52
	PM2	0.93	0.63	0.11	8.22	0.40
ξ4	QMP7	0.72	0.59	0.10	7.35	0.35
	Design1	100	0.83			0.68
	Design2	0.60	0.60	0.08	7.45	0.37
ξ5	PM1	1.00	0.90			0.80
	PM3	0.85	0.72	0.07	12.44	0.52

Fit indices for SCI construct: χ^2=142.039 (P=0.00), df=55, χ^2/df=2.583, GFI=0.915, AGFI=0.860, NFI=0.900, TLI=0.905, CFI=0.933, RMSEA=0.083.
Fit indices for QMP construct: χ^2=143.082 (P=0.00), df=66, χ^2/df=2.168, GFI=0.920, AGFI=0.872, NFI=0.912, TLI=0.931, CFI=0.950, RMSEA=0.072.

Assessment of the fit and unidimensionality

An evaluation of model fit, together with two diagnostics indicators modification indices, and standardised residuals will be used to assess unidimensionality. The overall fit of a hypothesised model can be tested by using the maximum likelihood χ^2 statistic provided in the AMOS output. This χ^2 is a function of both internal and external consistency. The p-value associated with this χ^2 is the probability of obtaining a χ^2 value larger than the value actually obtained under the hypothesis that the model specified is a true reflection of reality (Koufteros, 1999). As the significance levels of χ^2 are sensitive to sample size and departures from multivariate normality, this statistic must be interpreted with caution in most applications (Jöreskog and Sörbom, 1989; Byrne, 2001). Therefore, we also use other measures of model fit in assessing model adequacy (Jöreskog and Sörbom, 1989). Such indices include the ratio of χ^2 to degrees of freedom, the goodness-of-fit index (GFI) and adjusted goodness-of-fit index (AGFI), Bentler and Bonnet normed fit index (NFI), the Tucker-Lewis indices (TLI), comparative fit index (CFI) and the root mean square error of approximation (RMSEA). Researchers have recommended using X^2/df ratios of less than 5 to indicate a reasonable fit (Marsch and Hocevar, 1985). Most current research suggests the use of χ^2/df ratios less than 2 as indication of a good fit (Koufteros, 1999). The recommended value for RMSEA should be less than 0.05 as an indication of a good fit while values between 0.08-0.1 indicate a reasonable fit (Hair *et al.*, 1995). The result of our analysis in Table 3.3 and Table 3.4 with regard to constructs SCI and QMP of both models showed that all of our indices have met the criteria. Further analysis was made of the full measurement model of the two constructs together.

Overall, the measurement models for both upstream and downstream pork chain had a very satisfactory fit. The fitness for the upstream measurement model are as follows: χ^2=46.897 (with d.f.=26), χ^2/df=1.804, GFI=0.956, AGFI=0.925, NFI=0.951, TLI=0.969, CFI=0.977, RMSEA=0.059, while the downstream measurement model has the following fitness values: χ^2=70.386 (with d.f.=33), χ^2/df=2.133, GFI=0.940, AGFI=0.899, NFI=0.929, TLI=0.946, CFI=0.960, RMSEA=0.070.

Diagnostic indicators such as modification indices (MI) and standardised residuals can be used to assess the model fit. The MI are measures of the predicted decrease in the Chi-square value that results if a single parameter (fixed or constrained) is free (relaxed) and the model re-estimated, with all other parameters maintaining their present values (Jöreskog and Sörbom, 1996). Typically small modification indices (i.e. approximately 4.0, $P<0.05$) provide an insignificant improvement in model fit relative to the loss of one degree of freedom from estimating the additional parameter (Anderson, 1987). However, the judgment as to how small the MI should be is quite different in the book of Byrne (2001). Most of the values were well above the recommended 4.0 by Anderson (1987). A careful check of other fit indices should be made before deleting the large MI. The standardised residuals (normalised) represent the differences between the observed correlation/covariance and the estimated correlation/covariance matrix. Residuals with values larger than 2.58 in absolute terms are considered statistically significant at the 0.05 level (Hair *et al.*, 1998). Significant residuals indicate the presence of a substantial error for a pair of indicators. Our analysis with regard to MI and standardised residuals shows the following results: the MI for items of constructs SCI and QMP of the upstream model ranged from 4.04 to 12.98 and 4.25 to 11.67 respectively. The MI for items of the downstream SCI and QMP constructs ranged from 4.08 to 9.05 and 4.07 to 9.23 respectively. According to Byrne (2001), both models indicated a good fit and need not be re-estimated. The results also show that none of the standardised residual values exceeded 2.58 in absolute terms. Therefore, the check on the two diagnostic indicators MI and standardised residuals provides additional evidence of model fit and of no apparent misspecifications.

Discriminant validity

Discriminant validity measures the extent to which items referring to the same construct are distinguishable from each other. In this study, discriminant validity is established by using CFA. Models were constructed for all possible pairs of latent variables (constructs) and run on each selected pair, (1) allowing for correlation between the two constructs, and (2) fixing the correlation between the two constructs at 1.0. A significant difference in chi-square values for the fixed and free solution indicates the distinctiveness of the two constructs (Bagozzi *et al.*, 1991). A chi-square difference is above 3.84 at a significance level of 0.05 and above 6.63 at a significance level of 0.01, meaning that discriminant validity between two measurement variables exists (Anderson and Gerbing, 1988; Steenkamp and van Trijp, 1991). For the 9 scales of the two constructs of the upstream model, a total of 72 different discriminant validity checks were conducted at the significance level of $P=0.05$. Half of the tests set the correlation between the pairs of scales to be 1 and the other half presented no constrained correlation. We found significant lower χ^2 values for all the models not constrained to unit. The same method was applied to the two constructs of the downstream models. This result provides strong evidence of discriminant validity among the theoretical constructs.

3.4 Result of structural modelling

In accordance with the structural equation modelling analysis step, we can come to hypothesis testing once the measurement model has been established. The structural equation model was tested by applying AMOS version 4.01. The theoretical framework illustrated in Figure 3.1 has three hypothesised relationships for the two models respectively among the variables SCI, QMP and firm performance. The results of the structural equation modelling analyses based on the four performance indicators for both upstream and downstream models did not provide us with a satisfactory fit. The fit indices for upstream model are: $\chi^2=224.120$, χ^2/df=3.615, GFI=0.863, AGFI=0.800, NFI=0.855, TLI=0.860 and CFI=0.889, RMSEA=0.107. The fit indices for downstream model are: $\chi^2=242.238$, X^2/df =3.364, GFI=0.864, AGFI=0.801, NFI=0.846, TLI=0.855 and CFI=0.885, RMSEA= 0.102. Though they were reasonable compared with the results of some research, such as Li *et al.* (2007), the χ^2/df value was 3.642.

The RMSEA indicated a less than optimal recommended value of 0.05. When the market share indicator was deleted from both models, the re-estimated models showed an improvement of fit indices. The upstream model had the following fit indices: χ^2=133.852, χ^2/df=2.646, GFI=0.903, AGFI=0.852, NFI=0.902, TLI=0.917 and CFI=0.938, RMSEA=0.085. The downstream model had the following fit indices: χ^2=149.136, χ^2/df=2.486, GFI=0.908, AGFI=0.860, NFI=0.894, TLI=0.913, CFI=0.933, RMSEA=0.081. The path diagram and the results of the SEM are presented in Figure 3.4 and Figure 3.5. It should be noted that even though all the t-values of the measurements are significant at 0.05 level, their loadings to the corresponding second-order construct are different among the sub-dimensions. As far as the upstream model is concerned, the internal integration showed the highest factor loading. The other three factors of supply chain integration have low factor loadings, indicating that they may not be strong indicators of supply chain management practices compared to internal integration. This may be true in line with the results of our in-depth multiple case studies. In quality management practices, indicators 'employee involvement' and 'quality design' have lower factor loadings as compared with the other three indicators in this construct. The downstream model showed some different results. The degree of external integration, integrated information technology and logistics management between the focal firms and their most important customers was higher than that with their most important suppliers in the upstream model. However, the degree of customer quality management was lower than that of supplier quality management in addition to the degree of 'employee involvement in QM' and 'quality design', which is the same with the findings for the upstream model.

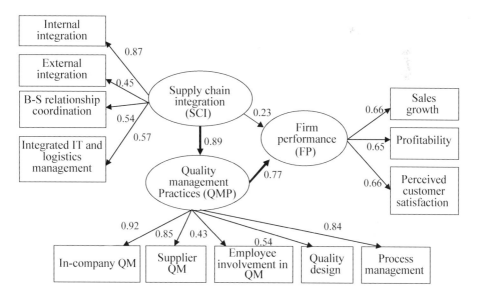

Figure 3.4. Path diagram for the upstream model (pork processors – suppliers).

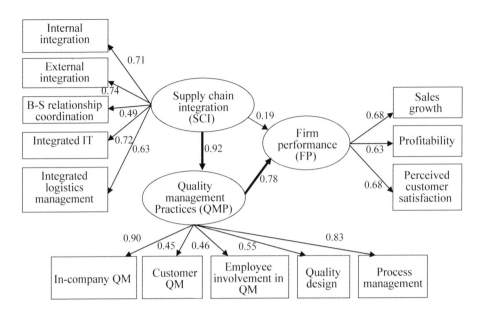

Figure 3.5. Path diagram for the downstream model (pork processors – customers).

We also tested the hypotheses based on the model as shown in Figure 3.1. Table 3.5 and 3.6 summarise the specified relationships among the variables supply chain integration, quality management practices and firm performance for the two models. As far as the upstream model is concerned, hypothesis 1 was not supported by the data, as indicated by an insignificant critical ratio (C.R. = 1.303), indicating that the significant positive relationship between SCI and firm performance was not significant. However, supply chain integration had an indirect impact on firm performance through QMP. The indirect effect[19] was 0.69. Our analysis showed strong evidence that the second and the third hypotheses were supported. Significant positive relationships have been found between QMP and firm performance (C.R. = 4.369, $P<0.001$) and between SCI and QMP (C.R. = 8.056, $P<0.001$).

By looking at Table 3.6, we also found similar results for the downstream model. While the direct impact of SCI on firm performance was not significant, it had a statistically significant influence on firm performance via the intermediate mechanism of QMP. The indirect effect is 0.72. This indirect impact of SCI on firm performance in our study corresponds with the findings of Vickery *et al.* (2003). Their research showed that customer service was found to mediate the relationship between SCI and firm performance for first tier suppliers in the automobile industry. The second and third hypotheses were also supported in the downstream model. The second hypothesis proposed a positive relationship between QMP and firm

---

[19] The indirect effect is the effect of a construct on a construct via another construct. The indirect effect of SCI on firm performance is 0.69 (direct effect of SCI on QMP 0.89×direct effect of QMP on FP 0.77) for the upstream model.

Table 3.5. Results of hypothesis testing (upstream model).

Variables	Estimates	S.E.	C.R.	P	Hypothesis
SCI→FP	0.403	0.309	1.303	0.193	Not supported
QMP→FP	0.635	0.145	4.369	0.000**	Supported
SCI→QMP	1.904	0.236	8.056	0.000**	Supported

*P<0.05; **P<0.001.

Table 3.6. Results of hypothesis testing (downstream model).

Variables	Estimates	S.E.	C.R.	P	Hypothesis
SCI→FP	0.143	0.183	0.783	0.433	Not supported
QMP→FP	0.675	0.211	3.198	0.000**	Supported
SCI→QMP	0.805	0.077	10.513	0.000**	Supported

*P<0.05; **P<0.001.

performance. This relationship was supported since the standardised coefficient was 0.78 (C.R. = 3.198, $P<0.01$). This indicates that the QMP of the focal firms had a significant positive impact on firm performance. The third hypothesis was also supported. The standardised coefficient was 0.92 (C.R. = 10.513, $P<0.001$). This indicated that the level of the focal firms' SCI with their most important customers contributed significantly to the focal firms' QMP.

The support for the second and third hypotheses in the two models (upstream and downstream) corresponds with the findings of several previous empirical studies. For example, Tracey and Tan (2001) examined the relationship among supplier involvement on design teams and in continuous improvement programs, and four dimensions of customer satisfaction (competitive pricing, product quality, product variety and delivery service) and overall firm performance. The empirical analysis showed that selecting suppliers based on product quality, delivery reliability and product performance has significant positive total effect on all four dimensions of customer satisfaction and on firm performance. Kaynak (2002) presents the relationship between supplier integration and firm performance (return of investment, sales growth and market share growth). The study finds that supplier integration positively influences firm performance and product quality.

3.5 Discussion and conclusions

Supply chain management represents one of the most significant paradigm shifts of modern business management by recognizing that individual businesses no longer compete as solely autonomous entities, but rather as whole supply chains (Lambert and Cooper, 2000). Although there are a number of interlocking ideas and propositions which constitute the theory and prescription of supply chain management, the central underpinning ideas relate to alignment and integration (Storey *et al.*, 2006). Our research attempted to study the interrelationships among supply chain integration, quality management practices and firm performance on the basis of data collected from the pork processing sector in China. We will discuss our findings below.

The most important results of the present study are that quality management practices are directly linked to firm performance, while supply chain integration was indirectly linked to firm performance through quality management practices. The confirmed positive effect of quality management practices on firm performance is very encouraging for practitioners. It reaffirms the role of quality management in improving firm performance and provides impetus to managers on various levels in the pork processing industry to continue adopting quality management practices in their organizations. As many companies put it *'Quality is the life of the enterprise'*. Firms that wish to improve their performance should therefore invest in quality management. Equally interesting is the indirect link between supply chain integration through quality management and firm performance. To improve the quality of the products and reduce uncertainty in hog supply chains, companies should therefore develop more integrated chains with their suppliers and customers. In the survey, we found (especially large) pork processors paying more attention to building strategic relationships with their most important suppliers and customers in order to provide high quality pork products to the consumers.

However, the direct effect of supply chain integration on firm performance was not significant in our study. This is in contrast to some earlier studies. For example, Kim (2006) studied the interrelationships among level of supply chain integration, implementation of supply chain practices and the organizational performance of 668 manufacturing corporations in Korea and Japan. He found that both the level of supply chain integration and SCM practices had a positive relationship to firm performance. The results of Li *et al.* (2006) in 196 American manufacturing industries also supported the hypothesis that firms with high levels of SCM practices had high levels of organizational performances. Nevertheless, a literature review also highlighted some contradictory results. Handfield and Nichols (1998) indicated that there were in practice few examples of truly integrated supply chains even though SCM has become popular. Few companies have succeeded simultaneously with strategic supplier-buyer partnerships, outsourcing non-core competencies and customer relations practices. Agricultural chains are still suffering from fragmentation, especially in developing countries (Boger, 2001a). China is in a transitional period. Although its economy is in rapid development, its agri-food industry is still dominated by small companies with limited implementation of information technology and logistics integration (Chen, 2003). Chen suggested information centres be established to facilitate supply chain integration. By taking a look at the results of our analysis, we found that factors like 'external integration', 'buyer-supplier relationship coordination' and 'integrated information technology and integrated logistics management' in relations between the pork processors and their suppliers contributed poorly to firm performance compared with the contribution of internal integration. In relations with the downstream customers, the pork processors paid more attention to information technology and logistics management. These findings may indicate that the integrated information technology and logistics management contributed more to the firm performance of the processors in their relationship with the downstream customers. However, the Chinese pork processors need to make a concerted effort to integrate with their upstream suppliers in information technology and logistics management.

3.6 Suggestions for further research and management implications

The present study focuses on the relationships both between the pork processing firms and their most important upstream suppliers and between the firms and their downstream customers in the pork supply chain. Since the unit of analysis in this study was at the chain level, information should be collected from the suppliers and customers from the focal firms. Although difficulties arise when empirical research is based on data collected from both the buyer and the supplier side, validation can be ensured through cross checking. Further efforts can be made in gathering data from multiple respondents per company in order to increase the validity of the data. The second limitation is related to the generalization of our results which must be carefully considered. The causality of the relations in this study requires further investigation in other research settings to see whether the findings can be generalised.

There are several opportunities for further research. Firstly, previous research suggests that buyer-supplier relationships in supply chains might be affected by characteristics of the firms, for example size of the firm. Studies carried out by Taylor and Wright (2003) and Powell (1995) found that firms that have discontinued quality management were predominantly small in size. Kim (2006) found out that supply chain integration had a significant effect on firm performance in both large and small firms. However, the direct effect of supply chain integration in small firms is stronger while the indirect effect of supply chain integration on performance is dominant in large firms. In large firms, the degree of supply chain integration is already high. Therefore, SCM practice and competition capability have significant direct effects on firm performance. This is therefore an opportunity for us to further investigate whether there are differences for large and small pork slaughterhouses and processors in implementing supply chain integration and quality management practices and whether these contribute differently to firm performance.

Secondly, previous studies have investigated the impact of strategic choices of pure cost, pure differentiation, or a combination on financial performance of third party logistics. For example, Yeung *et al.* (2006) found that companies which adhered to the combined strategy of cost and differentiation perform best, followed by pure differentiation companies, which in turn outperformed pure cost and commodity driven companies. Then we ask ourselves whether companies that apply product differentiation strategy are more integrated in supply chains than those that apply cost leadership strategy.

Thirdly, many studies have emphasised a connection between performance and the fit or alignment of the firm within its external environment (Miller, 1988; Powell, 1992; Strandholm *et al.*, 2004). The general environment in which agri-food supply chains operate includes socio-cultural, economic and governmental pressures, as well as technology perspectives. Since food quality and safety is related to the well-being of the consumers, the involvement of government authorities in formulating laws and regulations is common. Firms increasingly respond to food quality requirements and ask their suppliers and customers to comply with certain regulations. To facilitate food quality and safety, government authorities also launch programs to support R&D in meat research. Will institutional support make a difference with regard to firm performance? This question will be dealt with in Chapter 6.

The present study has provided several important implications to both academics and pork supply chain managers in China.

This paper proposed to study the interrelationship between supply chain management, quality management practices and firm performance. The main theoretical contributions are as follows:
- The supportive effect of supply chain integration on firm performance through quality management practices contributes to supply chain management theory. This result also highlights the assertion that supply chain management initiatives alone cannot improve profitability (Tan *et al.*, 1999), which further confirms the interaction between supply chain management and quality management practices. This finding makes an important contribution to literature. As Robinson and Malhotra (2005) mentioned, the interlinking of supply chain management with the quality management perspective is often limited and tangential in nature even though much attention has been focused on supply chain management concepts in recent years. Academics need a more focused approach to evaluating quality management issues within the internal and external supply chain contexts. The significant impact of supply chain integration on quality management practices and the indirect relationship between supply chain integration and firm performance enriched the concept of supply chain quality management.
- The empirical evidence of the significant positive impact of quality management on firm performance contributes to quality management theory. Our study indicated that quality management forms a second-order construct composed of the first-order constructs of in-company quality management, supplier/customer quality management, employee

involvement in quality management, quality design and process management – the five major components of quality management practices. It is worth nothing that the data analysis showed a profound impact of long-term quality strategy, policy goals and quality assurance systems on firm performance on one hand, and the important contribution of supplier/customer quality management on firm performance on the other. Aligned with quality management practices, other important perspectives are employee involvement and quality design. Our empirical study showed that employee involvement in quality management and quality design contributed less than the other three dimensions. Further investigation is therefore needed.

The empirical evidence has several implications for practitioners in pork supply chains in a transition economy like China:

- The results show that there is a direct relationship between quality management and firm performance. The attention to quality management turns out to be critical for generating sales growth, improve customer satisfaction and provide profits for the company. Therefore, pork processing firms in China should implement these practices and combine them with strategic supply chain partnerships so as to develop closer relationships with their suppliers and customers. In addition to these efforts, quality management requires a clear vision from the management team and participation by all employees of the company.
- The indirect relationship between supply chain integration through quality management and firm performance reveals the important role of quality management for the success of firms in the competitive business environment. Firms have to integrate their processes with suppliers and customers more tightly to deal with complex quality management pressures. If consumers lose confidence in the safety and quality of food, this affects all the stakeholders in the supply chain.

Chapter 4. Integrated information and logistics management, quality management and firm performance[20]

4.1 Introduction

In Chapter 3, we found that supply chain integration had an indirect significant impact on the performance of the pork processing firms in both upstream and downstream models. However, integrated information technology and integrated logistics management had higher loadings to the second order construct 'supply chain integration' in the downstream model than in the upstream model. We ask ourselves this question: 'will they significantly contribute to the firm performance in the relations between the pork processors and their downstream customers'? This is one of the purposes of this chapter. The following part of this introduction serves to explain this objective in more detail as well as illustrate the other objectives of this chapter.

In the last decade, intense competition has drastically changed the way companies operate their production and distribution systems. These changes include the application of the integrated logistics management concept to the analysis and design of their supply chains and, most importantly, the extensive use of information technology (IT) to gain a competitive edge (Chiu, 1995). Introducing IT for integrated SCM could lead to better efficiency and effectiveness compared to existing logistics systems (Goldhar and Lei, 1991). Information technology and logistics systems form the structural and infrastructural processes relating to the transformation of materials into value-added products, and the delivery of finished products through appropriate channels to customers and markets so as to maximise customer value and satisfaction (Narasimhan and Kim, 2001). Therefore, the introduction and utilization of integrated IT for managing the supply chain would not only enhance quality and reduce delivery time and costs, but also eventually enhance the company's competitiveness and position it for further growth (Huggins and Schmitt, 1995). To support the transfer of information between supply chain partners requires utilizing technology in an effective way. Enterprise resource planning (ERP) system is an IT infrastructure that facilitates the flow of information between the processes of an organization (Al-Mashari and Al-Mudimigh 2003). The Internet has also brought about a revolution in supply chain thinking (Davenport and Brooks 2004). This means that IT should be used not only within the company, but more importantly across company boundaries. However, the IT and information systems utilised by most companies are separate and meant to be used in such areas as procurement, production

---

[20] This is the extended version of the paper 'Integrated information and logistics management, quality management and firm performance of pork processing industry in China' published in the British Food Journal, Vol.111 No. 1, 2009, 9-25. Authors: J. Han, J.H. Trienekens and S.W.F. (Onno) Omta.

and sales, which lowers the effectiveness and efficiency of these systems (Narasimhan and Kim, 2001).

As with ERP and other information technologies, total quality management is a practice that continues to have an enormous effect on business. Quality management and IT implementations are strategic business initiatives that aspire to improve firm performance (Laframboise, 2002). As far as agri-food supply chain is concerned, the ultimate goal is to gain accurate information and a smooth, continual high-quality product flow between partners to maximise buyer satisfaction (Van der Vorst, 2000). Regarding quality management systems, information exchange by information and communication technology facilitates the exchange of large quantities of quality data between suppliers and buyers (Trienekens and Van der Vorst, 2003). Many quality management systems include requirements for receiving in-process and final inspection data of every stage of the supply chain (Petersen *et al.*, 2002). The current literature investigating the impact of information technology and logistics management on pork quality management in China is scarce. This is one of the rationales for this chapter.

Previous research on the applications of IT and integrated logistics management has emphasised the importance of each element to firm performance (Stank *et al.*, 2001; Wang *et al.*, 2006). Furthermore, studies have mainly focused on manufacturers not in the agri-food processing business or on processing companies for which agri-food is a non-dominant business (Laframboise and Reyes, 2005; Narasimhan and Kim, 2001; Daugherty *et al.*, 1996). In addition, more emphasis was given to the integration of suppliers in IT or logistics management (e.g. Laframboise and Reyes, 2005; Han *et al.*, 2007). Unfortunately, information about China's readiness to participate in integrated logistics management is limited (Daly and Cui, 2003). Therefore, the current study intends to expand the body of knowledge on the food processor-customer dyadic relationship involving the interactions of integrated IT, integrated logistics management and quality management practices as well as their impact on firm performance. We draw on information management, logistics management and total quality management perspectives to develop the hypotheses of our conceptual framework.

The empirical evidence was collected from pork slaughtering and processing companies in China. With increasing incomes and changing life-styles generated by rapid economic and social development, the pork industry will be driven to emphasise safety, quality and convenience. Reacting to these developments, some leading meat processing companies like Shineway and Yurun Co. Ltd. have invested heavily in developing cold chains and IT to provide consumers with branded products (Han *et al.*, 2007). Some leading national and regional companies have also developed ERP and used the Internet to facilitate information sharing and data processing. Will the application of IT facilitate logistics management? Will the level of IT and logistics integration facilitate quality management practices as well as firm performance? Does higher quality management bring higher performance to pork processors in China? By exploring the interrelationships between these perspectives, we can assist managers of pork processing firms with their market-oriented business operations.

In the sections to follow, we discuss the elements of the conceptual framework of our study and present the hypotheses in Section 4.2. The research design is presented in Section 4.3 and a review of the findings from a sample of pork processors is described in Section 4.4. Elaboration on the conclusions and discussions follows in Section 4.5 and the article concludes with managerial implications of the study in Section 4.6.

4.2 Theoretical framework: a structural model

As can be seen from the introduction, there have been no scholarly research attempts in China that link integrated information technology and integrated logistics management with quality management and firm performance. The research herein will test the linkages between these constructs by using a structural equation model (as shown in Figure 4.1). Hypotheses will be developed in the following part of this section.

4.2.1 Integrated information technology, integrated logistics management and firm performance

The literature suggests that there are two interrelated forms of integration that manufacturers regularly employ. The first type of integration involves coordinating and integrating forward physical flow of deliveries between suppliers, manufacturers, and customers (Saunders, 1997; Trent and Monczka, 1998). It has been pointed out by Saunders (1997) and Gattorna (1998) that the importance of delivery integration was for using third-party logistics. The other prevalent type of integration involves the backward coordination of information technologies and the flow of data from customers to suppliers (Trent and Monczka, 1998). Information technologies allow 'multiple organizations to coordinate their activities in an effort to truly manage a supply chain' (Handfield and Nichols, 1998). Information technologies include electronic data interchange (EDI) (Jayaram and Vickery, 1998; Narasimhan and Carter,

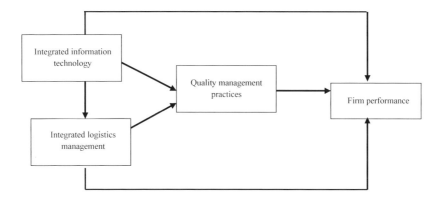

Figure 4.1. The conceptual model.

1998), ERP (Laframboise and Reyes, 2005) as well as sharing data from traditional planning and control systems (Bowersox and Daugherty, 1995). A small number of empirical studies have examined the relationship between IT and firm performance. Among those, Bharadwaj (2000) compared the performance of firms recognised by Information Week magazine as being IT leaders in their industry to the performance of a control group. She found that firms with high IT capabilities outperformed the firms from the control group. Therefore, we hypothesise:

> *H1: There is a positive relationship between integrated IT and performance of pork processing firms in China.*

As defined by the Council of Logistics Management, logistics is that part of the supply chain process that plans, implements, and controls the efficient, effective flow and storage of goods, services, and released information from the point of origin to point of consumption in order to meet customers' requirements. Successful integrated logistics management ties all logistics activities together in a system which simultaneously works to minimise total distribution costs and maintain desired customer service levels (Kenderdine and Larson, 1988). Best logistics practices embrace the transaction trade-offs that allow simultaneous improvement in economic performance and service quality (Stank *et al.*, 2001). For example, effective and efficient production and distribution system can reduce cost (Chiu, 1995). Previous literature review efforts revealed only a small handful of studies that touch on Chinese logistics issues (Daly and Cui, 2003). They examined the reality of issues surrounding e-commerce and logistics in China. Interviews were conducted with government, business and academic leaders in Qingdao, a coastal city in the east of China. They defined logistics as 'the design and operation of physical, managerial and information systems needed to overcome time and space' (Daskin, 1985) and investigated nine major e-commerce and logistics challenges that fall under these three systems, e.g. transportation, logistics warehousing, information infrastructure, data quality, logistics knowledge. The qualitative research indicated that the rise of e-commerce has opened an entirely new front with which the Chinese economy must catch up. The shortage of quantitative studies on the relationship between logistics management and firm performance challenge us to propose the following hypothesis:

> *H2: There is a positive relationship between integrated logistics management and performance of pork processing firms in China.*

Information technology has been important to the development of the logistics activity, not only because costs have decreased and accuracy and frequency have become accepted, but possibly more importantly, information offers the facility to coordinate activities. This has enabled management to focus upon managing the core business and delegating the management of the support infrastructure to specialists who have developed the necessary expertise and can apply the benefits of economics of scale (Gattorna and Walters, 1996). Previous studies have indicated a close relationship between integrated IT and integrated logistics management. For example, Chiu (1995) states that IT is an important prerequisite to good logistics management integration. Integrated IT and information systems can lead to higher quality products, enhanced productivity and ultimately increase logistics efficiency and flexibility (Narasimhan and Kim, 2001).

H3: Integrated IT facilitates the application of integrated logistics management.

4.2.2 Integrated information technology, integrated logistics management and quality management practices

Due to the complexity of agri-food supply chains, the role of information technology and logistics management in quality management is especially important. By using IT and information systems, companies are able to integrate similar functions spread over different areas as well as curtail unnecessary activities, thus enhancing their capacity to cope with the sophisticated needs of customers and meet product quality standards (Bardi *et al.*, 1994). As far as pork production chain is concerned, tracking and tracing of the whereabouts of the animals and the activities undertaken in the whole supply chain proved to be essential in preventing the further spread of diseases and in gaining consumer trust (Van der Vorst and Beulens, 2002). An overall flow of materials from raw materials, manufactured parts in pork processors and packaging materials expanded the responsibilities of management into a broader logistics concept. The systematic gathering and sharing of the large amount of quality data along these flows are extremely important for pork processors to guarantee quality, product composition and origin of their products (Trienekens and Beulens, 2001). Information technology enables the pork processors to monitor the process. We thus draw the following hypotheses:

H4: Integrated IT has a positive impact on quality management practices.

H5: Integrated logistics management has a positive impact on quality management practices.

4.2.3 Quality management practices and firm performance

To cope with a competitive environment, many companies have applied quality assurance systems. The importance of quality and its associated benefits such as improvements in customer satisfaction is well documented (e.g. Hendricks and Singhal, 1997). Madu *et al.* (1995) studied quality management practices in Taiwan's manufacturing firms. They found a significant causal relationship between quality dimensions (i.e. customer satisfaction, employment satisfaction, and employee service quality) and organizational performance. Most quality management practices are related to one form or another of performance improvement, e.g. productivity, customer service, profitability and competitiveness. Kuei *et al.* (2001) noted that the focus of the quality-based paradigm has shifted from the traditional company-centered setting to complete supply chain systems. A number of articles offer insights into the critical success factors for achieving quality management in a broader supply chain context. The sub-measurements of quality management practices were mainly drawn from Saraph *et al.* (1989). They consist of the following four sub-measurements: management leadership, supplier/customer quality management, quality design and process management. Some research has also showed failures in implementing quality management practices. A survey by A. T. Kearney of 100 British firms and a survey of executives in US manufacturing and service firms revealed that only 20-30% believed that quality management made them more competitive (Mathews and Katel, 1992). Dooyoung *et al.* (1998) also reported estimates of quality management failure rates as high as 60-67%. These mixed findings put forward the necessity to study the quality management practices-performance link in companies of various sizes, not only in big companies. We therefore draw the following hypothesis:

> *H6: There is a positive relationship between quality management practices and performance of pork processing firms in China.*

4.2.4 Firm performance

In Section 3.2.4 of Chapter 3, we have introduced the performance indicators we use in our study. The same indicators are used in this chapter, namely growth rate, market share, profitability and perceived customer satisfaction. Their operationalisation and the sources of measures can be found in Table 3.1.

4.3 Research design

4.3.1 Construct measures

A valid and reliable construct is very crucial for research. The following factors are considered in designing the constructs of this research. Firstly, multiple measures for each construct were used to overcome the shortcomings of a single item and ensure more robust conceptualizations of complex variables, thereby reducing measurement error (Segars, 1997). Secondly, existing literature with elements of our research model were searched to obtain validated questions that have been successfully applied in previous studies (Van Plaggenhoef, 2007). Thirdly, quasi perceptual measures for firm performance were used as it was impossible to get exact financial performance figures from the pork processors. Finally, we followed the suggestion of Churchill (1999) that including more items in the scale will increase its reliability. A seven-point Likert scale was used in our analysis, in which 1=not agree at all, 4=neutral and 7=totally agree. Following these principles, we designed our constructs in the research model. The scale development for integrated IT and integrated logistics management was mainly adapted from Chen and Paulraj (2004) and Segars (1997). Information technology can facilitate supply chain coordination, particularly when the technologies are used to span the traditional boundaries of supply chain firms (Hill and Scudder, 2002). As the pork chain is concerned, well-developed information management systems will facilitate the information exchange between the pork processors and their suppliers and customers. For example, if the pork processors and their retailers can share point-of-sales data, pork processors can react more promptly to market signals and economise on inventories. This can reduce uncertainty in business management. Recently there has been a recognition that logistics activities should be integrated more within the entire domain of the business, not simply related to a narrow functional role within each specific department of the firm (Greis and Kasarda, 1997). Integrated logistics management would be reflected by the extent to which the logistics activities of a firm are integrated with those of its suppliers and customers (Stock *et al.*, 2000). For example, indication of higher levels of logistics integration in our research includes greater coordination of the pork processors' logistics activities with those of their most important suppliers and customers. The operational concepts of dimensions of the construct 'quality management practices', their sources and measures are listed in Table 3.1. Items on firm performance were mainly from Tan *et al.* (1998), Vickery *et al.* (1999), Tracey and Tan (2001), Frohlich and Westbrook (2001) and Claro (2004). Based on their studies and through interviews with practitioners, the items for the sub-measurements of the constructs were developed.

The scale was evaluated by practitioners and academicians in a formal pre-test study in order to establish construct validity. In addition, the scales were pilot tested in 10 pork processing companies through structured interviews. Based on suggestions by the managers, items were added, changed, or deleted to form a revised instrument that contained 23 items for the constructs integrated IT, integrated logistics management and quality management practices and 4 items for firm performance. The measurement items and indicators for this study are shown in Appendix A.

4.3.2 Data collection and study population

The same data base as Chapter 3 is used for the quantitative analysis of this chapter. For a detailed description of data collection process, please refer to Section 3.3.2 of Chapter 3.

4.3.3 Methods

Before running the research model with the data collected, the validity and reliability of the constructs in the study should be obtained. The constructs in this study are of a reflective nature. Reflective constructs represent latent variables that cannot be measured directly, but are computed from one or more items. Their validity and reliability were assessed by following the procedures described by Anderson and Gerbing (1988) and Steenkamp and Van Trijp (1991), within which content validity, convergent validity, discriminant validity and nomological validity should be achieved. Procedures conventionally used to assess the validity of reflective constructs are factor analysis (both explorative and confirmatory) and item-total correlation. Furthermore, it is necessary to assess the reliability of the constructs by means of Cronbach's α, composite reliability and variance extracted. Table 4.1 summarises the threshold levels of the evaluation criteria for the validity and reliability of the constructs in this study.

Table 4.1. Overview of the statistical evaluation criteria for constructs in this study (Anderson and Gerbing, 1988; Steenkamp and Van Trijp, 1991).

	Evaluation criteria		Threshold
Validity	Inter-item total correlation		≥0.50
	Exploratory factor analysis	Explained variance	≥60%
		Factor loading	≥0.60
	Confirmatory factor analysis	Standardised loadings	≥0.60
		t-value of the standardised loadings	≥1.96
Reliability	Cronbach's α		≥0.60
	Composite reliability		≥0.70
	Composite validity (variance extracted)		≥0.50

The items of the measurements were subjected to a purification process by using SPSS (Field, 2005) and Partial Least Squares (Wold, 1982). In the first step, exploratory factor analysis with oblique rotation was conducted to the construct 'quality management practices' as the other constructs only contained a single dimension. In the second step, factor loading, composite reliability, average variance extracted and item-to-total correlation were obtained from the measurement and structural models to show the validity and reliability of each construct. PLS was chosen to evaluate errors in the construct measurements and test the proposed hypotheses.

PLS regression (path) analysis is an alternative to ordinary least square (OLS) regression, canonical correlation or structural equation modelling (SEM) for analyzing dependent and independent variables. Although developed by Herman Wold (1981) for econometrics, PLS is increasing in popularity in social sciences as a second generation multivariate technique (Brown and Chin, 2004). PLS is a predictive technique which can handle many independent variables, even when these display multicollinearity. In PLS, one set of latent variables is extracted for the set of observed independents and another set of latent variables is extracted simultaneously for the set of observed dependent variables. Compared with the better known factor based-covariance fitting approaches (i.e. LISREL), the component-based PLS has some advantages. Firstly, it avoids two serious drawbacks: inadmissible solutions (e.g. negative variance) and factor indeterminacy (Fornell and Bookstein, 1982). Secondly, PLS estimation imposes substantially fewer conditions for its application. It requires only that the basic assumptions of least squares estimation are satisfied. PLS uses jack-knife or bootstrap (Efron and Gong, 1983) in combination with the traditional measures of goodness-of-fit (Bagozzi, 1981) to evaluate the model. Following Chin (1998), we ran 500 resampling bootstrapping. As this method cannot measure the second layer dimensions of quality management practices, we calculated the average weighted score of the construct's sub-dimensions.

4.4 Empirical results

4.4.1 Validity and reliability of measures and constructs

Following the criteria for evaluating the validity and reliability of constructs in Table 4.1, we examined the inter-construct correlation, composite reliability and average variance extracted for each construct. The result is shown in Table 4.2. Exploratory factor analysis for construct 'quality management practices' turned out to be five sub-dimensions instead of the original four identified. It was more appropriate to rename the first dimension as 'in-company quality management' (coded as QMP1, QMP6 and QMP8) and the new sub-dimension into 'employee involvement in quality management' (coded as QMP3, QMP4, QMP5 and PM2). When looking at the measurement items, they actually reflected the contents of the new dimension. It reconfirms the validity and reliability of previous studies on this dimension in construct 'quality management practices' (Saraph *et al.*, 1989; Kaynak, 2003). The remaining items in the three sub-dimensions basically loaded on their assigned factors, with QMP2 and QMP7 adding to the factor 'quality design'. Factor analysis indicated that all the loadings are ≥ 0.7 except the loadings of QMP2, QMP4 and FP3 which are lower than 0.7, indicating a high degree of item reliability. As the factor loadings of QMP is already presented in Appendix C2, only those of 'integrated information technology' and 'integrated logistics management' are listed in this chapter (Table 4.3). As FP3 (profitability) is an important item for firm performance, we keep this in our analysis. The other two items (QMP2 and QMP4) indicated

Table 4.2. Mean, standard deviation, composite reliability, variance extracted, and inter-correlation of constructs.

Variables	Mean	Standard deviation	Composite reliability	Integrated IT	Integrated logistics management	Quality management practices	Firm performance
Integrated IT	3.24	1.68	0.91	**0.92**			
Integrated logistics management	4.57	1.42	0.87	0.54	**0.91**		
Quality management practices	4.68	1.29	0.84	0.69	0.54	**0.84**	
Firm performance	4.23	1.34	0.87	0.55	0.48	0.71	**0.89**

Note: the **bold** numbers on the diagonal are the square root of the variance shared between the constructs and their measures (square root of average variance extracted). Off-diagonal are the correlations among the constructs.

Table 4.3. Measurement and factor loadings for each construct (N=229).

Variables	Items	Factor loading	Code
Integrated information technology	We have a good information management system covering different department.	0.85	Integ3
	Our most important customers share sales information with us through information management system.	0.83	Infods1
	Most of the time, we share information with our most important customers by using e-mail.	0.87	Infods2
	We have an ERP system in communication with our most important customers.	0.83	Infods3
Integrated logistics management	We organise production in an efficient way according to market information.	0.88	Logis
	Our logistics activities are well integrated with those of our most important customers.	0.86	Logisds1
	We work together with our most important customers to reduce logistics costs instead of the internal cost of the company.	0.76	Logisds2

All constructs are measured using 7 point Likert-scale (not true at all – totally true).

the role of managers in quality improvement processes and whether the employees were rewarded for quality improvement suggestions. Due to their weak contribution to the factor loadings, they were deleted in subsequent data analysis.

Internal consistency was assessed using composite reliability. A value of 0.7 or greater is reasonable for exploratory research (Nunnally, 1988). The composite reliability for all constructs of the current study exceeds 0.84 (Table 4.2), indicating a good internal consistency of the constructs.

We assessed the discriminant validity in two ways. First, the square root of the average variance extracted (AVE) should be greater than all construct correlations, as shown in Table 4.2. Second, all items should load higher to their associated construct than to the other constructs (Table 4.4). The results for both criteria indicate that the discriminant validity of the constructs used in this study is more than adequate.

Table 4.4. Construct to item measure loadings and cross loadings.

Variables	Constructs			
	Integrated IT	**Integrated Logistics management**	**Quality management practices**	**Firm performance**
Integ2	**0.86**	0.49	0.65	0.54
Infods1	**0.84**	0.45	0.53	0.41
Infods2	**0.85**	0.39	0.58	0.40
Infods3	**0.85**	0.51	0.60	0.49
Logis	0.45	**0.84**	0.46	0.36
Logisds1	0.39	**0.84**	0.36	0.33
Logisds2	0.49	**0.81**	0.49	0.48
In-company QM	0.62	0.50	**0.89**	0.67
Process management	0.57	0.49	**0.85**	0.64
Employee involvement in QM	0.43	0.31	**0.59**	0.41
Design	0.47	0.31	**0.68**	0.48
CQM	0.40	0.29	**0.56**	0.24
Growth	0.47	0.40	0.59	**0.89**
Market share	0.24	0.23	0.38	**0.74**
Profit	0.45	0.41	0.61	**0.73**
Satisfaction	0.50	0.41	0.58	**0.78**

The **bold** numbers indicate the loadings of the items to the corresponding construct.

4.4.2 Results of structural equation modelling

The structural equation model was tested by applying PLS4.01. The results of the structural model are provided in Figure 4.2. Only path coefficients that are significant at 1% and 5% levels are listed here. The average variance explained (R^2) for the overall model is 51%, indicating a robust explanatory power.

Table 4.5 summarises the results of partial least square analysis. The hypothesised H1 and H2 were rejected. The T-values of both hypotheses are lower than 1.96. This suggests that integrated IT and integrated logistics management (LM) does not bring about higher performance in pork processing firms. However, we found a significant indirect effect of integrated IT on firm performance through quality management practices (QMP). This mediating effect of quality management practices corresponds with the findings of Laframboise and Reyes (2005). In their study, ERP as an IT is a contingent resource, which interacts with another resource,

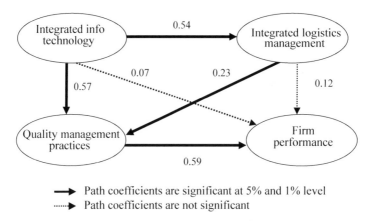

Figure 4.2. Results of the structural model.

Table 4.5. Results of hypothesis testing.

Path	Path coefficient	T-value	Indirect effect[1]	Hypothesis
H1: Integrated IT → Firm performance	0.07	1.33	0.34	Not supported
H2: Integrated LM → Firm performance	0.12	1.75		Not supported
H3:Integrated IT → Integrated LM	0.54	12.91**		Supported
H4: Integrated IT → QMP	0.57	12.62**		Supported
H5: Integrated LM → QMP	0.23	4.03**		Supported
H6: QMP → Firm performance	0.59	7.59**		Supported

*P<0.05; **P<0.01.

[1]Indirect effect is the effect of a construct on a construct via another construct. The indirect effect of integrated IT on firm performance is 0.34 (direct effect of integrated IT on QMP 0.57 × direct effect of QMP on firm performance 0.59).

such as quality management, to influence the competitive position and performance of the aerospace industry.

We found significant positive relationships in other hypotheses ($P<0.01$). The implementation of integrated IT can greatly facilitate integrated logistics management (H3, coefficient is 0.54, $P<0.01$). The positive relationship between integrated IT and logistics management was also supported by Butler *et al.* (2005). Their research findings showed advances in IT greatly facilitated data collection, manipulation and presentation, which in turn facilitated the building of decision supporting systems to support logistics management in the milk collection sector. The application of IT is also conducive to the application of quality management practices

(H4, coefficient is 0.57, $P<0.01$). This is identical to the findings of Laframboise and Reyes (2005), in which ERP application facilitated process improvement projects with better data than before and had a direct link to the quality program because of the increased information flow. Our results also supported H5 (coefficient is 0.23, $P<0.01$). There is a significant positive impact of integrated logistics management on quality management practices. In analysing the impact of quality management practices on firm performance, we find a significant positive relationship between them (coefficient is 0.59, $P<0.01$). Therefore, H6 is also supported.

4.5 Conclusion and discussions

The key findings of our research show that the application of integrated IT is positively related to integrated logistics management. Furthermore, the implementation of integrated IT and integrated logistics management have major impacts on the quality management of pork processing firms in China. We have looked at both internal and external integration of IT and integrated logistics management. Firms which have implemented integrated IT and integrated logistics management indicated more success in improving customer service, quality and profitability than in non-integrated firms but only through quality management. As two important elements in supply chain integration, the integration of IT and logistics management should contribute to higher firm performance. However, our findings did not support this hypothesis. This can be explained by the complexity of integrated IT, the existing logistics barriers as well as the underdeveloped logistics services in China. Zhang *et al.* (2003) found that the implementation success rate of ERP in China was significantly lower than in Western countries (10% versus 33% according to the authors). The empirical research on logistics barriers in China showed that 6 areas of logistics management posed barriers to strategic alliances: purchasing, transportation services, documentation/order processing, warehousing services, inventory control and import/export services. Among those, purchasing, transportation, documentation/order processing and import/export were categorised as very severe. Specifically, poor logistics services included carriers' lack of delivery dependability, inadequate transportation infrastructure and lack of communication infrastructure (Pearson *et al.*, 1998). These barriers hinder the improvement of firm performance.

The proposed relationship between quality management practices and firm performance is supported. It provides impetus to managers on various levels in the pork processing industry to continue adopting quality management practices in their organizations. Firms that wish to improve their performance should not only pay attention to internal quality management, which involves product quality assurance and employee empowerment in quality improvements, but also establish strategic partnerships with their customers in process management.

Though our results appear to be useful for managers involved in integrated customer management, two limitations of our study must be taken into account. First, further analysis should be undertaken to determine whether the impact of integrated IT and integrated logistics management on firm performance can be explained based on firm characteristics, e.g. firm size. Larger firms might be able to commit more resources to IT and integrated logistics management and thus achieve better performance. Second, the generalization of our results must be carefully considered. The causality of the relations in this study requires further investigation in other research settings to see whether the findings are robust. In addition to this, it is worthwhile for the future research to study the role of each sub-dimension of the construct 'quality management practices' to firm performance in view of the increasing importance of food quality and safety. This endeavour will help the company to make better use of quality management tools in business operation.

4.6 Managerial implications

The economic growth and huge market potential of China has attracted not only business attention, but also a growing amount of academic interest. Previous research already showed a lack of investigation into logistics in China (e.g. Peng *et al.*, 2001; Wang *et al.*, 2006). Furthermore, very little research has been conducted to address integrated logistics strategies and their operational priorities in relation to business performance (Yeung *et al.*, 2006) and the interaction between integrated IT and integrated logistics management and their relationships with firm performance. Therefore, the present study has provided several important implications for managers of the pork processing industry in a large transitional economy like China.

- Changes in IT and integrated logistics management will increasingly affect business processes, shaping the future of quality management through a need for increased effectiveness and efficiency. The pork processing industry will continue to update its technology and provide consumers with good quality products. As future quality management development will be influenced by increasingly competitive and global markets, it is critical for practitioners to be sensitive to the application of integrated IT and integrated logistics management, which leads to better quality management.
- Our findings didn't support the significant positive relationships between integrated IT and integrated logistics management and firm performance. With more professionalism in pork supply chain, more integration in logistics management can be foreseen in the future. For pork processing firms seeking to construct their IT applications after a comprehensive quality program is in place, it is important to consider the impact of integration of information on the product quality of its suppliers and customers. An inevitable trend in the future is the increasing importance of the integration of IT and logistics management. Such integrated systems enable processors and retailers to save on labour, increase accuracy, improve agility and cut costs, eventually leading to better firm performance. In China, whether IT can eventually directly lead to higher firm performance or whether it must integrate with quality management practices to contribute to higher firm performance requires further investigation.
- The results show that there is a direct relationship between quality management and firm performance. Attention to quality management turns out to be critical for generating

sales growth, improving customer satisfaction and providing profits for the company. In quality management practices, we found that in-company quality management, supplier/customer quality management, employee involvement, quality design and quality process management as a whole contributed to overall firm performance. Quality management requires a clear vision from the management team and participation by all employees of the company.

Chapter 5. Governance and quality management[21]

5.1 Introduction

In the past two decades, organizational arrangements in the agricultural sector in developed countries have been moving from spot market towards more close coordination. As far as the pork industry is concerned, the vertical coordination systems between livestock producers and processors in most Western countries have dramatically shifted toward long-term contract coordination or vertical integration (Lawrence and Hayenga, 2002). The major driving forces for this shift include the level of risks faced by agricultural producers, stringent quality requirements for processing and changes in technology (e.g. Fearne, 1999; Hobbs and Young, 2001). Moreover, more than ever before, consumers are demanding that food be healthy, safer and more environmentally friendly. This implies that the competitiveness of pork production in many cases depends more on the supply of safe and high-quality products than on quantity and prices.

Organizational arrangements and governance structures have been studied by the theory of transaction cost economics (TCE). Characteristics of transaction-specific investments, frequency and uncertainty have been examined in light of their impact on governance mechanisms. The general proposition of TCE is that managers align the governance features of interorganisational relationships to match known exchange hazards, particularly those associated with specialised asset investments, difficult performance measurement, or uncertainty (Williamson, 1985, 1991). In response to exchange hazards, managers may craft complex contracts that define remedies for foreseeable contingencies or specify processes for resolving unforeseeable outcomes. When contracts are too costly to craft and enforce, managers may choose to vertically integrate (Poppo and Zenger, 2002). However, some researchers argue that in practice, given that transaction specific investments (TSI) are necessary, many transactions exist outside the realm of vertical integration or contracts (Bensaou and Anderson, 1999). They postulate that one possible reason for this is that relationships based on trust make vertical integration to protect TSI less important. An ongoing relationship generally fosters trust and enables partners to adopt more flexible models of cooperation (such as alliances), create value together (that is, mutual benefits or reciprocity), and eventually, induce exchange partners to make TSI (Yu *et al.*, 2006). This is the major view of relational exchange theory (RET, MacNeil, 1978, 1980). This kind of relational perspective offers a different, less explicit set of governance mechanisms, such as trust, cooperation and joint

---

[21] A shorter version of this chapter was submitted to the Journal of Production Economics in September 2008. The revised version was accepted to publish on May 12, 2009. A part of this chapter was published as: 'Quality management and the role of organization in the pork processing industry in China', published in: R. Ruben, M. van Boekel, A. van Tilburg and J. Trienekens (ed.) (2007), Tropical Food Chains, Wageningen, Wageningen Academic Publishers, the Netherlands, pp. 133-151.

planning. Though in the last decade, studies have been done to investigate interfirm exchange relationships by using both transaction cost economics and relational exchange theory (e.g. Zhou *et al.*, 2003; Ferguson *et al.*, 2005; Yu *et al.*, 2006; Zhou *et al.*, 2008), empirical evidence informing this issue in Chinese context is scarce and mixed (Zhou *et al.*, 2008). For example, Guthrie (2001) documents that many Chinese firms are now less likely to use informal and network-based practices. Economic strategies and practices that resemble foreign firms are more likely adopted by these firms. In contrast, Zhou *et al.* (2003) from their survey of 620 firms in 1999/2000, show that social relations still play a critical role in interfirm relationships in addition to the use of contracts in China. Yu *et al.* (2006) find that calculative trust acts as a moderating factor in the relationship between formal governance mechanisms and TSI. Furthermore, Styles and Ambler (2003) also argue that there is a coexistence of transaction and relational marketing in the Chinese business context. Furthermore, while the impact of transaction attributes on governance mechanisms has been devoted significant attention, there is a lack of a comprehensive framework to explain the alignment of governance mechanisms in the presence of transaction characteristics in the pork supply chain in both transaction and relational relationships. Therefore, one of the purposes of this study is to develop a framework that integrates TCE and relational exchange theory (RET, MacNeil, 1978, 1980) to explain the impact of transaction attributes on governance mechanisms in the context of pork processing industry. In addition to this, the trade-off between formal contracts and relational governance mechanism (e.g. long-term cooperation and trust) will also be examined.

Another driving force for this study is the concern about the impact of governance mechanisms on quality management. During the time spent designing this study, quality management in the meat industry was a very hot topic in China. Though China is the largest pork producer in the world, it exported less than 1% of its domestic production volume in 2007 (China Meat Association, 2008). It is widely recognised that the quality and safety of pork products are not up to the standard of importers. With rapid economic development in China, food safety and quality is increasingly becoming an issue of concern to its consumers. This poses challenges for the organization of pork supply chains in China. Pork processing firms are endeavouring to establish closer cooperative links with their suppliers and downstream customers in order to be competitive in the market. Past studies in industrial organization theory have focused on the relationship between transaction attributes and the selection of different organizational arrangements. Relatively little research has been done with regard to the influence of different organizational arrangements on the implementation of quality management practices. Therefore the second aim of this study will be to attempt to find empirical evidence of this relationship.

The layout of the chapter is as follows: the next section introduces the theoretical perspectives used in this research. This is followed by an explanation of the research model, together with the development of hypotheses in Section 5.3. The research method is described in Section 5.4. The results of empirical tests are presented in Section 5.5 and Section 5.6 draws conclusions and presents some discussions. Finally, the chapter concludes with implications for the managers of pork processing firms in China, identifying the limitations of the study and offering some recommendations for future research in Section 5.7.

5.2 Theoretical background

5.2.1 Transaction cost economics perspective

Transaction cost economics (TCE) is an analytical paradigm whose primary subject matter is the design of efficient governance mechanisms[22] for supporting exchange (Heide and John, 1992). The original framework, as developed by Williamson (1975), views the governance decision as fundamentally a choice between a 'market', based on governance through a price mechanism, and a 'hierarchy', implying governance through a unified authority structure. The term 'governance' traditionally has been defined very broadly as a 'mode of organizing transactions' (Williamson and Ouchi, 1981). It is a multidimensional phenomenon, encompassing the initiation, termination and ongoing relationship maintenance between a set of parties (Heide, 1994). A 'governance structure' is the organizational form in which a transaction is carried out (Williamson, 1985).

The main approach of TCE is, as Williamson (1989) suggested, to assign attribute differentiated transactions to governance structures in a transaction-cost-minimizing manner. Transaction cost was interpreted broadly as the 'comparative costs of planning, adapting, and monitoring task completion under alternative governance structure'. Transaction costs arise *ex ante* and *ex post* of transferring goods or services between technically separable phases of production or distribution. *Ex ante* transaction costs arise *before* the transaction, such as searching and screening potential exchange agents and bargaining. *Ex post* transaction costs arise *after* the transaction such as monitoring the product quality, enforcing payment and breaches of contractual promises. The important exploratory elements for the existence of transaction costs are two behaviour assumptions – bounded rationality and opportunism (Williamson, 1975). *Bounded rationality* refers to human behaviour that is intentionally rational, but limited by the capacity to collect and evaluate information as well as barriers related to language and communication. Bounded rationality becomes important in combination with uncertainty. In the presence of *opportunism*, however, the risk of contractual hazards occurs. Opportunism is defined as the individual's 'self-interest seeking with guile,' including all kinds of conveying biased or incomplete information to exploit a situation to one's own advantage (Boger, 2001a).

As described by Williamson (1975), certain dimensions of transactions give rise to transaction costs and combine to create 'market failure' in the sense that the market mechanism becomes an inefficient means of mediating exchange. There are three dimensions for TCE: transaction specific investments, uncertainty and frequency (Williamson, 1985). The *transaction specific investment* dimension is most frequently used to explain the optimal governance mechanism

---

[22] 'Governance mechanism' or 'governance form' has been used in TCE instead of 'governance structure' (Hesterley *et al.*, 1990: 430). They will be used interchangeably in our study.

for transactions. It involves physical or human assets that are dedicated to a particular relationship and which cannot be redeployed easily. Its idiosyncratic nature gives rise to a safeguarding problem, in the sense that mechanisms must be designed to minimise the risk of subsequent opportunistic exploitation (Klein *et al.*, 1978; Williamson, 1985). Before contract execution, many potential buyers and sellers exist but as soon as the contract is concluded, a bilateral monopoly may emerge. The party having made the specific investment is vulnerable to post contractual opportunistic behaviour by the other party in attempting to appropriate quasi-rents of the specialised assets (Klein *et al.*, 1978). When asset specificity increases, administrative control and coordinated adaptation of hybrids and hierarchies gain importance. This implies a relatively greater growth of transaction costs in markets than in hybrids and hierarchies when asset specificity increases. The *frequency* with which a transaction occurs can be a relevant determinant of which governance structure the cost economizing solution will be. It usually affects governance only in conjunction with the asset specificity involved in the transaction (Boger, 2001a). As TCE researchers have been largely unsuccessful in confirming the hypothesised effects of frequency on the governance model, frequency has received limited attention in TCE literature (Rindfleisch and Heide, 1997). It is thus not one of the transaction attributes under our study. *Uncertainty* and complexity are central problems of transactions. Without uncertainty, transactions would be fully predicted ex-ante. Uncertainty comprises unforeseen, exogenous disturbances as well as behavioral uncertainty (Williamson, 1985). When behavioral uncertainty is in conjunction with asset specificity, it affects the efficiency of governance structures. Although the efficiency of all governance structures deteriorates in the face of great uncertainty, the hybrid forms are held to be the most susceptible given their typical contractual relationships (Williamson 1996). This leads to a shift of the transaction cost function of the hybrid mode. In summary, the following alignment of transactions with governance structures can be made to minimise transaction costs (Table 5.1): market governance with classical contracts for non-specific transactions; trilateral governance with neo-classical contracts for occasional transactions of mixed and highly idiosyncratic nature; bilateral governance with relational contracting for reducing mixed idiosyncratic transactions; and unified governance with relational contracting for recurring highly-specific transactions Williamson (1979).

Table 5.1. Matching governance structures with commercial transactions (Williamson, 1979).

		Investment characteristics		
		Non-specific	**Mixed**	**Idiosyncratic**
Frequency	Recurrent	Market governance (Classical contracting)	Bilateral governance (Relational contracting)	Unified governance (Relational contracting)
	Occasional	Market governance (Classical contracting)	Trilateral governance (Neo-classical contracting)	

In buyer-supplier relationships in China's pork processing sector, spot market transaction, hybrid forms (including written contracts and relational exchange based on long-term cooperation and trust) are the two major governance forms. Vertical integration is not the focus of our study. One reason is that the percentage of firms using this governance form is rather small when compared with spot market and contractual governance. For example, our survey showed that the hogs from the production farms of the second largest pork processor only accounted for one percent of the slaughtered hogs. The other reason is to follow the suggestion of Heide (1994): more recent research on transaction cost analysis calls for vertical control in the market as a practical alternative to vertical integration. The assumption is that the costs associated with vertical control in the market are less than the sum of the bureaucratic costs and the production costs associated with vertical integration inside the firm (Ryu *et al.*, 2008). Therefore, our study will focus on three main governance structures: spot market, contracting governance and relational governance.

5.2.2 Relational exchange theory perspective

Although formal contracts are mechanisms that attempt to reduce risk and uncertainty in exchange relationships (Lusch and Brown, 1996), legal contracts cannot explicitly state how potential situations will be handled in the future (MacNeil, 1980). Buyer and seller are incapable to write *a priori* comprehensive agreement that covers future contingencies (Williamson, 1975). The buyer-supplier exchange performance can be enhanced by embedding private and public information flows in a matrix of social ties rather than by resorting to a contract or its enforcement by a third party such as courts (Uzzi, 1999). Therefore relational governance mechanisms in interfirm exchange relationships are considered important by many researchers (e.g. MacNeil, 1980, 2000; Lusch and Brown, 1996; Poppo and Zenger, 2002; Ferguson *et al.*, 2005).

Relational governance is often referred to as '*relationalism*' (Noordewier *et al.*, 1990; Artia and Frazier, 2001) and '*social embeddedness*' (Uzzi, 1999). It is a set of relational norms that develops over time. Norms represent important social and organizational mechanisms for controlling the exchange (Gundlach and Achrol, 1993). Actually, shared norms and values are the hallmark of relational exchange (Brown *et al.*, 2000), and they essentially develop through a socialization process in which the parties understand and endorse each other's expectations (Gundlach and Achrol, 1993). The theories of bilateral governance are important because they identify a form of governance that differs in many aspects from the ones implied in other theoretical frameworks (Heide, 1994). Specifically, TCE historically has been criticised for failing to account of the social structures within which exchange is 'embedded' (Granovetter, 1985).

Trust is a key feature of relational governance. The need for trust between partners has been identified as an essential element of buyer-supplier relationships (Anderson and Narus, 1990). As an important social component, trust is the basis of relational exchange. Relational governance mechanisms (such as trust) are regarded as a means to enhance transaction specific investments associated with less monitoring and bargaining (Barney and Hansen, 1994). The existence of trust between two partners can help to facilitate collaboration (Claro *et al.*, 2003) and can help to create a stable and committed relationship (Lu, 2007). Holm *et al.* (1996) also posits that increased levels of understanding in a relationship will increase the overall commitment level of the relationship.

Although both TCE and RET are developed to complement classical contract theory (Cannon and Perreault Jr., 1999), they have some difference in the notion of contract. In TCE, a contract between a buyer and a supplier means that the specific transactions, agreements, and promises, and the terms of the exchange are defined by price, asset specificity, and safeguards, under the assumption that quantity, quality and duration are all specified (Williamson, 1996). The concept of contract in RET is expanded to refer to relationships between people who have exchanged, are exchanging, or expect to exchange in the future (MacNeil, 2000). In this theory, formal contracts represent promises or obligations to perform particular actions in the future (MacNeil, 1978). Moreover, RET describes a set of relational contracting norms, which are adaptations of the norms common to all contracts (MacNeil, 2000). Evidently, the popular and legal notion of contract is more compatible to the concept of contract in TCE than in RET (Ferguson *et al.*, 2005). To distinguish between TCE and RET approaches to contract, researchers have referred to contracts as hard and soft, explicit and normative, formal and informal, and written and unwritten (Antia and Frazier, 2001; Lusch and Brown, 1996). There is a risk of oversimplification when using such dichotomous classifications as legal ties interwoven with various social norms in the actual business to business exchanges (Ferguson *et al.*, 2005). However, the operationalisation of contractual governance in terms of hard, explicit, formal and written contracts fits the purpose of our study. Therefore by 'contractual governance', we mean formal written contacts between buyers and suppliers of the pork chain.

5.2.3 Formal contracts and relational governance

With regard to the interaction between contractual governance and relational governance, several studies tried to distinguish whether the two governance forms function as substitutes or are complementary. 'Substitutes' means that the presence of one governance device (relational governance in particular) obviates the need for the other (Gulati, 1995; Dyer and Singh, 1998). Informal self-enforcing agreements which rely on trust and reputation often supplant the formal controls characteristic of formal contracts (Dyer and Singh, 1998). Gulati (1995:93) posits '....trust avoids contracting costs, lowers the need for monitoring, and facilitates contractual adaptation. Trust counteracts fears of opportunistic behaviour and as a result, is likely to limit the transaction costs associated with an exchange....'. Another reason for substitution is that formal contracts may actually undermine the formation of relational governance. Ghoshal and Moran (1996) argue that the use of relational, formal control has a pernicious effect in cooperation.

The logic for viewing relational governance and contractual governance as complementary appears equally compelling. In settings where hazards are severe, the combination of formal and informal safeguards may deliver greater exchange performance than either governance choice in isolation (Poppo and Zenger, 2002). Relational governance becomes a necessary complement to the adaptive limits of contracts by fostering continuance and bilateralism when change and conflict arise (MacNeil, 1978). Regardless of the duration of an exchange, vast dimensions of the exchange may prove impossible to contractually specify; managers are clearly constrained in their capacity to foresee and contractually resolve potential future contingencies. As a result, when unforeseen disturbances arise, contracts are obviously unable to maintain the continuity of the relationship. Thus, managers choose relational governance to safeguard specific investments from premature and costly termination. Relational governance may also promote the refinement of formal contracts. As a close relationship is developed and sustained, the buyer and seller can work together to learn from the prior experiences and revise the contract on mutual agreement. Exchange experience, patterns of information sharing, and evolving performance measurement and monitoring may all enable greater specificity (and complexity) in contractual provisions (Poppo and Zenger, 2002). In reverse, the contractual governance also complements relational governance mechanism. Through clearly articulated clauses that specify requirements and punishments, formal contracts have the advantage of formal specifications of a long-term commitment to exchange (Baker *et al.*, 1994). Thus, the specification of contractual safeguards promotes expectations that the other party will behave cooperatively and thus complements the informal limits of relational governance. Cooperative behaviour in the present then reinforces an expectation of cooperation in the future. Formal contracts help ensure that the early, more vulnerable stages of exchange are successful (Poppo and Zenger, 2002).

5.2.4 Quality management under transaction cost perspective

Because quality is a major competitive priority of manufacturing firms worldwide, much discussion has been devoted to defining the quality construct (Forker *et al.*, 1996). For example, Garvin (1984) classified his viewpoints about quality into the following five categories of approaches: transcendent-based (innate excellence), product-based (quality of desired attributes), user-based (satisfaction of consumer preferences), manufacturing-based (conformance to requirements) and value-based (affordable excellence). Researchers and practitioners from economics, marketing and operations management have also made great efforts in operationalising the construct. For example, Saraph *et al.* (1989) reported that eight critical factors could be used for quality management assessment, namely the role of the quality department, training, product/service design, supplier quality management, process management, quality data and reporting, and employee involvement. In our study, we didn't use a single item construct for the 'quality of pork products'. In our view, the 'quality of pork products' is achieved through multidimensional quality management practices involving the efforts from both the focal firms themselves and the efforts of their suppliers and customers. Therefore, the construct was structured mainly based on the studies of Saraph *et al.* (1989)

and Kaynak (2003) and consisted of the following four sub-measurements: management leadership, supplier/customer quality management, quality design and process management.

Following transaction cost economics' framework (Williamson, 1991, 1996), we expect to find an alignment between quality management practices used in transactions in interfirm exchanges and the governance of transactions between these firms. More specifically, pork processing firms pursue a good reputation in producing good quality pork products. Quality pork products and the reputation of the processing firms are specific assets of the firms. To safeguard the specific assets, the firms tend to adopt hybrid forms or vertical integration rather than spot markets to cope with the need for greater control over the steps of the vertical chain that affect product quality (Raynaud *et al.*, 2005). Due to the nature of the agri-food supply chain, final quality of the products depends on different stages of the vertical chains, from input suppliers to the final consumers (Trienekens and Zuurbier, 2008). Developing efficient information and monitoring systems in intermediate transactions is therefore an important issue for the pork processors, especially when asymmetric information on the quality of intermediate products is a challenge. The production of quality products must follow a set of specifications, namely a quality standard. Pork processing firms may need to invest or carefully design their production process in order to meet this quality standard. These quality and safety requirements may increase transaction specific investments, for instance, specific characteristics of the raw materials, good facilities, advanced technologies etc. Thus, the pork processing firms must institute inventive control mechanisms in the interfirm exchanges. This can take the form of contractually restricted sets of input (or even providing input themselves), monitoring the quality at several stages and providing bonuses for high quality hogs (meat). According to TCE typology of governance structure (Williamson, 1991), a shift from market-like governance to 'hybrid' mode or even vertical integration is observed to safeguard the specific investments and protect from the opportunistic behaviour of the exchange partners.

In addition to the TSI, the degree of uncertainty in quality on various stages of the pork chain also shapes governance choice. A salient aspect of processed pork products is the strong heterogeneity of raw materials. At the same time, the supply of raw material is still largely fragmented with sometimes thousands of suppliers and many small slaughterhouses. This can pose serious problems for evaluating and assessing each supplier's separate contributions to the final quality or individual responsibility in case of food-related diseases. The issue here is related to the problems of evaluating individual performance (Alchian and Demsetz, 1972) and measuring products or asset characteristics (Barzel, 1982). This calls for mechanisms to deal with this uncertainty about quality in order to reduce observability and traceability problems (Spiller and Zellner, 1997; Ménard, 2004). The processing firms may apply quality management systems to reduce and manage quality uncertainty (Barzel, 1982). Furthermore, they can go a step further and directly try to control critical steps of the production chain by vertically integrating or by contractually specifying restraints on its suppliers/retailers' behaviour (for example, a particular technology, production methods, and sales promotion of the retailers). Sometimes, there is more than just uncertainty on quality along the chain.

The processing firms must also react to several kinds of unpredicted external 'shocks' like a safety crisis, a new strategy or marketing campaign trigger by its competitors and so on. The combination of specific assets and the need to adapt to new external circumstances raises important coordination problems (Muris *et al.*, 1992; Raynaud *et al.*, 2005). Here again, TCE predicts a shift from market transaction governance to a more hierarchical one.

To summarise the above description, the implementation of a quality management system will affect attributes of transactions within the chain and modify the nature and/or the extent of coordination problems (what Williamson, 1996, called contractual hazards). By committing their reputation capital to protect quality, and creating a quality standard to cope with suppliers and customers in the supply chain, the pork processing firms risk increased contractual hazards in transactions. The firms have therefore strong incentives to implement governance structures that can mitigate these hazards (Hobbs and Young, 2000).

5.3 Conceptual model and hypotheses

As can be seen from the literature review, this study is one of the few attempts to integrate transactional and relational governance regimes to study interfirm exchanges and quality management in the pork supply chain in China. Here we will test the linkages among them. The conceptual model for our research is developed in accordance with the literature review in Section 5.2 (Figure 5.1). This part will focus on hypotheses development with regard to the constructs under study.

5.3.1 Transaction attributes and governance structure

Asset specificity and governance structures

In Williamson's pioneering work (1979), the characteristics of transactions were linked to the governance structure from 'classical contracting' (spot markets) at one end of the spectrum, to unified governance (vertical integration) at the other. Transaction cost analysis predicts that market governance will be cost-efficient as long as the level of asset specificity is modest. As TSI pose a contractual hazard for any investor, either the suppliers or the buyers, the exchange partner can exploit such assets because they are not re-deployable, or at least they

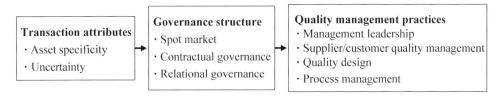

Figure 5.1. The conceptual model.

have a reduced value in an alternative exchange relationship. Therefore, the hybrid mode will come into play when asset specificity does rise substantially. Under such circumstances, hybrid governance is warranted for the purpose of enhancing the utility of specific productive resources (Williamson, 1991a).

According to TCE logic, 'failures of alignment' occur when one part of the buyer-supplier relationships choose a governance structure that is inappropriate for a given level of asset specialization (Dyer, 1996). In the presence of the complicated and turbulent transaction environment, the appropriate alignment is not an easy task. However, despite all pitfalls and constraints, much effort has been put on empirically investigating the influences of the transaction attributes on organizational efficiency since the early 1980s. The major results of some empirical studies on transaction costs in the agri-food sector can be found in Boger (2001b). The recent relevant studies on the Chinese context include Lu (2007) and Zhou et al. (2008). Lu (2007) found out that the vegetable processing firms are more likely to use contracts to conduct transactions with the downstream customers while the degree of TSI is high. However, a significant negative relationship has been found between these two variables when the vegetable processing firms conduct business with the farmers. It is also interesting to notice that Zhou et al. (2008) didn't find empirical evidence on the significant positive relationships between the level of TSI and the application of contractual governance in commercial machinery, computer equipment, and electronic component manufacturing. Their explanation is that these companies tend to more relational ties when the degree of TSI is high. We therefore propose the following hypotheses:

> H1: When asset specificity is low, pork processing firms will use spot market transaction in their exchanges with upstream suppliers (H1a) and downstream customers (H1b).

> H2: With the increase of asset specificity, pork processing firms will use formal contractual governance mechanism to trade with their upstream suppliers (H2a) and downstream customers (H2b) to safeguard their investments.

Uncertainty and governance structures

Uncertainty has been a prominent factor in using the transaction cost approach (e.g. Anderson and Schmittlein, 1984). TCE implies a discriminating match between the type of purchasing arrangements employed and the level of uncertainty (Noordewier et al., 1990). The transaction cost logic advances that, for simple exchanges, markets efficiently coordinate adaptation, since 'price' serves as a sufficient mechanism. That is, the future is expected to confirm to the present, such that 'price' can reflect the change in demand or supply. However, contracts become more tailor-made with relevance to duration, expectations, processes, and procedures aimed at preserving the cost, quality, and service of the product (Williamson, 1996). Compared with spot market transaction, contracts function better in making monitoring less difficult and adjustment easy to be facilitated when uncertainty arises (Zhou et al., 2008). They provide a safeguard, albeit not perfect, from the uncoordinated, self-interested actions that may increase with uncertainty (Williamson, 1996).

The TCA literature holds that performance will be enhanced when there is a 'match' between the governance structure employed and the uncertainty surrounding the exchange. In practice, the construct of uncertainty has proved controversial due to contradictory empirical findings (Noordewier *et al.*, 1990; Heide and John, 1990). Balakrishnan and Wernerfelt (1986) once argued that the conflicting claims are due to rather distinct aspects of uncertainty that have been confounded previously in broad definitions of the construct. Heide and John (1990) isolate three different forms of uncertainty, volume unpredictability, technological unpredictability and performance ambiguity, and analyse the effect of each individually. In addition to the failure in finding significant relationships between the volume unpredictability and tighter interfirm linkages to facilitate adaptation, their results support the other two hypotheses. Noordewier *et al.* (1990) operationalise uncertainty as behavioral uncertainty and find negative relationships between uncertainty and degree of quasi-integration. Studies on the alignment of governance structures and uncertainty in less developed countries and emerging countries are more in favour of the relationship. For example, according to a World Bank report (2005), higher prices, avoidance of price uncertainty and guaranteed product sales are the most important arguments for contracts in countries such as Hungary, the Czech Republic and Slovakia. Schultze *et al.* (2007) also concluded that contracts are a highly preferable option for farmers in developing and transformational countries to reduce (price) risks, to safeguard specific investments, and to overcome market failures and poor public institutions for governing market transactions. Our operationalization of uncertainty follows the lines of Williamson (1996) and focus on the unpredictability of cost, quality and service of the product. To find out the impact of uncertainty on the selection of governance structures in China, we hence hypothesise:

> H3: *When uncertainty is low, pork processing firms will use spot market transaction in their exchanges with upstream suppliers (H3a) and downstream customers (H3b).*

> H4: *With the increase of uncertainty, pork processing firms will use formal contractual governance mechanism to trade with their upstream suppliers (H4a) and downstream customers (H4b).*

Relational governance and transaction attributes

Relational arrangements as a personal institution govern transactions through repeat dealing, shared values, and a lack of third-party enforcement (North, 1990). The emphasis in the relational paradigm is on long-term, mutually beneficial relationships between buyers and suppliers and industrial networks, interaction to develop and build cooperation, commitment, and dependence (Zaheer and Venkatraman, 1995; Styles and Ambler, 2003). Cooperation through long-term interactions helps to develop mutual understanding. After dealing with buyers for a long period of time, suppliers will have greater confidence in making specialised investments, owing to their knowledge of buyers' reputation and intent (Yu *et al.*, 2006). And with long-term cooperation, exchange partners are more likely to trust one another and to develop specialised methods of communication. A supplier may acknowledge that a long-term relationship can be regarded as a relational safeguard, because the manufacturing firm would hesitate to jeopardise it (Bensaou and Anderson, 1999). Therefore, more specifically, cooperative norms enable partners to act as if the expected value of the exchange were stable, even in the presence of specific assets (Uzzi, 1997). Relational governance may also mitigate adaptation problems arising from uncertainty because of their underlying shared norms (Zhou *et al.*, 2008). With cooperative norms, parties can act with greater confidence because they share joint expectations about how each party will behave in the future (Uzzi, 1997).

Previous studies have supported the positive relationship between transaction attributes and the use of relational governance mechanism. For example, Brown *et al.* (2000) studied the effectiveness of three alternative governance mechanisms – ownership, transaction specific investment and relational exchange in the relationship between the hotel brand headquarters and the hotels. They argue that hotel investments in transaction specific assets represent potential sanctions that hang over the relationship between brand headquarters and its hotels. The hotels are therefore provided with incentives not to behave opportunistically. Relational exchange, in contrast, emphasises the building and sustaining of the brand headquarters – hotel relationship through behavioral norms rather than potential sanctions. Therefore, relational exchange is a more positive form of governance. When behavioral norms and relational exchange are used jointly, relational exchange enhances the effectiveness of transaction specific investment by focusing on the benefits of the relationship rather than the potential damage to it from opportunism. Alternatively, transaction specific investment heightens the effect of relational exchange by providing a 'stick' that reinforces the latter's 'carrot' approach to governance. Zhou *et al.* (2008) find that managers in commercial machinery, computer equipment and electronic equipment manufacturing firms in China rely on relational ties to govern their more complex exchanges (e.g. higher levels of asset specificity and uncertainty). To test whether our study is consistent with Peng and Luo's (2000) proposition 'relational ties characterise economic activities in emerging economies, and are the lifeblood business conduct in Chinese society', we propose:

> H5: With the increase of asset specificity, pork processing firms will use relational governance mechanisms to trade with their upstream suppliers (H5a) and downstream customers (H5b) to safeguard their investments.

> H6: With the increase of uncertainty, pork processing firms will use relational governance mechanisms to trade with their upstream suppliers (H6a) and downstream customers (H6b) to respond to market changes.

5.3.2 Relational governance mechanism and contractual governance mechanism

As described in Section 2, the academic world holds two different views on the relationships between relational governance and contractual governance mechanisms: substitution and complementarity. We hold the second view that both coexist and are complementary with each other in the Chinese context (Styles and Ambler, 2003; Yu *et al.*, 2006). The reasoning is as follows: although contracts are explicitly drafted with provisions to promote the longevity of exchanges, unexpected disturbances may place considerable strain on an exchange relationship (Williamson, 1991). Contracts that shift from merely specifying deliverable outcomes to providing frameworks for bilateral adjustments may facilitate the evolution of highly cooperative exchange relations. In addition, the process of contracting may itself promote expectations of cooperation consistent with relational governance. The activity of creating complex contracts requires parties to mutually determine and commit to processes for dealing with unexpected changes, penalties for non-compliance, and other joint expectations of trade (Poppo and Zenger, 2002). Long-term relations established between exchange partners will facilitate the process of contract making. As MacNeil (1978) posits, formally specified processes for adapting to change promote longevity in the exchange, but don't guarantee continuance or a mutually acceptable, bilateral resolution. Thus, contracts alone may serve simply to facilitate termination of an exchange as courts use it to review the broken aspects of the contract and then allocate assets between the parties on some basis deemed equitable.

Some research findings have supported the complementary role of these two mechanisms. For example, Poppo and Zenger (2002) find empirical support for the proposition by using data from a sample of information service exchanges in the USA. Bunduchi (2008) proposes that the nature of inter-organizational relationships depends on the interaction between the logic of transaction cost economics and the need for trust and interdependencies between exchange partners. We thus propose:

> *H7: There is a positive relationship between formal contractual governance mechanisms and relational governance mechanisms in the buyer-supplier relationship between the pork processing firms and their suppliers (H7a) and their customers (H7b).*

5.3.3 Governance structure and quality management practices

TCE offers one perspective on the relationship between market organization and product quality. One class of transaction costs are measurement or information costs (Hobbs, 1996). These include costs of searching for information about buyers or sellers in the market, inspecting goods prior purchase, and assigning a price. Markets may be organised to reduce measuring costs that are associated with assuring a closer correspondence between product value and price, or actions and rewards (Williamson, 1985). When hog quality attributes are difficult to measure the producer may engage in opportunistic behaviour to exploit private information by failing to perform as agreed, such as shirking or cutting corners on quality, also referred to as moral hazard. This is expected to lead to contracts with added security features to mitigate the hazard (Martinez and Zering, 2004). In this regard, two packer surveys in the USA in 1996 and 2001 respectively showed that related to hog quality and consistency, contract forms of governance performed better than spot market forms of governance (Martinez and Zering, 2004).

The same goes for Europe, where agri-food chains have been experiencing increasing concern about product quality and/or food safety (e.g. the 'mad cow' and 'Belgian chickens' crises in the European meat industry) with significant impacts on consumers' willingness to pay (Raynaud *et al.*, 2005). This poses challenges to the organization of meat supply chains. Stronger vertical ties within agri-food chains have been proposed by many researchers (e.g. Hobbs, 1995; Den Ouden *et al.*, 1996; Hobbs and Young, 2001). The underlying assumption behind this argument is that with higher market segmentation the need for processors to define stricter governance structures grows (Schulze, *et al.*, 2007). Serving special market segments may require specific investments and/or a high collaborative adaptability of the supply chain. The Japanese pork market, for instance, is famous for its specific consumer demands concerning taste, marbling, cutting and the like (Makise, 2002). Since vertically disintegrated chains do not provide the required quality, the Japanese market has mainly been served by contractually bound or vertically integrated pork producers from Denmark or the United States.

Consider the example of a processor who implements new quality standards for a specific buyer (e.g. a supermarket). The new quality standards might require new knowledge about production techniques, handling processes and packaging facilities. Based on the request of the buyer, hog producers might need to invest in new feed and learning new production techniques, all of which are specially tailored to meet the processor's requirements (Dyer, 1996).

Empirical evidence supporting TCE hypotheses has been obtained in various studies. Den Ouden *et al.* (1996) identify customers' growing quality requirements as a major impetus behind contracts and vertical integration. In particular, product differentiation in order to meet changing consumer demands regarding credence attributes, such as animal welfare, food safety and environmental issues, is considered a main driver of closer ties in the meat supply chain. Boger (2001a) also argues that production contracts in the Polish pork market are applied as an instrument to establish high quality markets without appropriate grading systems.

In addition to the transactional perspective, the RET perspective also illustrates the impact of long-term relationships and interpersonal trust on quality management. The parties to these relationships have achieved mutual benefits from quality performance in previous transactions (Frazier, 1983), have come to understand each other's preferences and capabilities, and see good prospects for satisfying exchanges in the future. The parties are not bound contractually in the classical sense (MacNeil, 1980), but share expectations for continued beneficial exchange (Dwyer and Oh, 1987). Hakansson (1982) also proposed long-term relationships offer better opportunities to reduce waste, and promote quality in business-to-business relationships. In the case of the pork supply chain, if the suppliers fail to comply with the processing firms' requirements on quality and other delivery conditions, it will greatly harm the trust in the buyer-supplier relationships and thereafter influence future transaction opportunities. The same argument relates to the relationships between the processing firms and their customers in the downstream supply chain.

Based on the above description, we thus propose the following hypotheses:

> *H8: Spot market transaction cannot guarantee good quality management practices of the pork processing firms when the firms are trading with their upstream suppliers (H8a) and downstream customers (H8b).*

> *H9: Formal contractual governance mechanism is positively related to quality management practices of the pork processing firms in buyer-hog (meat) supplier relationships (H9a) and in buyer-supplier relationships of the downstream pork chain (H9b).*

> *H10: Relational governance mechanism is positively related to quality management practices of the pork processing firms in buyer-hog (meat) suppliers (H10a) and in buyer-supplier relationships of the downstream pork chain (H10b).*

5.4 Research methodology

The buyer-supplier relationships in pork supply chains constitute the unit of analysis in this study, and the data was collected from pork slaughtering and processing firms in China. In this part, we will describe the standard procedures of the empirical research, e.g. data collection, construct development, measurement validation and statistical tools for data analysis.

5.4.1 Samples and data collection

As the same data set as that in Chapter 3 and Chapter 4 is used for our analysis, we will omit the procedures of sample development and data collection.

5.4.2 Measurement

All the questionnaire items were measured using a 7-point Likert scale in which '1' represented 'strongly disagree' or 'totally untrue' and '7' represented 'strongly agree' or 'totally true'.

Asset specificity

Williamson (1985) identified site, physical, human and dedicated asset specificity as distinct types of transaction-specific investments. As the concentration degree of either hog production or pork processing is rather low, a slaughterhouse or processor depends on many suppliers. Furthermore, the slaughterhouses/processors usually have diversified marketing channels, for example, supermarkets, specialised stores, wholesale markets, and wet markets. The majority of the processing firms do not have a dominant retail market. Therefore, the site specificity and dedicated asset specificity are not the focus of our study. We follow the operationalization of Buvik (2002) for asset specificity: the magnitude of the investments and/or adaptations made by the buyer in physical assets, production facilities, tools and knowledge tailored to the relationships. The construct was measured with three questionnaire items (see Appendix A). This instrument was developed based on the previous studies of Heide and John (1988) and Claro (2004).

Uncertainty

Uncertainty may rise from rapidly changing technology, markets, and consumer preferences, etc. In the last two years, pork production in China has been experiencing enormous market turbulence and buy-supply related uncertainties. Due to rapid economic development, some farmers have quit hog production and migrated to other businesses or urban areas. The outbreak of blue ear diseases was another reason contributing to the shortage of hog supply. The pork price reached the highest in history at the end of 2007 (http://www.yangzhi.com/news/200801/2008_01_31_116227.html). Price and volume uncertainties are key aspects of this construct's domain (Noordewier *et al.*, 1990). In addition to price and volume uncertainty, we also consider quality uncertainty and the impact of unstable supply on pork production. This construct was therefore measured with 4 items, based on the previous studies of Noordewier *et al.* (1990) and Buvik (2002).

Spot market

This market governance arrangement is the traditional form of most agricultural produce transactions in China. It is also the most common governance structure in buyer-supplier relationships in pork production and marketing (Zhou and Dai, 2005). Farmers sell hogs to the slaughterhouses or deliver their hogs to brokers or traders based on instant transactions. This is a single item construct, measuring the percentage of hogs (or meat) procurement in the upstream model and percentage of pork products marketing through spot market transactions.

Contractual governance

The contract usually involves indications of price, quantity, quality, delivery time, rights and obligations. No contract would be complete due to the bounded rationality. Therefore, clear clauses with regard to the above-mentioned items in the contract play a very important role in regulating buyer-supplier transactions. In addition to these, the conflict settlement mechanism should also be stated in the contract to save renegotiation cost. As we used a single item to measure this construct, we requested our respondents to answer the questionnaire item on the basis of the completeness of clauses in the contract. This means that availability of such clauses with relevance to price, quantity, quality, delivery time and place, rights and obligations, and way of conflict settlement in the contract determine the degree to which the focal firm and its most important suppliers or customers created a formal contract. This instrument was adapted from the study of Poppo and Zenger (2002).

Relational governance

In this study, relational governance is defined as recurrent transactions that are completed based on long-term relationships between two parties with mixed or idiosyncratic specific investments. Collaborative relationships, long-term cooperation, sharing long- and short-term goals and plans, as well as trust between the processing firms and their most important suppliers or customers were the four questionnaire items used for this study. We developed this instrument based on the studies of Poppo and Zenger (2002) and Claro (2004).

Quality management practices

As described in Section 3.3.1 'Construct measures' of Chapter 3, this construct was measured mainly based on the studies of Saraph *et al.* (1989) and Kaynak (2003) and consisted of the following four sub-measurements: management leadership, supplier/customer quality management, quality design and process management. Each sub-measurement has multiple questions. 'Management leadership' is measured by 8 items, including top and middle level management's performance in implementing quality strategies, quality assurance schemes, employee empowerment in standard operations. 'Supplier quality management' has four items, emphasizing the pork processors' attention to selecting suppliers and the quality of the hogs (meat). For example, we have questions like 'our most important suppliers are selected based more on quality than on price of the hogs (meat) they offer' and 'we pay our most important suppliers with a premium for good quality hogs (meat)'. For the sub-measurement 'customer quality management', we used 3 items, including 'we involve our most important customers in the quality improvement process' and 'our most important customers pay more attention to quality than to price of the pork products'. With 2 and 3 items respectively, 'quality design' and 'process management' paid attention to the quality element in the design of pork products and services as well as work-floor management.

All the questionnaire items can be found in Appendix A.

5.4.3 Methods

The standardised procedure is used to assess the validity and reliability of the constructs under study in this chapter. It has been described in detail in Section 4.3.3 'Methods' of Chapter 4. Please refer to Table 4.1 for an overview of the statistical evaluation criteria for constructs in our study. In addition, the statistical method 'partial least squares' is used again for our data analysis. An introduction to this method is also given in Section 4.3.3.

5.5. Empirical results

5.5.1 Result of construct reliability and validity

Following the criteria for evaluating the validity and reliability of constructs in Table 5.2, we examined the inter-construct correlation, composite reliability and average variance extracted for the construct 'asset specificity', 'uncertainty' and 'relational governance mechanism'. The results are shown in Table 5.2, Table 5.3 and Table 5.4. The corrected item total correlation for Asset1 is 0.48 and 0.45 respectively for the upstream and downstream models. They are deleted for subsequent analysis. For the construct 'uncertainty', the corrected item total correlation for Uncertainty4 of the upstream model is -0.20. It was therefore deleted for subsequent analysis.

Table 5.2. Measurement and factor loadings for each construct (N=229).

Variables	Indicator	Upstream model (relationship with the suppliers)			Downstream model (relationship with the customers)		
		CITC*	Factor loading	Cronbach's alpha	CITC*	Factor loading	Cronbach's alpha
Asset	Asset1	0.48	-	0.73	0.45	-	0.75
specificity	Asset2	0.63	0.89		0.60	0.89	
	Asset3	0.58	0.89		0.60	0.89	
Uncertainty	Uncertainty1	0.55	0.81	0.71	0.64	0.83	0.76
	Uncertainty2	0.51	0.78		0.61	0.81	
	Uncertainty3	0.56	0.81		0.52	0.74	
	Uncertainty4	-0.20	-		0.51	0.72	
Spot market (single item)	Spot	-	-	-	-	-	-
Contractual governance mechanism (single item)	Contract	-	-	-	-	-	-
Relational	Relational1	0.51	0.79	0.70	0.53	0.80	0.71
governance	Relational2	0.42	-		0.25	-	
mechanism	Relational3	0.52	0.78		0.52	0.79	
	Relational4	0.55	0.81		0.53	0.80	

Note: CITC refers to 'corrected item-total correlations'.
All constructs are measured using 7-point Likert-scale (totally untrue or strongly disagree – totally true or strongly agree).

Table 5.3. Mean, standard deviation, composite reliability, variance extracted, and inter-correlation of constructs (upstream model).

Variables	Mean	Standard deviation	Composite reliability	Asset	Uncertainty	Spot	Contract	Relational	QMP
Asset specificity (Asset)	3.86	1.49	0.88	**0.89**					
Uncertainty	4.53	1.20	0.84	0.39	**0.80**				
Spot market (Spot)	4.96	1.60	1.00	-0.26	-0.39	**1.00**			
Contractual governance mechanism (Contract)	4.59	2.13	1.00	0.29	0.40	-0.45	**1.00**		
Relational governance mechanism (Relational)	5.00	1.27	0.83	0.17	0.23	-0.37	0.35	**0.79**	
Quality management practices (QMP)	4.77	1.26	0.88	0.24	0.25	-0.54	0.48	0.44	**0.78**

Note: the **bold** numbers on the diagonal are the square root of the variance shared between the constructs and their measures (square root of average variance extracted, referred to as AVE). Off-diagonal are the correlations among the constructs.

Table 5.4. Mean, standard deviation, composite reliability, variance extracted, and inter-correlation of constructs (downstream model).

Variables	Mean	Standard deviation	Composite reliability	Asset	Uncertainty	Spot	Contract	Relational	QMP
Asset specificity (Asset)	4.16	1.55	0.89	**0.89**					
Uncertainty	4.27	1.37	0.85	-0.33	**0.77**				
Spot market (Spot)	4.31	1.58	1.00	0.36	-0.51	**1.00**			
Contractual governance mechanism (Contract)	4.67	1.83	1.00	-0.35	0.48	-0.72	**1.00**		
Relational governance mechanism (Relational)	5.01	1.27	0.80	-0.22	0.16	-0.26	0.24	**0.76**	
Quality management practices (QMP)	4.68	1.29	0.84	-0.37	0.46	-0.58	0.53	0.48	**0.73**

Note: the same as in Table 5.3.

The corrected item total correlation for Relational2 of the construct 'relational governance mechanism' is 0.42 and 0.25 respectively for upstream and downstream models. They were also deleted from the construct. The corrected item-total correlations, factor loadings and Cronbach's Alpha for constructs 'asset specificity', 'uncertainty' and 'relational governance mechanism' is presented in Table 5.2. The exploratory factor analysis for the construct 'quality management practices' was the same as that in Section 3.3.3. Please refer to this section for more details. The corrected item-total correlations, factor loadings and Cronbach's Alpha for the construct 'Quality Management' is in Appendix C1 (upstream model) and Appendix C2 (downstream model).

Internal consistency was assessed using composite reliability. A value of 0.7 or greater is reasonable for exploratory research (Nunnally, 1988). The composite reliability for all constructs of the current study exceeds 0.80 (Table 5.3 and Table 5.4), indicating a fairly good internal consistency of the constructs.

We assessed the discriminant validity in two ways. First, the square root of the average variance extracted (AVE) should be greater than all construct correlations, as shown in Table 5.3 and Table 5.4. Second, all items should load higher to their associated construct than to the other constructs (see Appendix D1 and Appendix D2). The results for both criteria indicate that the discriminant validity of the constructs used in this study is more than adequate.

5.5.2 Results of structural equation modelling

The structural equation model was tested by applying PLS4.01. The results of the structural model for upstream and downstream pork chain are provided in Figure 5.2 and Figure 5.3 respectively. The average variance explained (R^2) for the upstream and downstream models are 40.7% and 48% respectively, indicating robust explanatory powers. Since PLS provides standardised path coefficients, we can compare the direction and the magnitude of the impacts based on the path coefficients. Table 5.5 and Table 5.6 summarise the results of partial least squares for both upstream and downstream pork chain respectively. The next part will describe the result of hypotheses testing.

Asset specificity and governance structure

The results indicate a positive significant impact of the degree of asset specificity on the selection of governance structures for both upstream and downstream models. There is strong support for both H1a (β=-0.12, $P<0.05$) and H2a (β=0.13, $P<0.05$) in the upstream model, and the same results are found for H1b (β=-0.21, $P<0.01$) and H2b (β=0.20, $P<0.01$) in the downstream model. These findings indicate that the focal firms have to make transaction specific investments to develop buyer-seller relationship. As the degree of asset specificity increases, the firms opt for formal contractual governance mechanism to safeguard against the opportunistic behaviour of suppliers and customers, and also effectively support resources and

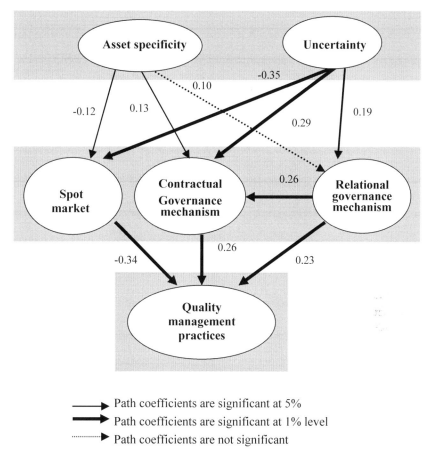

Figure 5.2. Results of the structural model (for relationship between pork processors and upstream suppliers).

efforts in developing relationships with upstream and downstream exchange parties. However, while the significant relationship between the degree of asset specificity and relational governance mechanism is supported in the downstream model (H5b: β=0.19, P<0.01), we do not find support for H5a in the upstream model (β=0.10, t=1.56). This result might imply that the focal firms pay more attention to long-term collaborative relationships with their downstream customers to safeguard their specific investment.

Uncertainty and governance structure

In Table 5.5 and Table 5.6, we find that H3a and H4a are both supported in our empirical study. This indicates that the focal companies apply spot market transactions with their upstream suppliers when uncertainty is low (H3a: β=-0.35, P<0.01), while using formal contract governance mechanism when uncertainty is higher (H4a: β=0.29, P<0.01). The

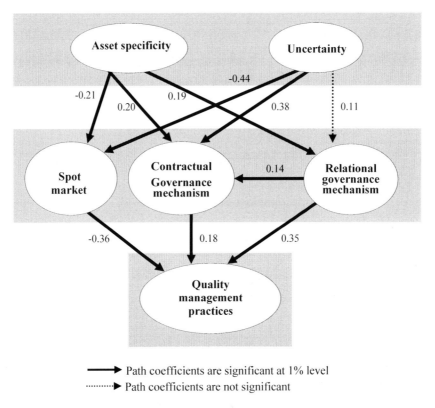

Figure 5.3. Results of the structural model (for relationship between pork processors and downstream customers).

Table 5.5. Results of hypotheses testing (upstream model).

Path	Path coefficient	t-value	Hypothesis
H1a: Asset specificity → Spot market	-0.12	-2.01*	Supported
H2a: Asset specificity → Contractual governance	0.13	2.14*	Supported
H3a: Uncertainty → Spot market	-0.35	-5.55**	Supported
H4a: Uncertainty → Contractual governance	0.29	4.85**	Supported
H5a: Asset specificity → Relational governance	0.10	1.56	Rejected
H6a: Uncertainty → Relational governance	0.19	2.73**	Supported
H7: Relational governance → Contractual governance	0.26	4.50**	Supported
H8a: Spot market → QMP	-0.34	-5.52**	Supported
H9a: Contractual governance → QMP	0.26	4.48**	Supported
H10a: Relational governance → QMP	0.23	3.66**	Supported

*$P<0.05$; **$P<0.01$.

Table 5.6. Results of hypotheses testing (downstream model).

Path	Path coefficient	t-value	Hypothesis
H1b: Asset specificity → Spot market	-0.21	-3.53**	Supported
H2b: Asset specificity → Contractual governance	0.20	3.25**	Supported
H3b: Uncertainty → Spot market	-0.44	-7.94**	Supported
H4b: Uncertainty → Contractual governance	0.38	6.82**	Supported
H5b: Asset specificity → Relational governance	0.19	2.44**	Supported
H6b: Uncertainty → Relational governance	0.11	1.57	Rejected
H7: Relational governance → Contractual governance	0.14	2.31**	Supported
H8b: Spot market → QMP	-0.36	-4.79**	Supported
H9b: Contractual governance → QMP	0.18	2.60**	Supported
H10b: Relational governance → QMP	0.35	7.53**	Supported

*$P<0.05$; **$P<0.01$

same applies to the downstream model. Both hypotheses are supported, which indicates that the focal companies depend on formal contractual governance mechanism as a response to high degrees of uncertain markets (H3b: β=-0.44, $P<0.01$; H4b: β=0.38, $P<0.01$). While we find a significant impact of uncertainty on relational governance mechanism in the upstream model (H6a: β=0.19, $P<0.01$), we do not find support for H6b in the downstream model (β=0.11, t=1.57). Although not significant, the coefficient was positive in accordance with our hypothesised sign. It is generally accepted that developing long-term partnerships in the supply chain is critical for focal firms to deal with uncertain markets. However, we find different impacts of relational governance on upstream suppliers and downstream customers for focal firms in the pork chain in China.

Relational governance and contractual governance mechanism

The complimentary role of relational governance on formal contractual governance mechanism is very obvious for the focal firms to manage upstream and downstream transactions. Our results support H7a for the upstream model (β=0.26, $P<0.01$) and H7b for the downstream model (β=0.14, $P<0.01$), suggesting that the focal firms may use both governance mechanisms in their interfirm exchanges. In a long-term collaborative and trusting relationship, the focal firms are more likely to conduct transactions based on contracts and comply with the requirements of the trading partners regarding quantity, quality, price, delivery condition, rights and responsibilities as well as compromises in conflict settlement.

Governance structure and quality management practices

The hypothesised relationships between governance structures and quality management practices for both upstream and downstream pork supply chains are positive and significant. As shown in Table 5.5 and Table 5.6, the spot market transaction has a negative impact on the implementation of quality management practices in China's pork processing firms for upstream model (β=-0.34, P<0.01) and downstream model (β=-0.36, P<0.01), which supports both H8a and H8b. Consistent with H9a (β=0.26, P<0.01) and H9b (β=0.18, P<0.01), formal contractual governance mechanism has a significant positive impact on quality management practices for both upstream and downstream pork chain relationship. This implies that contracts may facilitate the implementation of quality management practices in managing buyer-supplier relationships in China. Our empirical results also support H10a (β=0.23, P<0.01) and H10b (β=0.35, P<0.01), indicating the significant positive impact of long term collaboration and trust on implementing quality management practices in the pork processing industry in China.

5.6 Conclusion and discussions

The main purpose of our research was to develop an integrated framework that combines both transaction cost economics and relational exchange theory to explain the relationship between transaction attributes and governance arrangements and between governance arrangements and quality management. Specifically, the analysis involves the alignment between transaction attributes and governance structures, the interaction of interorganisational relationships between the logic of TCE and the need for trust and long-term cooperation between exchanging parties, and the impact of governance arrangements on quality management practices. Data was collected from 229 pork processing firms in China. Overall, the estimated upstream and downstream models show relatively good support for our hypotheses, with the exception of the impact of transaction attributes on relational governance mechanism.

5.6.1 Transaction attributes and governance structure

Our study provides empirical evidence that the degree of asset specificity and uncertainty does matter in the alignment of governance structures in the pork chain. This is consistent with transaction cost logic. Through formal contracts, managers specify penalties for early termination, and this formal record facilitates, if need be, the court 'picking up the pieces' and resolving termination issues (MacNeil, 1978). This result confirms the non-triviality of specialised assets and its importance in the governance decision (Poppo and Zenger, 2002). We also find that managers tend to use formal contracts when faced with greater uncertainty – presumably because formalised agreements facilitate necessary adaptation (Zhou *et al.*, 2008). When uncertainty increases, contracts should be more detailed in order to make monitoring and adjustment less difficult. Managers therefore craft more customised contracts to provide a safeguard, albeit not perfect, from the uncoordinated, self-interested actions that may increase with uncertainty (Williamson, 1996). Thus our empirical test is identical to transaction cost theory as the construct of uncertainty is significantly related to governance choice, and to some of the previous empirical studies. For example, Buvik's (2002) empirical findings demonstrated the positive effective impact of hybrid governance on industrial purchasing relationships when buyers and suppliers encountered substantial asset specificity and unpredictable or changing conditions.

Relational governance appears to offer transaction efficiencies, such as perceptions of stability to ease adaptations arising from uncertainty or decreased risk of opportunistic behaviour arising from specific investments (Zhou *et al.*, 2008). However, our study shows mixed findings in the impact of asset specificity and uncertainty on the use of relational governance. In relationships with customers, the focal firms appear more concerned about long-term cooperation and trust in the presence of asset specificity, which is in contrast to the relationships with hog or meat suppliers in the upstream model. This might mean that managers of focal firms do not appear to select relational governance in response to increasing levels of specialised assets in their relationship with suppliers. While increased asset specificity may facilitate long-term cooperation between focal firms and their downstream customers, it does not appear to be an effective means of maintaining a cooperative and trusted relationship between the focal firms and their suppliers.

Contrary to the significant positive relationship between the focal firms and their most important suppliers in the presence of uncertainty, our empirical findings indicate a non-significant relationship between uncertainty and relational governance between the pork processors and their downstream customers. This might be explained by the different environments the pork processors are in when trading with their suppliers and their customers. A more unstable environment with regard to hog (meat) supply, and price uncertainty was witnessed in the upstream pork chain than in the downstream chain. To gain stable hog (meat) supply for sustainable business development, it is critical for the pork processors to use relational governance in trading with suppliers. As Williamson (1991) states, relational norms are necessary to facilitate adjustments to high market disturbances, which are likely to occur with high levels of changes in hog (meat) supply and the large variance in quality due to many small suppliers. The other explanation might be the nature of relational ties in Chinese context. The building of relational networks is associated with longer term considerations. The relational ties take time to develop, but once formed, are difficult to break, even in turbulent environments. As our research does not focus on the nature and values of relational ties, we won't go further into this aspect.

5.6.2 Relational governance and contractual governance mechanisms

Within the tradition of strategic management, most empirical and theoretical work on relational governance couches it as a self-enforcing mechanism. Some scholars ignore the role of formal contracts (e.g. Saxton, 1997), while others view formal contracts as a more costly substitute for relational governance (Gulati, 1995; Dyer and Singh, 1998). Strong argument also indicates that the combined use of relational governance and formal contracts is fundamentally problematic, since formal controls signal distrust and relational governance is based on trust (Ghoshal and Moran, 1996). Contrary to this substitution view, our empirical analysis supports the conclusion that contracts and relational governance function as complements. This finding is consistent with previous empirical studies. For example, Burchell and Wilkinson (1997) have highlighted the complementary nature of formal contracts and interfirm social cooperation in the two industrial sectors of mining machinery and kitchen furniture in Britain, Germany and Italy. Ferguson *et al.* (2005) found out that there appear to be sufficient relational norms that mitigate any substantial negative effect of contractual governance in commercial banking exchanges in North America. Taking the research of the Chinese context as an example, our finding is also consistent with Yeung's (2006) observation that ethnic Chinese businesses in Southeast Asia employ both social networks and more formal (bureaucratic) forms of firm control. In addition, Lu *et al.* (2008) also found a significant impact of interpersonal trust on buyer-seller relationships in China's vegetable sector as complementary to more formal governance forms.

5.6.3 Governance structures and quality management practices

The shift from spot market and wholesale purchase towards preferred supplier arrangements is strongly induced by changes in consumer preferences and adjustments for supermarket formats (Ruben *et al.*, 2007). Once rapid economic development and urbanization have increased the income of farmers and the proportion of urban consumers, quality and safety attributes will be appreciated by consumers in selecting pork products. Retailers, especially the supermarkets look for a certain number of suppliers to meet quality demand. Contracts are developed with these suppliers. More franchised and specialised stores are established by large pork processing firms. The governance arrangements are developing toward hybrid and vertical supply chain management. As the institutional setting for obtaining a reward for quality production can be subject to a high degree of uncertainty in evolving markets (Boger, 2001a), it is even more important for firms in China to develop more integrated governance arrangements in their relationships with suppliers and customers. Meanwhile, long-term cooperative interfirm exchange relationships have to be established and maintained for the efficiency and continuity of exchanges. Our empirical test supports the positive relationships between more integrated governance forms and use of quality management practices in pork processing firms in China. This is in line with the findings of Martinez and Zering (2004) in the USA. Contracting between pork packers and producers in the USA has increased considerably since the 1990s. Marketing contracts accounted for approximately 69% of hogs sold in 2004, compared with less than 2% in 1980. One of the main reasons is the changing emphasis on pork quality by consumers. Den Ouden *et al.* (1996) also identified increasing quality requirements of customers as a major driving force for contracts and vertical integration in the Netherlands.

In summary, we find the following identical and different relationships between the pork processors and its upstream and downstream partners in the two models. (1) With the increasing degree of transaction specific investments and uncertainty, the pork processors tend to use contractual governance mechanisms to manage buyer-supplier relationships. The finding is the same between the two models. (2) If the pork processors intend to implement good quality management practices, they may not depend on spot transaction with their upstream suppliers and downstream customers. The buyer-supplier relationship management on the basis of contractual and relational governance mechanisms may help the companies to exert higher degree of control and monitoring on their exchange partners. Together with long-term cooperation established in trusted relationships, they contribute to better quality management of the pork processors. These identical findings can be understood in the context of the similar industrial structures in hog production, distribution and marketing (see Figure 2.2 for more details). Due to very low concentration degree in the sector, the pork processors need to face many suppliers and buyers. They usually apply spot market transactions with the small suppliers and sellers. Contracts are usually used in transaction with specialised hog producers and commercial producers in the upstream chain and with supermarkets and business agents in the downstream chain. Though similar structure exists in the pork chain, the pork processors do face different transaction characteristics in the upstream and downstream supply chains. They are confronted with more uncertainty than transaction specific investments in managing relationships with the suppliers. Therefore, they need to establish long-term cooperative relationships with the suppliers to secure raw material supply. The degree of uncertainty thus has a significant impact on the selection of relational governance mechanism in the upstream chain. In the downstream chain, there is less uncertainty involved. To expand market and generate sales growth, the pork processors need more specific investments with the downstream customers, e.g. training employees of the customers in product management, investments in cold chain facilities in the retail outlets. The time investment in getting to know the customers is also very critical for business operation.

Like any other, our study also has certain limitations. First, although our approach towards getting data from the most knowledgeable informant is consistent with some prior research on vertical relationships (e.g. Heide and John, 1990; Poppo and Zenger, 2002), the dependence on a single respondent for data on buyer-seller relationships suggests the possibility of common method bias. Using multiple sources in data collection would improve the reliability of the measures and increase the confidence in the results. Second, the generalisability of our results must be carefully considered. The sample of China's pork slaughtering and processing firms may reflect some unique characteristics of this specific sector. It is imperative to replicate the present study in other research settings. Third, some authors have investigated the relative importance of contractual and relational governance on exchange performance and the influence of the boundary spanner of these governance mechanisms and the exchange performance (e.g. Poppo and Zenger, 2002; Ferguson *et al.*, 2005). The impact of hybrid governance mechanisms on the performance of interfirm exchanges has not been studied in this article. Future study on this aspect will generate important implications for business to business exchanges in the Chinese context.

5.7 Managerial implications

As emerging economies move toward a market-based economy, a central issue is whether governance of market exchanges will evolve toward impersonal, contract-based institutions. Some propose that as economic transactions grow in scope and complexity, governance shifts from personal, reciprocal relational ties to more impersonal institutions such as contract law (North, 1990; Peng, 2003). As business transactions become more complex, characterised by high levels of asset specificity and uncertainty, managers are more likely to employ relational ties or contracts as safeguards for such complex exchanges (Zhou *et al.*, 2008). This research has been motivated to integrate economic and non-economic perspectives to understand both spot market transaction and two hybrid forms of interorganisational exchanges, namely formal contractual governance and relational governance mechanism. Therefore, our study makes a contribution to the organizational economics literature by offering operationalisations and empirical investigations of both market and hybrid transactions as well as of the role of long-term collaboration and trust in interfirm exchanges. The study on the impact of both transactional and relational governance on quality management practices is also deemed valuable as not much empirical study has been done in the sector so far. The empirical findings generate several important implications for the managers in the sector.

First, the analysis of governance forms and their relationships with transaction attributes highlights some basic strategies for establishing and managing channel relationships in pork supply chains. In the current Chinese setting, there is coexistence of different dimensions along the interfirm relationship spectrum. As there are many small hog producers and plenty of processing firms in China's pork production industry, spot market transaction is perhaps a popular selection for the commodity markets for the time being. However, firms have to make appropriate alignment between the nature of procurement and marketing situations at hand and the features of selected governance mechanisms when the transactions become more complex with high degrees of asset specificity and uncertainty. For example, specifying details on various transaction dimensions in a contract, the firms can execute high degrees of control over their suppliers and customers and induce them to make specialised investments to create exit barriers.

Second, our research finding shows the importance of both transaction specific investments and relational governance mechanism characterised by trust in determining long-term oriented interfirm collaborative relationships. Ganesan (1994) indicates the different focus of transaction specific investments and relational governance mechanism in developing the buyer-supplier relationships. The transaction specific investments achieve the realization through creating dependence and locking in exchange partners by getting them to invest in transaction-specific assets. However, with trust, the relational governance focuses on the perception of a fair division of the resources in the future. Relational exchanges obtain transaction efficiencies through joint synergies resulting from investment in and exploitation of idiosyncratic assets and risk sharing. Both have the ultimate objective of maximizing the outcomes obtained by channel members and do not imply any altruistic motives on the part of channel members. However, the trust in buyer-supplier relationships affects the long term orientation of a business company in three ways: (1) it reduces the perception of risk associated with opportunistic behaviour by the focal firms' suppliers or customers; (2) it increases the confidence of the focal firms that short-term inequalities will be resolved over a long period, and (3) it reduces the transaction costs in an exchange relationship (Ganesan, 1994). Because of bounded rationality and the costs of writing, negotiating, and implementing a contract, a comprehensive contract involving a long-term relationship is not possible. The hazards of opportunistic behaviour in long-term relationships can be mitigated or removed if there is trust between the two parties. Incomplete contracting in a trusting relationship means that the two parties agree to adapt to unanticipated contingencies in a mutually profitable manner. In such trusting relationships, the focal firms and their suppliers and customers are likely to respond to inequalities through solutions over the long run instead of short-term opportunistic behaviour. This suggests that trust reduces the risk of opportunistic behaviour in a long-term exchange relationship. Thus, when trust exists, the focal firms and their exchange partners in the supply chain can make idiosyncratic investments. Both parties will refrain from using their power to renege on contracts or use a shift in circumstances to obtain profits in their favour (Zaheer and Venkatraman, 1995).

Third, it is important for managers to opt for appropriate governance arrangements to ensure quality management in the pork chain. Quality control is of a specific nature in the case of pork products, since focal firms regularly face problems in monitoring the quality and safety of raw materials. Drug residues and disease aspects are difficult to detect but influence business relationships. Equally true is that for the retailers it is also difficult to detect the processes of pork production. Furthermore, processed pork products consist of heterogeneous ingredients. In order to guarantee reliable supply of quality pork products, the managers of pork processing firms in China should not only develop more integrated governance regimes, but also search for sustainable partnerships with suppliers and customers that reduce information and screening costs and reinforce mutual trust amongst chain members (Hueth *et al.*, 1999; Ruben *et al.*, 2007a).

The implications of our study are viewed best within the context of a practice-oriented approach and in light of the constraints of the study. Since the empirical analysis is conducted in the pork sector by using cross sector data, the generalization of the relationships awaits longitudinal studies in the sector and more investigations in other sectors in this emerging economy.

Chapter 6. Competitive strategy, quality management and government support

6.1 Introduction

One of the predominant challenges of this age is the production of safe food. Due to the far-reaching effects of food-borne diseases on food consumption in all parts of the world, food safety is one of the central issues for the food industry, governments, traders and consumers alike (FAO/WHO, 2002). In the food industry the quality management paradigm has been advocated in a wide range of research projects on the relationships between specific practices in quality management and the firm's performance (Flynn *et al.*, 1995). In Chapter 3, we examined the relationship between quality management practices (QMP) of pork processors in China and firm performance and found that QMP was positively associated with firm performance. However, as QMP is analysed as a higher order construct, we are not clear about which practices have significant positive contributions to firm performance. Therefore, one of the purposes of this chapter is to investigate the relationships between specific quality management practices and firm performance.

Quality management has often been advocated as being universally applicable to organizations. This is in contrast to the contingency approach of Operations Management that calls for internal and external consistency between strategy choices (Sousa and Voss, 2001). Though some of the studies have empirically supported the proposition that QMP are contingent on a firm's manufacturing strategy (e.g. Reed *et al.*, 1996; Sousa and Voss, 2001), the question as to whether the effects of QMP on firm performance are monotonic across different strategies has not been fully investigated (Matsuno and Mentzer, 2000). In this regard, this chapter investigates the moderator effect of competitive strategy on QMP-firm performance relationships. Therefore, the second purpose of this chapter is to propose and test the hypothesis that competitive strategy will moderate the relationship between QMP and firm performance.

The third purpose of this study is to examine the relationship between government support and firm performance of pork processors and the moderating effect of strategy in this relationship. Government authorities at various levels are of the utmost importance in the provision of the appropriate legislative framework to safeguard all aspects of food production, processing and sales to consumers (Griffith, 2005). The support of the technology infrastructure by the government and the conduciveness of the industrial and national technology climate is a catalyst for firms to achieve full technological potentials and improve firm performance. In this study, we will focus on the financial and technological support of the Chinese government authorities in managing food supply chains, for example training employees in quality management and facilitating scientific research in the pork processing sector.

The insights obtained from this empirical study help the pork processing firms not only to manage their environment more effectively but also to improve their organizational performance. Similarly, government authorities can examine national as well as international environmental conditions to understand how best to adapt or manage those conditions to improve the effectiveness of technological legislation and provide right incentives for better quality management in the pork processing sector.

To address these issues, we employ data from a sample of 229 pork processing firms in the east of China for empirical analysis. In the next section, the major theories used in this chapter will be introduced and the research framework will be developed, along with the hypothesizing of the relationship between quality management practices and firm performance and between financial and technological support of the government authorities and firm performance. Furthermore, the moderating effect of competitive strategy on the above-mentioned relationships will be examined. Then, the methodological issues associated with empirically testing of the hypothesised relationships are presented in Section 6. 3. The results are presented and analysed in Section 6.4. This is followed by a discussion and research implications in Section 6.5. The paper concludes with identification of the weaknesses of this study and recommendations for future research in Section 6.6.

6.2 Theoretical framework and hypotheses

In this section, we first discuss contingency theory and strategic management theory. Afterwards, elements of the framework will be detailed and hypotheses will be developed.

6.2.1 Contingency theory

The fit that organizations must achieve between their external environment and the elements and structure of their processes is the starting point of Contingency Theory (Lawrence and Lorsch, 1967; Boyd and Fulk, 1996). Many contingency studies have emphasised a connection between performance and the fit or alignment of the firm within its external environment (Miller, 1988; Strandholm et al., 2004). This view means that performance is determined not so much by the environment or the firm's actions as by the congruence of the two (Child et al., 2003).

As Clark et al. (1994) proposes, an important debate in the Contingency Theory is the question to what extent the external business environment determines organizations (environmental determinism) and decision-makers and the other way around: the degree to which organizations and decision-makers determines environments (strategic choice). The underlying point for this debate is which kind of environment is aimed at. Yasai-Ardekani and Nystrom (1996) make a distinction between the *general* environment and the *task* environment. The *general* environment includes socio-cultural, economic and governmental pressures, whereas the *task* environment encompasses product-market environment and factor-market pressures. As we understand it, the *general* environment is identical to external fit while the *task* environment is identical to internal fit.

In the past decade, companies have begun to recognise not only the need for continual quality improvement and meeting the needs of their immediate customers, but also the necessity of competing quickly and efficiently in ever-changing global markets (Robinson and Malhotra, 2005). Therefore, there should be a more focused approach to studying quality management issues within the internal and external supply chain contexts. Contingency Theory stresses the necessity of maintaining close and consistent linkages between the firm's strategy and the business environment (Venkatraman, 1989). The theory is important to our study for linking the company's strategy and external environment (government support in this study) to the relationships between QMP and firm performance.

6.2.2 Strategic management theory

Strategy is an essential part of any effective business plan. By using an effective competitive strategy, a company finds its industry niche and learns about its customers (Porter, 1980). The Miles and Snow (1978) and Porter (1980) typologies of business strategy are the two dominant frameworks in the strategic management literature. Miles and Snow (1978) developed a comprehensive framework that addresses the alternative ways in which organizations define and approach their product-market domains and choose structure and processes to achieve success in those domains (Slater and Olson, 2000). They suggested four strategic types: defenders, analysers, prospectors and reactors. Prospector's prime capacity is that of finding and exploiting new product and market opportunities. For a prospector, maintaining a reputation as an innovator in product and market development may be as important as, if not more important than, high profitability (Miles *et al.*, 1978). At the other end of the spectrum, defenders attempt to seal off a portion of the total market to create a stable set of products and customers. Analysers occupy an intermediate position between the two extremes by combining the strengths of both the prospector and defender to cautiously follow prospectors into new product-market domains while protecting a stable set of products and customers. The fourth type, the reactor, does not have a consistent response to the entrepreneurial problem (Mile and Snow, 1978; Slater and Olson, 2000). The first three enjoy similar degrees of success, while the last is a strategic failure (Segev, 1987). The implication of this proposition is that the strategy types do make a difference in performance. This implicitly indicates the importance of strategy implementation for firms in their competitive environment.

While Miles and Snow were studying strategy as part of a broader holistic approach to the organization-environment adaptation cycle, other researchers were addressing the same question from a different point of view, and developing a parallel typology to describe the strategy-making process. For example, Mintzberg (1973) suggested three modes of strategy-making: the Entrepreneurial, the Adaptive and the Planning. The process by which strategies emerge was emphasised rather than their contents. In the Entrepreneurial mode, strategy making is characterised by actively searching for new opportunities. Power is centralised in the hands of the chief executive, dramatic forward leaps are made in the face of uncertainty, and growth is the dominant goal of the organization. Of the four strategic types suggested by Miles and Snow (1978), the prospector strategy is most compatible with the Entrepreneurial mode of strategy-making (Burgelman, 1983).

The strategy literature provides numerous theories, research methodologies, and ideas on the strategy-performance relationship (Allen and Helms, 2006). But the literature has remained largely at the conceptual level in discussing the link between the business strategies and firm performance. Researchers have not determined which specific strategic practices are critical to achieve organizational goals (Allen and Helms, 2006). More importantly, there is a lack of studies with regard to the link in transitional economies like China. There is a recognised need for empirical work in this area. Therefore this study fills the gap.

6.2.3 Quality management practices and firm performance

In Chapter 3, we examined the joint impact of supply chain integration (SCI) and quality management practices (QMP) on firm performance of pork processors in China. The construct 'quality management practices' included five indicators: in-company quality management, supplier/customer quality management, employee involvement in quality management, quality design and process management. The empirical findings not only indicated a strong positive relationship between QMP (the higher-order construct) and firm performance, but also that QMP mediated the relationship between SCI and firm performance. Therefore, QMP (as a high order construct) plays a very critical role in achieving firm performance. In this research, we make a step further to explore the relationship between specific quality management practices and firm performance. This will provide more practical information to the managers of pork processors as to which practices contribute significantly to firm performance. In addition, we also examine the moderating effect of competitive strategy in the relationship between QMP and firm performance.

Several articles have reviewed and identified relationships between various quality management practices and firm performance. For example, Forker *et al.* (1997) concluded that suppliers quality management, role of the quality departments, training, quality data and reporting and product/service design are practices that resulted in positive performance. Ulusoy (2003) investigated operational performance in terms of logistics, supplier relations, customer relations, and production in a survey of manufacturing firms in Turkey, and concluded that the closer a company is to the best practices in the industry, the more likely it is for that company to achieve higher business performance. Van Plaggenhoef (2007) investigated the integration of quality management in meat, vegetable and flower supply chains. The empirical findings indicate that the best way for firms to cope with external pressures (such as change of societal demands for better quality products) is to integrate their quality management activities with both suppliers and customers.

The impact of quality management programs, such as hazard analysis and critical control points (HACCP), ISO 9001 and QS-9000[23], on some aspects of performance has been well acknowledged. Johnson (2002) and Terziovski *et al.* (2003) explored the adoption and benefit of ISO 9001 and QS-9000 implementation. Their research generated different results. Terziovski *et al.* (2003) found a positive relationship between these quality management certifications and firm performance while Johnson (2002) discovered conversely that QS-9000 actually would still allow the production of poor quality products and unacceptable delivery performance. Yeung *et al.* (2003) reported on ISO 9001 as an operational program that creates a foundation not only for improved internal operations and quality systems, but also as a practical conduit to supplier and customer processes. As these studies reported a promising picture of the relationship between the quality management programs with firm performance, it is necessary to further investigate the relationship.

Employee involvement in quality management is another critical factor for firms to achieve good performance. Human resource development is at the heart of all the quality management programs (Rao *et al.*, 1999). To achieve world class quality, it is imperative that a company empowers its workers and makes the best use of the talents and abilities of a company's entire workforce. Rao *et al.* (1999) conducted an empirical research in three newly industrialised countries (India, China and Mexico) to assess the practices in the human resource development dimension of quality management. Their findings reveal that companies in these countries score high on quality concepts, training in work-related skills, and continuous quality awareness building. However, their research indicates the low effectiveness of employee involvement and participation in quality management.

In quality management, quality design is an important dimension. The greatest source of product failure often lies in design weakness, with failure costs multiplying when discovered in the field (Cole, 1981). As one of the important dimensions of quality management practices, quality design is less studied with regard to its relationship with firm performance when comparing other dimensions of quality management practices. A meta analysis of the relationship between quality management practices and firm performance conducted by Nair (2006) could not examine the relationship of quality design and management to financial performance and customer service due to an insufficient number of papers investigating these relationships. It revealed that quality design and management was positively correlated with operational performance, but failed to conclude a positive correlation with customer service. Only Kaynak (2003) had relevant information on the relationship between quality design and firm performance.

---

[23] QS-9000 is a quality system standard that focuses on helping automotive suppliers ensure that they are meeting/ exceeding automotive customer requirements. ISO 9000 is the core of this standard, for example, document control, corrective action, auditing, etc., but adds quite a few other requirements. QS-9000 is now being replaced by a newer related standard called ISO/TS 16949. TS is much more process-oriented than QS or ISO. It defines the business as a set of processes with inputs and outputs that need to be defined, controlled, improved/optimized, etc. (http://www.isixsigma.com/dictionary/QS-9000-528.htm, accessed on Feb. 25, 2009).

Process management focuses on managing the manufacturing process so that it operates as expected, without breakdowns, missing materials, fixtures, tools, etc. (Flynn *et al.*, 1994). Quality management places a great deal of emphasis on the maintenance of quality process control (Forza and Filippini, 1998). There is evidence that some studies have shown that about 50% of quality problems are due to incoming materials (Crosby, 1979). By eliminating the input variance, the process control techniques become much more efficient because it is possible to concentrate on the variables which can be controlled internally, such as the conduct of both the machinery and the workforce.

Based on the above descriptions, we thus propose the following hypotheses:

> *H1: In-company quality management is positively related to firm performance of the pork processors in China (H1a for the upstream model;H1b for the downstream model).*

> *H2: Supplier/customer quality management is positively related to firm performance of the pork processors in China (H2a for the relationship with suppliers of the upstream model; H2b for the relationship with the customers of the downstream model).*

> *H3: Employee involvement in quality management is positively related to firm performance of the pork processors in China (H3a for the upstream model; H3b for the downstream model).*

> *H4: Quality design is positively related to firm performance of the pork processors in China (H4a for the upstream model; H4b for the downstream model).*

> *H5: Process management is positively related to firm performance of the pork processors in China (H5a for the upstream model; H5b for the downstream model).*

6.2.4 The moderating effect of prospector strategy in the QMP – firm performance relationship

The strategy of a firm provides its overall direction by specifying the firm's objectives, developing policies and plans to achieve these objectives and allocating resources to implement these policies and plans (Johnson and Scholes, 1999). When the strategy of the firm is strongly focused on supporting and improving quality management in the firm, the firm will allocate resources in its effort and becomes a forerunner of effective integration of quality management with its suppliers and buyers (Van Plaggenhoef, 2007). Although plenty of empirical studies in strategic management have examined firm-level strategy-performance relationships (Capon *et al.*, 1990), the investigation of the impact of competitive strategy on quality management and firm performance is limited. Sousa and Voss (2001) empirically investigate whether quality management practices are contingent on a plant's manufacturing strategy context, by examining the use of process quality management practices – a critical and distinctive subset of the whole set of quality management practices. The statistical analyses suggest that the pattern of use of process quality management practices is strongly influenced by a plant's overall strategic context. Reed *et al.* (1996) develop a contingency model of quality management according to which quality management effectiveness depends on the degree of fit between firm orientation (with the associated quality management practices) and environmental uncertainty. They found out that firms with different strategic orientations achieve financial performance through different routes with which different quality management practices are associated.

Most of the previous empirical testing of the strategy framework has been carried out in large countries and particularly in the USA (Christiansen *et al.*, 2003). Limited studies are available for small developed countries and the large developing world. As far as the pork processing industry in China is concerned, multiple strategies exist due to differences in factors such as organizational goals, strategies, and collections of resources. Although China's pork slaughtering industry is in a consolidation process, there are still a large number of pork slaughterhouses driven by low-cost strategy. Some of them even survive by offering facilities to the other small slaughterhouses. However, with rapid economic development and income growth, the structure of Chinese food expenditure is changing. The top tier of urban households in China devote expenditure to higher quality food: better cuts of meat, processed and packaged food, meals away from home and food that is safer, convenient, or healthier (Gale and Huang, 2007). To respond to this market sector, some large and medium-size firms are offering high-quality products to the Chinese consumers. They differentiate themselves by investing in brand construction and bring a wide range of products into the market. We expect that this type of prospector strategy will strengthen the relationship between quality management practices and firm performance. Therefore, the following hypotheses are proposed:

> H6: *The relationship between the in-company quality management and firm performance is moderated by the prospector strategy employed by the pork processors in China (H6a for the upstream model; H6b for the downstream model).*

> H7: *The relationship between supplier/customer quality management and firm performance is moderated by the prospector strategy employed by the pork processors (H7a for the relationship with suppliers of the upstream model; H7b for the relationship with customers of the downstream model);*

> H8: *The relationship between the employee involvement in quality management and firm performance is moderated by the prospector strategy employed by the pork processors (H8a for the upstream model; H8b for the downstream model).*

H9: The relationship between the quality design and firm performance is moderated by the prospector strategy employed by the pork processors (H9a for the upstream model; H9b for the downstream model).

H10: The relationship between the process management and firm performance is moderated by the prospector strategy employed by the pork processors (H10a for the upstream model; H10b for the downstream model).

6.2.5 Government's financial and technological support[24] and firm performance

It is well acknowledged that government agencies and public policies play a very important role in the national innovation system in any country (Nelson, 1993). China is making a transition from an economy in which growth is based on labour intensive production and imported ideas and technology to one in which growth is driven by domestic innovation. If China wants to make this transition, we would expect to see institutions that promote the technological advance and firms that develop new capabilities, technologies and products (Dobson and Safarian, 2008). The Chinese government has realised the problem of its weak technological development and innovative capacity. Investment in R&D has increased. China's R&D intensity (R&D spending as a ratio of GDP) reached 1.6% in 2006 compared to 2.5% and 3.2% in the United States and Japan, respectively (OECD, 2006). R&D spending was mainly allocated to industry in 2004 (67%), with 10% going to higher education institutions. United Nations (2006) also reports China's heavy investments in human resources in science and technology. As far as government support to the pork processing sector is concerned, the Ministry of Science and Technology (MOST) launched a series of programs five years ago to support companies working together with universities and research institutions to promote improved pig breeding and reproduction, swine breed conservation, slaughtering facility innovation and further processing of pork by-products. The Ministry of Agriculture (MOA) invested heavily in constructing disease-free zones. The State General Administration of Quality Inspection invested in standardised swine production zones and certified hog production farms. It is worth mentioning the following important programs launched by the Chinese government to promote scientific and technological development: the Key Technologies R&D Programs (launched in 1982), the Spark Program (launched in 1986), the High-Tech Research Development Program (launched in 1986), the Torch Program (launched in 1988) and the National Key Basic Research (launched in 1997). The main missions of these programs are to facilitate industrial upgrading and economic development through advanced science and technology, stimulate R&D in industries that would result in original innovations and improve the industries' international competitiveness (Sigurdson,

---

[24] We originally used the 'perceived government support' construct to examine its relationship with firm performance. The construct included two sub-dimensions: (1) 'the effectiveness of quality assurance schemes' and 'quality inspection systems', and (2) the 'financial/technological support from the government authorities'. Due to the insignificant effect of the first sub-dimension on firm performance, we deleted it from our current analysis.

2004). Pork processing firms can stand on the same platform as the other sectors and apply for these national projects together with universities and research institutions. In addition to the financial and technological support from the central government, local authorities also provide support to stimulate the development of the pork processing industry. For example, Nanjing municipal government in Jiangsu province provided a subsidy of € 10,000 for the consolidation of a slaughterhouse and € 20,000 for a slaughterhouse to apply mechanical operation[25]. The financial institutions also provide financial support to large-scale pork processors. For example, the Agricultural Bank of China provided € 10 billion to agri-food companies including Shineway in 2006 (the largest pork processor in China)[26].

In the present era of deregulation, privatization and fierce market competition, most industrialists in developing countries have come to the realization that better technology is needed for the survival of both public and private sector enterprises (Sharif, 1994). Technology not only enables necessary transformation operations, but also provides the vital underpinning for survival and prosperity of the enterprise in an increasingly globalised and interlinked world economy (Fusfeld, 1989). More and more the value of a product is determined by the technology that goes into it, and not by the raw material that constitutes it (Bolwijn and Kumpe, 1990; Kleindorfer and Partovi, 1990). As some of the most important members of the national innovation systems, governments at various levels play a critical role in establishing norms and regulations to promote technological innovation. We thus propose the following hypothesis:

> *H11: The financial and technological support of the government authorities are positively related to firm performance of the pork processing firms in China (H11a for the upstream model; H11b for the downstream model).*

6.2.6 The moderating effect of the prospector strategy on the relationship between government support and firm performance

Current literature includes many papers on business strategies, which have looked into the causes of superior performance and the process by which competitive advantages are created (Prahald and Hamel, 1990; Schroeder, 1990). However, there is a lack of clear understanding of options and opportunities in technological management in developing countries (Sharif, 1994). Therefore there is a strong suggestion that technological considerations must be properly incorporated into overall business strategies. Sharif (1994) examined the relationship between four commonly practiced business strategies (price, value, niche and image leadership) with the four evolving technology strategies (technology leader, follower, exploiter and extender). It is proposed that being a technology leader requires that firms are fast, fearless, facilitative and flexible to a very high value market, and spend heavily on research and development.

---

[25] Report of the Nanjing Municipal Designated Pork Slaughtering Administration, 2005.

[26] http://finance.sina.com.cn/roll/20071106/01171771927.shtml, accessed on Oct. 25, 2008.

Technology follower can reap benefits if they could buy state-of-the-art facilities or modify products and processes through reverse engineering. They need to be very good at quickly adapting advanced technologies to join the high value market at the beginning of the growth phase of the product life cycle. When the market is growing, exploitation of standardised technologies may give rise to rapid growth (a strategy successfully implemented by the newly industrialised countries like Korea, and Singapore). Technology extenders cater for the low value price-sensitive markets which have been vacated by the industry leaders.

For developing countries, firms are almost exclusively dependent on imported mature technologies to take advantage of relative abundant endowment of either natural resources or unskilled labour, or both. When competition for quality products is becoming more fierce, firms need capability to acquire better technologies and also capability to maintain and adapt imported technologies. Although not all firms need to be able to engage in major product and process innovation, they must at least have the capacity to undertake incremental improvements in existing technologies, as competition is increasingly based on product differentiation and value addition. To move from this follower strategy into the leader category, innovation capability becomes a most important prerequisite and entrepreneurship is often the critical bottleneck in many countries (Sharif, 1994). Therefore, strategy formulation should be guided by a firm's existing technological capabilities (e.g. Hayes, 1985), which means a firm's competence in manufacturing technology or quality processes is a 'springboard' for development strategy (Parthasarthy and Sethi, 1992). However, the extent to which firms in general coordinate their decisions about strategy and technology is an open question (Dean and Snell, 1996). Empirical study will enable a better understanding about the financial/technology-strategy-performance linkages. We thus propose:

> H12: The relationship between support of the government authorities and firm performance is moderated by prospector strategy (H12a for the upstream model; H12b for the downstream model).

Figure 6.1 summarises the previous discussion and provides the integrated conceptual framework for this study. The control variables will be discussed in Section 6.3.

6.3 Research design

As the same data collected in 229 pork processors in eastern China is used for analysis, we won't introduce the sample frame and data collection procedure. The remaining part of this section is devoted to the development of measures, control variables and the statistical method.

6.3.1 Measures

As the construct development of 'quality management practices' and 'firm performance' has been presented in Section 3.2, we will focus on the measures of prospector strategy and the

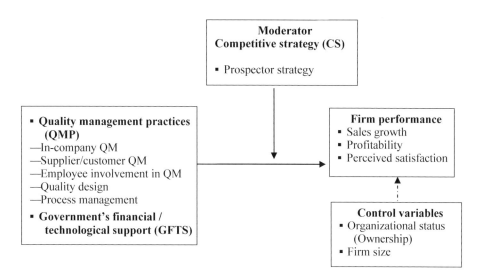

Figure 6.1. Theoretical framework.

government's financial and technological support. The detailed items of the new constructs are listed in Appendix A.

Prospector strategy

Snow and Hambrick (1980) distinguish between four broad approaches for identifying and measuring strategies: (1) self-typing; (2) objective indicators; (3) external assessment; and (4) investigator inference. The most widely employed method to operationalise Miles and Snow's strategic typology is that the respondents are asked to classify their organization as defender, prospector, analyser or reactor based on paragraph descriptions of the four strategic types (Conant *et al.*, 1990). As our study only focuses on prospector strategy, we follow the recent attempts to measure and operationalise the variable using multi-item scales. In our study, the prospector strategy refers to the pork processors focusing on a strategy of seeking competitive advantage by distinguishing themselves from their competitors through a wide range of product offerings and sound company image. This strategy was measured using an amended form of the studies by Miller (1988), Conant *et al.* (1990) and Slater and Olson (2000).

Government's financial and technological support

This construct refers to the financial and technological support provided by both central government and local government to promote the competitiveness of the industry and manage food quality and safety. In strategic quality management, Chinese government has recognised there is a lack of awareness in the pork processing sector on quality management and therefore encourages firms to build partnerships with overseas industries and universities (Li and

Willborn, 1990) to learn advanced technology and managerial experiences. Investment into science and technology has been increased. To improve the innovation capability of the processing firms is one of the very important elements in government funded programs. Pork processing firms can apply for financial support to buy foreign production lines, to invite foreign experts in employee training programs. This construct includes two scale items, indicating the extent of financial and technological support pork processors could get from the government authorities.

Firm performance

This construct uses both financial and operational indicators to measure the firm performance of pork processors. Originally there were four items including sales growth, market share, profitability and customer satisfaction. In the structuring equation modelling of Chapter 3, the item 'market share' was deleted due to its poor contribution to the goodness-of-fit of the model. Therefore the 'firm performance' construct in this study uses the unweighted composite score of three items including 'sales growth', 'profitability' and 'perceived customer satisfaction'.

Control variables

In addition to the focal theoretical variables mentioned above, two control variables are included in the study, namely organizational status and company size. The rationale for these control variables is explained as follows.

Organizational status (ownership)

China has experienced radical enterprise restructuring since the mid-1990s. Ownership forms have evolved from mostly state-owned enterprises (SOEs) to a mix of SOEs, collectively owned and non-state enterprises that often include government and private investors, as well as private and foreign-owned enterprises (Dobson and Safarian, 2008). There is a sharp decline in the share of SOEs in terms of total value added for large and medium-size enterprises in the manufacturing sector, from 73.3% in 1995 to 34.5% in 2002. Behind the substantial decline of the SOEs, a large increase is found among the shareholding enterprises, whose share of value added in the total for all types of ownership rose from 6.8% in 1995 to 33.1% in 2002. Foreign enterprises also gained in share during the same period, increasing from 7.0% to 15.9%. In addition, similar to SOEs, the collectives are a shrinking segment within Chinese industry (Motohashi, 2008). This is also reflected in the picture of the organizational status of the pork processors in China. The diversity of ownership has been presented in Table 3.2. With 150 private and private shareholding processors, we witness the dominant position of this ownership in the pork processing sector in China (65.5% of the total respondent companies in 2005). It is interesting to examine whether different types of companies perform differently in QMP. We used dummy variables in the regression analysis. Three categories of ownerships are examined in our analysis: state and collectively owned firms (reference variable), foreign joint ventures and private firms.

Firm size

Firm size is a contingency variable and may affect the resources and networking of a firm (Scholten, 2006). It has been noted that larger firms have more resources than smaller firms (Boyer *et al.*, 1996). It is believed that larger firms have more flexibility to devote resources to strategic purchasing activities, while smaller firms do not have the same flexibility (Carr and Pearson, 1999). Previous research on the impact of firm size on quality management is diverse. Authors such as Powell (1995) and Taylor and Wright (2003a) found that firms with discontinued quality management were predominantly small in size. Large firms are better in quality management practices due to more market power, capital resources and professional and managerial experience. Another view is that smaller firms have flatter organizational structure and more informal communication channels. As a result quality management systems may be more effectively implemented in small firms (Van Plaggenhoef, 2007). However, some researchers did not find any impact of size on quality management (e.g. Ahire and Dreyfus, 2000; Ahire *et al.*, 1996). In this research, the size of the firms was measured by the number of employees of the pork processor. The respondents were requested to report the number of employees in 2004.

6.3.2 Method

Multiple regression is used to test our hypotheses. Regression analysis is popular among researchers because it allows for an evaluation of the degree (i.e. coefficient size), nature (i.e. coefficient sign) and optimization (i.e. coefficient of determination R^2) of association between variables (Hair *et al.*, 1998). The regression model is a linear combination of independent variables that corresponds as closely as possible to the dependent variables (Lattin *et al.*, 2003). In a two-dimensional example this means that regression analysis estimates the line of best fit by minimizing the vertical distances between the points used to estimate the line. The line of the best fit is called the regression line. The vertical distances between the points and the estimated lines are squared and used as measurement of the total sum of error. In fitting the line, the ordinary least squares procedure minimises the sum of the square error. A general multiple regression equation has the following form (Hair *et al.*, 1998):

$$Y = \beta_0 + \beta_1 X_1 + \beta_2 X_2 + ... + \beta_k X_k + \varepsilon$$

In this equation, Y is the dependent variable and the X_k are the independent variables and ε is the error term of the prediction. β_0 is the intercept of the regression line. The coefficient β_k is the relative contribution of the independent variable X_k to the overall prediction of the dependent variable and represents the standardised partial regression coefficient (Churchill, 1999).

The coefficient of determination (R^2) is one of the most important measures. This coefficient represents the proportion of variation in the dependent variable that is accounted for by the co-variation in the predictor variables. The adjusted coefficient R^2 takes into account the number of independent variables and the sample size. This measure gives an insight into what certain independent variables significantly influence the dependent variable. The adjusted R^2 ranges from 0 to 1 and the higher the value, the better the explanatory power of the regression equation. The significance of R^2 adjusted is assessed by the magnitude of the F statistics.

Another important item in multiple regression is the Variation Inflation Factor (VIF) which can be used to assess multicollinearity within the data. If multicollinearity is present, the independent variables are highly correlated and are interchangeable. When a multiple regression is carried out with variables showing high levels of multicollinearity it will not be clear which variable accounts the most for the variation in the dependent variable (Field, 2003). As our study investigates the moderating effect of the prospector strategy, we use the mean centering technique in our analysis to remove the multicollearity between the predictors and the interactions containing these predictors (Lai *et al.*, 2005).

By computing the unweighted average of the items reflecting each construct, we regressed the firm performance on QMP, including the moderator and the control variables. We standardised the variables to reduce multicollinearity between the multiplicative terms (moderator variable) and their constituent variables.

6.4 Results

6.4.1 Validity and reliability of measures and constructs

As the constructs 'prospector strategy' and 'government's financial and technological support' (GFTS) have multiple items, we use factor analysis to check their validity and reliability. Following common practice (Fornell and Larcker, 1981), we examine the individual item reliability (factor loading) and the value of Cronbach's alpha for construct reliability. We first examined the loadings of the measures on their corresponding constructs. The result in Appendix E reveals that all loadings are greater than 0.7 for the two constructs, indicating a high degree of individual item reliability. The Cronbach's alpha for the two constructs 'prospector strategy' and GFTS is 0.77 and 0.81 respectively, higher than 0.7 as recommended by Hair *et al.* (1998).

We then test the unidimensionality of our measures. Means, standard deviations, and correlation matrix for all the measures of the prospector strategy and QMP-firm performance link in the upstream model (the relationship between pork processors and their suppliers) and the downstream model (the relationship between the pork processors and their customers) are reported in Table 6.1 and Table 6.2 respectively. The unidimensionality for the prospector strategy and QMP-performance link was also checked. The results show that all of the intercorrelations are below 0.80, indicating sound unidimensionality of the measures in this study. Researchers have commonly used a cut-off of 0.80 for correlations among independent variables for dismissing serious multicollinearity problems (Hair *et al.*, 1998).

Test for multicollinearity by examining variance inflation factors (VIF) also showed no problem. The largest of the resulting VIF scores in all the regression models in this study is 4.057. Most of the VIF scores were below 2.0, well below the maximum level of 10.0 suggested by Mason and Perreault (1991), indicating that multicollearity shouldn't be a problem with our data.

6.4.2 Test of the hypotheses

The hypotheses were tested using moderated hierarchical regression analysis. The approach recommended by Cohen and Cohen (1983) was followed. Three regression equations are considered:

$$Y=a+b_1X \tag{1}$$

$$Y= a+b_1X+ b_2M \tag{2}$$

$$Y= a+b_1X+ b_2M+ b_3 X^*M \tag{3}$$

Where Y is the dependent variable, X is the independent variable and M is the potential moderating variable. As per Sharma *et al.* (1981), M can be deemed as a pure moderator, if Equations (1) and (2) should not be different but should be different from Equation (3) i.e. $b_2=0$ but $b_3 \neq 0$. However if $b_2 \neq b_3 \neq 0$, then, M is a quasi moderator. Such a variable is both a predictor as well as a moderator (Sharma, *et al.*, 1981; Purani and Sahadev, 2008).

The following steps are used to estimate the above equations. In Step 1 (Model 1[27]), the main effects of QMP, GFTS, and two control variables (firm ownership and firm size) were entered as a block. The explained variance is marginally significant (Upstream model: $R^2=0.629$, F=46.349, $P<0.01$; Downstream model: $R^2=0.669$, F=48.990, $P<0.01$). In Step 2 (Model 2), the main effects of QMP, GFTS with the moderator 'prospector strategy' as well as the control variables were entered as a block. The explained variance is significant (Upstream model: change in $R^2=0.071$, F=50.528, $P<0.01$; Downstream model: change in $R^2=0.019$, F=47.953, $P<0.01$). Finally, each of the six interaction effects of QMP and GFTS as well as the prospector strategy was added to the base model 'Model 2', each time with one interaction effect[28]. Therefore another 6 models were generated (Model 3-Model 8). Only models with

---

[27] As the regression result of Model 1 is similar to that of Model 2, the result of this model is not presented in Table 6.3 and Table 6.4.

[28] This method has been applied by Dean and Snell (1996).

Table 6.1. Means, standard deviations and intercorrelations (Upstream model, n=229).

Variable*	Mean	SD	1	2	3	4	5	6	7	8	9	10
1. In-company QM	4.600	1.270										
2. Supplier QM	4.846	1.204	0.765									
3. Employee	4.795	1.350	0.369	0.313								
4. Design	4.786	1.208	0.476	0.435	0.282							
5. Process	4.530	1.282	0.782	0.723	0.354	0.414						
6. GFTS	4.620	1.578	0.458	0.429	0.263	0.453	0.459					
7. Prospector	3.879	1.202	0.606	0.556	0.328	0.470	0.581	0.782				
8. Foreign JV	0.070	0.256	0.181	0.158	0.159	0.167	0.275	0.175	0.227			
9. Private	0.660	0.476	0.274	0.250	0.174	0.110	0.204	0.166	0.205	-0.381		
10. Size	4.649	16.03	0.268	0.234	0.206	0.195	0.277	0.147	0.203	-0.003	0.109	
11. Perform	4.169	1.060	0.716	0.707	0.406	0.463	0.690	0.615	0.714	0.258	0.226	0.267

Independent variables: 1=In-company quality management; 2=supplier quality management; 3=employee involvement in quality management; 4=quality design; 5=process management; 6=government's financial and technological support; 7=Prospector strategy; 8=control variable ownership foreign joint venture and 9=dummy variable ownership private companies and 10=control variable firm size.
Dependent variable: firm performance.

Table 6.2. Means, standard deviations and intercorrelations (Downstream model, N=229).

Variable*	Mean	SD	1	2	3	4	5	6	7	8	9	10
1. In-company QM	4.600	1.270										
2. Customer QM	4.397	1.357	0.394									
3. Employee	4.795	1.350	0.369	0.298								
4. Design	4.786	1.208	0.476	0.279	0.282							
5. Process	4.530	1.282	0.782	0.331	0.354	0.414						
6. GFTS	4.620	1.578	0.458	0.273	0.263	0.453	0.459					
7. Prospector	3.879	1.202	0.606	0.369	0.328	0.470	0.581	0.782				
8. Foreign JV	0.070	0.256	0.181	0.041	0.159	0.167	0.275	0.175	0.227			
9. Private	0.660	0.476	0.274	0.191	0.174	0.110	0.204	0.166	0.205	-0.381		
10. Firm size	4.649	16.03	0.268	0.220	0.206	0.195	0.277	0.147	0.203	-0.003	0.109	
11. Perform	4.169	1.060	0.716	0.257	0.406	0.463	0.690	0.615	0.714	0.258	0.226	0.267

Independent variables: 1=In-company quality management; 2=customer quality management; 3=employee involvement in quality management; 4=quality design; 5=process management; 6=government's financial and technological support; 7=Prospector strategy; 8=control variable ownership foreign joint venture and 9=dummy variable ownership private companies and 10=control variable firm size.
Dependent variable: firm performance.

significant interaction effects are presented in Table 6.3 (for upstream model) and Table 6.4 (for downstream model).

From Table 6.3 and Table 6.4, we find that the moderator 'prospector strategy' has a significant positive correlation with firm performance in both upstream and downstream models ($P<0.01$).

Results of the hypotheses test for the upstream model (relationship between pork processors and their suppliers)

We expected a positive relationship between each of the five dimensions of quality management practices and firm performance. From Table 6.3, we find that the following quality management practices have significant positive relationships with firm performance: in-company quality management ($t=2.065$, $P<0.05$); supplier quality management ($t=4.080$, $P<0.01$); employee involvement in quality management ($t=2.033$, $P<0.05$) and process management ($t=1.765$, $P<0.10$). However the positive relationship between quality design and firm performance is not supported ($t=0.220$, $P=0.826$). Therefore we can conclude that H1a, H2a, H3a, H5a are supported while H4a is rejected, indicating that the organizational performance of pork processors in China benefits from such quality management practices as in-company quality management, supplier quality management, employee involvement in quality management and process management. Quality design doesn't contribute to the firm performance of the pork processors.

In the second group of hypotheses (from H6a to H10a for the upstream model), we expected that the prospector strategy would moderate the relationships between the quality management practices and firm performance. From Table 6.3, we only find the significant increases in the change of R^2 value (from base Model 2) in Model 4 (change in R^2 =0.006, $P<0.05$), Model 6 (change in R^2 =0.004, $P<0.10$) and Model 7 (change in R^2 =0.005, $P<0.05$), indicating that the prospector strategy increases the strengths between three quality management practices and firm performance, namely supplier quality management, quality design and process management. Thus H7a, H9a and H10a are supported while H6a and H8a are rejected.

In H11a, we expected a significant positive relationship between government financial and technological support (GFTS) and firm performance. From Table 6.3, we find that this hypothesis is supported ($t=2.139$, $P<0.05$), indicating that the GFTS contributes significantly to firm performance of the pork processing industry in China.

We expected a moderating effect of the prospector strategy in the GFTS-firm performance link (H12a). However our empirical findings rejected this hypothesis (change in R^2 =0.002, $P=0.256$), indicating that firms with the prospector strategy may not present a stronger strength in the relationship between GFTS and firm performance.

Table 6.3. Results of hierarchical regression analysis for the Upstream model (the relationship between the pork processors and suppliers, N=229).

Independent variables	Dependent variable: firm performance			
	Model 2	Model 4	Model 6	Model 7
Main effect				
In-company QM	0.150 (2.065)**	0.144 (2.005)**	0.154 (2.134)**	0.148 (2.061)**
Supplier QM	0.257 (4.080)***	0.271 (4.314)***	0.253 (4.037)***	0.260 (4.152)***
Employee involvement	0.084 (2.033)**	0.082 (1.994)**	0.080 (1.940)*	0.085 (2.078)**
Quality design	0.010 (0.220)	0.015 (0.338)	0.020 (0.453)	0.017 (0.372)
Process management	0.115 (1.765)*	0.109 (1.686)*	0.110 (1.693)*	0.110 (1.710)*
Government's financial/tech support	0.142 (2.139)**	0.137 (2.086)**	0.140 (2.119)**	0.131 (1.991)**
Moderators				
Prospector strategy	0.228 (3.061)***	0.215 (2.897)***	0.230 (3.099)***	0.223 (3.003)***
Interaction items				
In-company QM×Prospector				
Supplier QM×Prospector		0.078 (2.033)**		
Employee involvement×Prospector			0.063 (1.659)*	
Quality design×prospector				
Process management×Prospector				0.077 (1.960)**
Government's financial/tech support×Prospector				
Control variables				
Ownership (foreign joint venture)	0.083 (1.856)*	0.087 (1.960)**	0.082 (1.846)*	0.076 (1.712)*
Ownership (private)	0.041 (0.925)	0.053 (1.186)	0.045 (1.013)	0.051 (1.152)
Company size	0.044 (1.121)	0.034 (0.869)	0.035 (0.876)	0.030 (0.764)
Model F	50.528	46.974	46.555	46.885
R^2	0.700	0.705	0.703	0.705
R^2_{Adj}	0.686	0.690	0.688	0.690
ΔR^2	0.071***	0.006**	0.004*	0.005**

Results of Model 1 are not presented as they are very similar to those of Model 2. The independent variables in Model 1 include the main effects of QMP, government's financial and technological support and the control variables.
The regression results for Model 3 (interaction items in-company quality management×Prospector), Model 5 (interaction item employee involvement into quality management×Prospector), Model 7 (interaction item financial and technological support×Prospector) are not presented as they are not significant.
*P<0.1, **P<0.05 and ***P<0.01; regression coefficients are standardized coefficients (β) and |t-test| within parentheses. The mean centering technique was used in models with interaction items to remove multicollinearity between the predictors and the interactions containing these predictors.

Table 6.4. Results of hierarchical regression analysis for the Downstream model (the relationship between the pork processors and customers, N=229).

Independent variables	Dependent variable: firm performance	
	Model 2	**Model 4**
Main effect		
In-company QM	0.303 (4.539)***	0.316 (4.726)***
Customer QM	-0.124 (-2.884)***	-0.148 (-3.301)***
Employee involvement	0.101 (2.379)***	0.103 (2.424)**
Quality design	0.032 (0.701)	0.038 (0.823)
Process management	0.179 (2.798)***	0.177 (2.788)***
Government's financial/tech support	0.127 (1.882)*	0.120 (1.780)*
Moderators		
Prospector strategy	0.280 (3.667)***	0.290 (3.813)***
Interaction items		
In-company QM×Prospector		
Customer QM×Prospector		0.073 (1.793)*
Employee involvement×Prospector		
Quality design×Prospector		
Process management×Prospector		
Government's financial/tech support×Prospector		
Control variables		
Ownership (foreign joint venture)	0.073 (1.595)	0.076 (1.685)*
Ownership (private)	0.054 (1.207)	0.058 (1.297)
Company size	0.055 (1.362)	0.042 (1.030)
Model F	47.953	44.330
R^2	0.688	0.693
R^2_{Adj}	0.674	0.677
ΔR^2	0.019***	0.005*

Results for Model 1 are not presented as they are very similar to those of Model 2. The independent variables in Model 1 include the main effects of QMP, government's financial and technological support and the control variables.

The regression results for Model 3 (interaction items in-company quality management×Prospector), Model 5 (interaction item employee involvement into quality management×Prospector), Model 6 (interaction item quality design×Prospector), Model 7 (interaction item process management×Prospector), Model 8 (interaction item financial and technological support×Prospector) are not presented as they are not significant.

*$P<0.1$, **$P<0.05$ and ***$P<0.01$; see Table 6.3.

Results of the hypotheses test for the downstream model (relationship between pork processors and their customers)

The regression results for the downstream model (the relationship between pork processors and the downstream customers) are presented in Table 6.4. The same as the upstream model, we expected a positive relationship between each of the five dimensions of quality management practices and firm performance. From Table 6.4, we find the same positive effects of the following quality management practices on firm performance with the upstream model: in-company quality management (t=4.539, $P<0.01$); employee involvement in quality management (t=2.379, $P<0.01$) and process management (t=2.798, $P<0.01$). The same insignificant effect of quality design on firm performance is also found (t=0.032, $P=0.484$). These findings find support for H1b, H3b and H5b, indicating that in-company quality management, employee involvement in quality management and process management contribute significantly to firm performance in the relationship between pork processors and the downstream customers. The rejection of H4b indicates that quality design doesn't have a direct significant correlation with firm performance. However, while supplier quality management contributes significantly to firm performance of pork processors, we find that customer quality management has a significant negative relationship with firm performance (t=-2.884, $P<0.01$), indicating H2b is rejected. This is unexpected; as customer quality management seems to negatively contribute to firm performance in pork processing firms.

In the second group of hypotheses (from H6b to H10b for the downstream), we expected that the prospector strategy would moderate the relationships between quality management practices and firm performance. From Table 6.4, we only find significant increases in the change of R^2 value (from base Model 2) in Model 4 (change in R^2 =0.005, $P<0.10$), indicating that the prospector strategy increases the strengths between customer quality management and firm performance. Thus, only H7b is supported. The other hypothesised positive relationships are denied. This finding indicates that we are not able to find a strong moderating effect of the prospector strategy in the relationships between such quality management practices and firm performance: in-company quality management, employee involvement in quality management, quality design, and process management. The moderating role of the strategy to the relationship between customer quality management and firm performance is significant, which will be discussed in the following sections.

In H11b, we expected a significant positive relationship between government's financial and technological support (GFTS) and firm performance. From Table 6.4, we find that this hypothesis is supported (t=1.882, $P<0.10$), indicating that the GFTS contributes significantly to firm performance of the pork processing industry in China.

In H12b, we expected a moderating effect of the prospector strategy in the GFTS-firm performance relation. However our empirical findings rejected this hypothesis (change in R^2

=0.002, *P*=0.200), indicating that firms with the prospector strategy may not strengthen the relationship between GFTS and firm performance.

By looking at Table 6.3 and Table 6.4, we find that the control variable private firms do not perform differently from the state and collectively owned firms (the reference group in our analysis), indicating that this control variable does not have a significantly different impact on firm performance. However, compared with the reference group, the foreign joint ventures perform better in managing the relationship with their upstream suppliers. Meanwhile they outperform the reference group in such quality management practices as supplier quality management, quality design and process management. When looking at the relationship between the pork processors and their downstream customers in Table 6.4, we cannot find the difference in performance of the three types of firms. However, we find that foreign joint ventures with prospector strategy outperform the state owned and collective firms in customer quality management. The empirical findings indicate that this group of pork processors is ahead of the national pork processors in quality chain management. The empirical research of Su *et al.* (2008) on 206 manufactures in China indicates that foreign owned firms have a remarkably higher level of supply chain management than the other types of firms which include state-owned, joint ventures, or private firms. However, there are no differences between state-owned companies and joint ventures.

Another control variable in our study is the firm size. From Table 6.3 and Table 6.4, we learn that larger size may not be related to better firm performance in pork processing industries. We find evidence in previous research that larger size may not be related to profitability as it is influenced by the insignificance of 'market share' variables in the profitability models (e.g. Kotha and Nair, 1995). In China, market share is commonly used to measure the firm performance in the pork processing sector. To gain larger market share, some companies may reduce product price. This may influence companies' profitability. As we take the unweighted score of 'firm performance' in our study, we do not know how the size of the companies is related to each scale of the construct. This may become one of the directions for our future research.

6.5 Discussion and conclusions

One of the major objectives of this research was to examine the relationships between quality management practices and firm performance and between the government financial and technological support and firm performance in the pork processing sector in China. The other important objective was to explore the role of prospector strategy in the above-mentioned two relationships. In this section, major results pertaining to these relationships are discussed.

6.5.1 Quality management practices and firm performance

The empirical results suggest that in-company quality management, employee involvement in quality management and process management have significant positive relationships with firm performance for both upstream and downstream models. This reaffirms the important role of quality goals and policies, quality standards and systems in ensuring the quality of products and firm performance and the importance attributed to the employee component of quality management practices. These findings are identical to several studies, such as Powell (1995) and Samson and Terziovski (1999). The positive impact of process management on firm performance is identical to the findings of Samson and Terziovski (1999). This could indicate that high firm performance of the pork processors depend largely on the quality conformance from the incoming raw material to production processes.

Supplier quality management has a positive association with firm performance. It can be reasoned that with an increasingly supply chain oriented business environment, improvements in quality management targeted at the supplier's end are important for improved firm performance. However, contrary to our expectations, the positive relationship between customer quality management and performance in the downstream model has not been found, which is opposite to the findings of Ahire and O'Sharghnessy (1998) and Samson and Tierziovski (1999). A focus on meeting and exceeding customer expectations allows firms to achieve customer satisfaction and higher firm performance. Therefore firms pay more attention to customer quality management. In our in-depth case studies, we found that pork processors had to make more investments in cold chain facilities and cleaning environment to guarantee high quality in distribution and marketing. If the pork processors deal with very strong wholesalers and retailers, they are not usually in an ideal position to negotiate a favourable profit margin. The low profit margin due to fierce competition might explain the negative relationship between customer quality management and firm performance.

Our research fails to find a positive relationship between quality design and firm performance in both models. In fact, several large scale empirical studies examining the impact of quality management on firm performance have found that some QMP did not have a significant impact on performance (e.g. Powell, 1995; Dow *et al.*, 1999; Samson and Terziovski, 1999). It has been suggested that this may be due to the context dependent nature of these practices (Powell, 1995; Dow *et al.*, 1999). This finding is identical with the meta-analysis result of Nair (2006), which fails to find a direct relationship between product design and management and product quality. Product design and management is aimed at improving design quality and in ensuring design for manufacturability (Flynn *et al.*, 1995). Scholars have argued that 80% of the manufacturing costs are determined at the design stage (Ulrich and Pearson, 1998) and these manufacturing costs are an important component of a firm's operational performance. Several quality management models underline that customer collaboration in product design is a key factor in obtaining quality performance, which can then at a later stage lead to customer satisfaction (e.g. Flynn *et al.*, 1994; Forza, 1995). Thus, it is suggested that the managers of pork processing firms should pay more attention to quality design.

6.5.2 Moderating effect of the prospector strategy in the QMP-firm performance link

Our empirical findings indicate that the prospector strategy applied by pork processors significantly affects the relationships between some dimensions of quality management practices and firm performance in both upstream and downstream models. Thus, it appears that decisions to emphasise particular dimensions of quality management practices should be made in the context of the firms' competitive strategies to maximise firm performance. Results and implications with regard to the effect of the moderator 'prospector strategy' on the upstream and downstream models will be discussed in the following.

One of the important findings of this study is the significant positive effect of the prospector strategy on the relationships between supplier quality management and firm performance and between customer quality management and firm performance. This is important as this empirical result is different from the finding of Section 6.2, which indicates a negative impact of customer quality management on firm performance in the downstream model. On the one hand, this clearly shows the importance of innovation, company image and product brand in strengthening the link between quality management practices and firm performance. On the other hand, this result not only provides empirical evidence that quality management should be studied and implemented from a supply chain perspective, but also sheds further light on QMP, strategy and firm performance measurement moving around a continuing shift from product-oriented internally driven quality management practices to externally focused process-based approaches, to supply chain quality management. Traditional quality programs based on approaches such as total quality management and international quality management standards must transfer to simultaneously make use of supply chain partner relationships and quality improvement gains essential to market-place satisfaction (Robinson and Malhorta, 2005).

The moderating effect of the prospector strategy on the relationships between quality design and firm performance and between process management and firm performance in the upstream model is very important to managers of pork processing firms. New product development through quality design efforts will lead to more varieties as well as the added value of the pork products. This will better tune to the increasing demands of the consumers. Together with quality design, process management is another core quality management practice to create inimitable capability (Nair, 2006). As far as a quality pork chain is concerned, quality conformance in every stage of production is critical in achieving good quality management practices. Quality conformance cannot be achieved if the firms cannot guarantee an input with steady, high quality levels. Some studies have shown that about 50% of quality problems are due to incoming materials (Crosby, 1979). By eliminating the input variance, the process control techniques become much more efficient (Forza and Filippini, 1998).

Our empirical results fail to find a significant moderating effect of prospector strategy on the relationship between in-company quality management and firm performance and between employee involvement in quality management and firm performance, for both upstream and downstream models. These two sub-dimensions measure the attention of management to internal quality management, particularly the availability of quality goals and policies, quality standards (HACCP, ISO9000 series or ISO14000), and employee empowerment in quality management. The results indicate that the prospector strategy may not strengthen the relationships between in-company quality management and firm performance and between employee involvement in quality management and firm performance. The quality management approach is characterised by an orientation towards quality which helps to prevent problems and make continuous improvement in quality management (Forza and Filippini, 1998). The importance of employee empowerment in quality management is underlined by many researchers that it can be identified as one of the fundamental dimensions in quality management (Flynn et al., 1995; Powell, 1995). The attention to quality goals and quality standards as well as employee empowerment should permeate all firms to survive in the marketplace, no matter what strategy type the firms employ.

In China, the pork processing sector is in a high growth phase. According to the China Meat Association, only about 10% of the pork processors were not profitable during the past five years. There is an increasing demand from consumers for more varieties of quality pork products. According to the five force model of Porter (1980, 1985), the threat of entry by new firms is highest during the high growth phase of the product life cycle. As demand increases, new market segments emerge, and new entrants stake a claim in the emerging market. At this point, the competitive focus shifts from primary to selective demand, and firms invest in new product development and differentiate their products on attributes deemed important by certain customer segments (Mansfield, 1993; Song et al., 2002). Firms with a prospector strategy thus may be frontrunners in these developments.

6.5.3 Government financial and technological support, the prospector strategy and firm performance

Our research findings reveal that the financial and technological support of government authorities has a significant impact on firm performance of pork processors. This is in line with the findings of Kotha and Nair (1995) that technology changes are positively related to growth in the Japanese machine tool industry. According to Van der Meulen and Van der Velde (2004), government authorities are quite dominant with a strong power position and clear interests in food safety and quality management. They influence food quality along two main lines, via rules and procedures and via inspection. Another line of government efforts is to promote R&D capabilities of the pork processing companies. As indicated in Section 6.2.3., nowadays, universities and research institutions are encouraged by the Chinese government to cooperate with meat processing firms to apply for government funded research programs. The firms are encouraged by government authorities to use more advanced technology. By introducing modern equipment and technologies from foreign countries, the firms are expected to achieve better performance. In addition, firms in the industry are strongly encouraged by government to focus on export markets by offering high quality products and services.

In summary, our results and analysis reveal important insights into the pork processing landscape in China. With a large population and rapid economic development, China has become one of the important countries to attract foreign investment in the world. To understand quality management issues in China is therefore important to the managers and researchers. The literature on the actual status of quality management and especially how quality is managed in China's pork processing sector is in most cases anecdotal. In particular, the discussion on the impact of financial and technological support of the government authorities on quality management is mostly qualitative.

The Chinese government has realised the utmost importance of technological innovation. One of the main goals of the 11th Five-Year Program (2006-2010) adopted in 2006 is 'scientific development' and a determined emphasis to encourage 'an innovation-oriented nation' (Dobson and Safarian, 2008). In the pork processing context, if China is making the transition from imitation to innovation, we expect to see institutions that not only promote technological advances, but also establish effective food safety and quality management systems.

6.6 Limitations and directions for future research

Our research is subject to the following limitations. First, the operationalization of competitive strategy is limited in scope. In addition to prospector strategy, there are three other strategies, Analyser, Defender and Reactor. A large number of studies that examine the relationship between strategic types and performance suggest that organizational performance will be (a) equal in Defender, Prospector, and Analyser organizations; and (b) lower in reactor organizations (Conant et al., 1990).

Previous research has indicated that the company's strategy should be aligned properly with the different development stages of the company (e.g. Sharif, 1994). Empirical findings also show that firms with a low-cost Defender strategy have the least benefits from using advanced manufacturing technology and total quality management.(e.g. Dean and Snell, 1996). Some studies also find significant positive relationships between a combined strategy with firm performance. As the largest developing country in transition, there is a coexistence of different markets in China. Future research might be directed to the relationship between other types of business strategy and firm performance as well as their moderating effects on the relationship between quality management practices and firm performance and between financial and technology support and firm performance.

Second, the generalisability of results is limited. The analysis is cross sectional in nature and provides only static snapshots of strategy – performance relationships (Capon *et al.*, 1990). It is very important to conduct longitudinal studies to evaluate the impact of competitive strategy on firm performance.

Chapter 7. Discussion and conclusions

In this final chapter, we discuss the results in light of the hypotheses, the research model and its theoretical bases. We provide answers to the research questions and assess whether the proposed hypotheses are confirmed or rejected in Section 7.1. The most important managerial implications are discussed in Section 7.2. In Section 7.3, the theoretical and methodological contributions of the present study are presented. The chapter ends with the limitations of this study and directions for future research in Section 7.4.

7.1 Answering of the research questions

The objective of this study is to investigate the key factors in supply chain integration and quality management that affect the performance of pork processing firms in China and how governance mechanisms align with quality management in the pork processing firms. The important elements of supply chain integration (SCI), quality management practices (QMP) and governance mechanisms in pork supply chains were defined with different theoretical perspectives. Supply chain management emphasises the foundational role of integration of key activities in buyer-supplier relationships, for example, internal integration within firm departments and external integration with upstream suppliers and downstream customers; buyer-supplier relationship coordination in the chain; integrated information technology and logistics management (Frohlich and Westbrook, 2001; Chen and Paulraj, 2004) within the chain and across the boundaries of pork processing firms. Total quality management stresses the important quality management practices in improving firm performance, for example, applying quality management systems in business operation; managing supplier/customer quality management, involving employee in quality management, improving quality design and process management (Flynn *et al.*, 1995; Kaynak, 2003). Transaction cost economics indicates the impact of asset specificity and uncertainty on the arrangement of governance mechanisms in pork chain management as well as the alignment of appropriate governance mechanisms with quality management practices. The effect of competitive strategy (prospector strategy in our study) on the relationships between quality management practices (the internal capabilities of the firms) and government support (external impact) and firm performance is underlined by contingency theory. From these theoretical foundations, we defined five research questions about the joint impact of supply chain integration and quality management on firm performance of pork processing industries in China as well as the governance mechanisms in the pork supply chain management. The answer to these five research questions will be discussed in Section 7.1.1 till Section 7.1.4. The interrelationships among the major constructs of our study are indicated in the following research model (Figure 7.1) that has been tested in this study.

The study was carried out in the pork processing sector in East China. We conducted a cross-sectional survey in 229 pork processors in Jiangsu province, Shandong province, and Shanghai municipality. Before the large-scale survey, pilot studies into 10 companies were conducted to

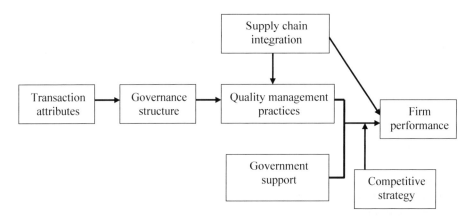

Figure 7.1. Conceptual model.

improve the validity and reliability of the questionnaire items. This preliminary study proved to be important to draw tentative conclusions with regard to the examined relationships between the pork processors and their most important upstream suppliers and downstream customers. After the large-scale survey, we conducted in-depth interviews in 5 pork processors from April to November 2007 to validate the hypothesised relationships in our quantitative data analysis and gain more insight into the issues under investigation.

Our empirical analysis is carried out in the upstream model (the relationship between the pork processors and their most important suppliers) and the downstream models (the relationship between the pork processors and their most important downstream customers). The results of most of the hypothesised relationships are identical in both models. However, we did find some contrast findings between the two models. Firstly, we found the different impact of transaction attributes (i.e. asset specificity and uncertainty) on relational governance mechanisms between the two models. In the presence of asset specificity in time and effort in developing buyer-supplier relationships, the pork processors tend to use more relational governance in the transactions with downstream customers than with upstream hog (meat) suppliers. When the pork processors encounter more uncertainty in quantity, quality, and price, there is a significant positive relationship between uncertainty and relational governance in the upstream model while the relationship in the downstream model is non-significant. Secondly, our research findings indicated a large difference in the impact of the competitive strategy (i.e. prospector strategy) in strengthening the link between quality management practices and firm performance in both models. While the prospector strategy strengthened the relationships between quality design and firm performance and between process management and firm performance in the upstream model, it failed to support this strengthening impact in the downstream model. The detailed explanation on the above different findings will be given in Section 7.1.3 and Section 7.1.4.

7.1.1 The joint impact of supply chain integration, quality management practices and firm performance

In Chapter 3, we addressed the first research question of this book:

> *What is the joint impact of supply chain integration and quality management practices on the firm performance in the pork sector in China?*

Firms are links in a networked supply chain. In response to rising international cooperation, e.g. through strategic alliances, along with a focus on core activities, the importance of supply chain management (SCM) is being recognised by the pork processing firms in China. Nevertheless, the practice of SCM is limited. Among the 229 respondents, only 44% had heard about SCM. The advantages of SCM to firm business competitiveness has been mentioned by many researchers (e.g. Mainardi *et al.*, 1999; Gryna, 2001; Christopher, 2000). However, the competitive performance of SCM can only be achieved by closely integrating the internal functions within the company and effectively linking them with the external operations of suppliers, customers and other supply chain members (Kim, 2006). We therefore focused on the key variable supply chain integration (SCI) in studying pork SCM in China. SCI is measured by 5 sub-dimensions: 'internal integration', 'external integration', 'buyer-supplier relationship coordination', 'integrated information technology' and 'integrated logistics management'.

Quality management is another hot topic in both academic and practitioner cycles. Many companies have adopted quality programs as a reaction to a changing and challenging competitive environment (Lee *et al.*, 2002). Most studies have analysed the relationship between QMP and firm performance, elements that affect quality management implementation and the major barriers to quality programs' success (e.g. Das *et al.*, 2000; Lee *et al.*, 2002; Soltani, 2005). However, little empirical research has been conducted in the area of quality management in Chinese manufacturing companies (Zhang *et al.*, 2000; Sun, 2006). The same situation holds true for the impact of QMP on firm performance. Our study fills this gap. We thus measure the other key construct QMP by 5 sub-dimensions: 'in-company quality management', 'supplier/customer quality management', 'employee involvement in quality management', 'quality design' and 'process management'.

The most important results of the present study were that QMP was directly linked to firm performance, while SCI was indirectly linked to firm performance through QMP. The empirical study also supported the positive significant relationship between SCI and QMP. The direct effect of SCI on firm performance was not significant in our study. This is in contrast to some earlier studies. For example, Kim (2006) studied the interrelationships among level of SCI, implementation of SC practices and the organizational performance of 668 manufacturing corporations in Korea and Japan. He found that both the level of SCI and SCM practices had a positive relationship with firm performance. By taking a close look at the result of our analysis, we found that the factors of 'external integration', 'buyer-supplier relationship coordination' and 'integrated information technology and logistics management' had lower impacts on firm performance compared to internal integration. In line with the study of Fronlich and Westbrook (2001), the highest level of integration with both suppliers and customers had the strongest association with performance improvement. Our findings may indicate that the Chinese pork processing industry still has a long way to go to further improve SCI.

To answer Research question 1, we conclude that quality management practices have a positive impact on firm performance and supply chain integration contributes to better quality management. However, there is only an indirect relationship between SCI and firm performance. This relationship is mediated by QMP.

7.1.2 Integrated information technology and logistics, quality management and firm performance

Seen in the light of the increasing role of information management and logistics management in agri-food industry, we proposed the second Research question:

How do integrated information technology (IT) and integrated logistics management (ILM) and quality management practices (QMP) influence the performance of pork processing firms in China?

To answer this question, several relationships were proposed (Figure 7.2). We first analysed the impact of integrated IT and ILM on QMP in the dyadic relationship between the processors and their most important customers[29].

The questionnaire survey supported the significant positive association of both with QMP. We also studied the relationship between integrated IT and ILM. The result indicated that the application of integrated IT contributed significantly to ILM of the pork processors. This finding further supports the strong emphasis in SCM literature that the enormous development of IT tools facilitates close cooperation in other processes of the chain (Cramer, 2004; Van der Zee, 2004), facilitating the successful integration of these processes in supply chains (Hill and Scudder, 2002; Lambert and Cooper, 2000).

Furthermore, we investigated the impact of integrated IT, ILM and QMP on firm performance. In contrast to our expectation, neither integrated IT nor ILM had significant contributions to

---

[29] The empirical study was only carried out for the relationship between the pork processors and their most important downstream customers. Our in-depth interviews indicated that the information technology was less applied due to the large-scale backyard producers in the upstream pork chain. Previous empirical studies also indicated that firms tend to be much more accommodating of the desires of their customers than of their suppliers in the use of information technology, such as electronic data interchange (Hill and Scudder, 2002).

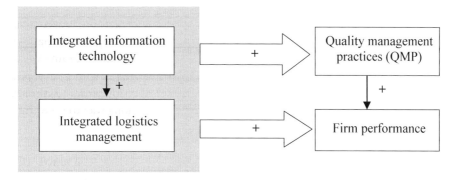

Figure 7.2. Proposed interactions among integrated information technology, integrated logistics management, quality management practices and firm performance.
Note: the '+' in this figure and the other figures of this chapter refers to the proposed positive relationships between the variables in our study developed on the basis of theory and literature review.

firm performance. This is in line with Chen's (2003) study. China is in a transitional period. Although its economy is in rapid development, its agri-food industry is still dominated by small companies with limited implementation of information technology and logistics integration (Chen and Luo, 2003). The positive significant impact of QMP on firm performance was supported.

7.1.3 Transaction attributes, governance structure and quality management

To support the transfer of information and materials between different stages of the supply chain it is required to manage the supply chain in an effective way. Coordination between actors in the chain may influence the bargaining power relationships, leading to different market selection choices and changing the value-added distribution amongst agents (Zúñiga-Arias, 2007). As mentioned by Williamson (1981; 1985), coordination in the chain will lead to different governance structures, depending on the presence of asset-specific factors, and uncertainties are specific for each commodity. Different commodities will have different transaction costs or dimensions, and values. Therefore, different governance structures emerge for coordinating actors throughout the chain from spot market, via contractual to relational governance mechanisms. We proposed the third research question:

> *What is the impact of transaction attributes on the governance structure and how will different governance structures influence quality management practices in China's pork processors?*

To answer this question, we defined the following conceptual framework (Figure 7.3).

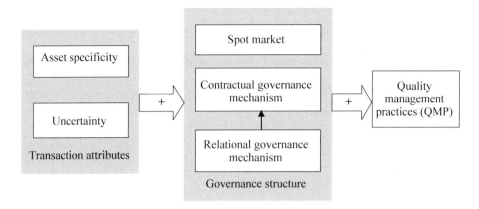

Figure 7.3. Proposed relationships between transaction attributes, governance structure and quality management practices.

This study provides empirical evidence that the degree of asset specificity and uncertainty does matter in the alignment of governance structures in pork supply chains. This is consistent with transaction costs logic. Through formal contracts, managers are in a better position to safeguard their investments in facilities and buyer-supplier relationship building. Penalties for early termination can be specified in formal contracts. When uncertainty increases, managers will craft more customised contracts to provide a safeguard, albeit not perfect, from the uncoordinated, self-interested actions that may increase with uncertainty (Williamson, 1996). Our finding is in line with the results in previous empirical studies. For example, Buvik (2002) found a positive impact of hybrid governance mechanisms, such as long-term economic and technological dependence on industrial purchasing relationships when buyers and suppliers used substantial asset specificity and were confronted with unpredictable and/or changing conditions.

Our study shows mixed findings as regards the impact of asset specificity and uncertainty on the use of relational governance in the upstream and the downstream models. In relationships with customers, the pork processors appear more concerned about long-term cooperation and trust in the presence of asset specificity, which is in contrast with the relationships with hog or meat suppliers in the upstream model. This might mean that managers of focal firms do not appear to select relational governance in response to increasing levels of specialised assets in their relationship with suppliers. While increased asset specificity may facilitate long-term cooperation between pork processors and their downstream customer, it does not appear to be an effective means of maintaining a cooperative and trusted relationship between the pork processors and their suppliers.

Contrary to the significant positive relationship between the pork processors and their most important suppliers in the presence of uncertainty, our empirical findings indicate a non-significant relationship between uncertainty and relational governance between the pork processors and their downstream customers. This might be explained by the different environments the pork processors are in when trading with their suppliers and with their customers. In the in-depth interviews with the managers of the pork processors, they expressed more concern on the unstable situations with regard to hog (meat) supply and price in the upstream pork chain. Comparatively speaking, the marketing channel operation is more stable compared with the upstream procurement of raw materials. The upstream hog (meat) supply is more susceptible to the uncertainty in both supply quantity and prices due to the rising cost of feed in the hog production chain. To gain stable hog (meat) supply for the firms' sustainable business development, it was critical for the pork processors to develop a long-term trusted cooperative relationship with the upstream suppliers. When the hogs were in serious shortage due to the outbreak of diseases in 2007, the supply of hogs (meat) became so important which again reaffirms the great importance of collaborations with the upstream suppliers established on the basis of long-term trusted relationships.

Contrary to the substitution view of Gulati (1995) and Dyer and Singh (1998) on the relationship between formal contracts and relational governance mechanisms, our empirical analysis supports the conclusion that contracts and relational governance function as complements. This finding is consistent with previous empirical studies. Taking the research of the Chinese context as an example, our finding is consistent with Yeung's (2006) observation that ethnic Chinese businesses in Southeast Asia employ both social networks and more formal (bureaucratic) forms of firm control. In addition, Lu (2007) also found the coexistence of interpersonal trust (relational governance) and more formal governance forms on buyer-seller relationships in China's vegetable sector.

Our empirical test supports the positive relationships between more integrated governance mechanisms and the use of quality management practices in pork processing firms in China. Previous empirical studies also identified increasing quality requirements of customers as a major driving force for contracts and vertical integration in the USA (Martinez and Zering, 2004) and in the Netherlands (Den Ouden *et al.*, 1996). As the institutional setting for obtaining a reward for quality production can be subject to a high degree of uncertainty in evolving markets (Boger, 2001b), it is even more important for firms in China to develop more integrated governance arrangements in their relationships with suppliers and customers. It has been repeatedly mentioned by the case study companies that the dynamic market in China needs a more integrated approach in upgrading quality management. To guarantee pork quality, one of the solutions for the firms was to establish production farms in the upstream part of the chain and specialised stores in the downstream part of the chain. Meanwhile, long term cooperative interfirm relationships have to be established and maintained for the efficiency and continuity of exchanges.

7.1.4 Quality management, government support, firm performance and the moderating role of competitive strategy

Though the fundamental importance of quality management practices on firm performance has been widely accepted and supported by this study in Chapter 3, important questions still remained open. For example, which specific practices contribute to higher firm performance? What role does government support play in improving firm performance as effort from both government and enterprises is needed to ensure food quality and safety? Are strategic configurations discussed in the current Western literature equally viable across different institutional settings, like China? We thus proposed relationships as depicted in Figure 7.4 and answer the fourth and the fifth research questions of this study:

> *What is the impact of quality management practices (RQ4) and government support (RQ5) on firm performance and will firm strategy moderate the relationships between quality management practices and firm performance and between government support and firm performance?*

Our quantitative analysis revealed several important findings:
- In-company quality management, employee involvement in quality management and process management have significant positive relationships with firm performance for both the upstream and the downstream model. This reaffirms the significant importance of quality goals and policies, quality standards and systems and employee involvement in quality management in improving the firm performance. The positive impact of process management on firm performance indicates that higher firm performance of the pork processors largely depend on the quality conformance from the incoming raw material to

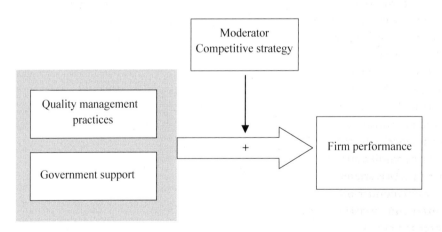

Figure 7.4. Proposed relationships between quality management practices, government support and firm performance, and the moderating role of the competitive strategy on these relationships.

production processes, including reducing input and process variation. For example, the mid-level management inspects the work floor on a regular basis to check all operational processes. If quality problems are identified, corrections can be made. These effective process management practices result in an increased percent-passed final inspection with no rework, contributing to competitive priorities (Ahire and Dreyfus, 2000; Kaynak, 2003).

- Supplier quality management showed a positive association with firm performance. However, in contrast to our expectation, the positive relationship between customer quality management in the downstream model has not been found, which is contrary to some of the previous studies (e.g. Ahire and O'Sharghnessy, 1998; Samson and Tierziovski, 1999). In our in-depth case studies, we found that pork processors had to make more investments in cold chain facilities and cleaning environment to guarantee high quality in distribution and marketing. In the face of very strong retailers, the pork processing firms are usually not in a position to negotiate a favourable profit margin. Therefore the pork processors may have low profitability in cooperating with strong retailers. However, the pork processors value greatly this business relationship as these retailers represent the modern marketing trend and help to promote the image of the processors. If they cooperated with small customers, they sometimes had to help the customers to invest in good facilities to ensure product quality. The increase in customer quality investment and low profit margin due to fierce competition might explain the negative relationship between customer quality management and firm performance.

- Our research fails to find a positive relationship between quality design and firm performance in both models. This finding is identical with the meta-analysis result of Nair's (2006), which fails to find a direct relationship between product design and management and product quality. Product design and management practices are aimed at improving quality design and in ensuring design for manufacturability (Flynn *et al.*, 1995). Several quality management models underline that customer collaboration in product design is a key factor in obtaining a quality performance, which can then at a later stage lead to customer satisfaction (e.g. Flynn *et al.*, 1994; Forza, 1995). Thus, our findings suggest that the managers of pork processing firms should pay more attention to quality design.

- Our empirical findings indicate that if a prospector strategy is applied by pork processors, this significantly affects the relationships between some dimensions of quality management practices and firm performance in both upstream and downstream models. (1) One of the important results of this study is the significant positive effect of the prospector strategy on the relationships between both supplier and customer quality management and firm performance. This result not only provides empirical evidence that quality management should be studied and implemented from a supply chain perspective, but also sheds further light on QMP, strategy and firm performance measurement moving around a continuing shift from product-oriented internally driven supply channel quality management practices to externally focused process-based approaches to supply chain quality management (Robinson and Malhorta, 2005). (2) We found the moderating effect of the prospector strategy on the relationships between quality design and firm performance and between process management and firm performance in the upstream model of pork processing firms. This different impact of the prospector strategy on the relationship between these two core quality management practices and firm performance in the upstream model and the downstream model might be explained by the different importance of these processes in pork supply chains. For improving firm performance, one of the critical factors for the firms is to manage the costs of raw material and production. As quality conformance in process management is concerned, quality conformance cannot be achieved if the firms cannot guarantee an input with steady and high quality levels. According to our in-depth interviews, the cost of hogs was about 90%~92% of the pork production cost while the cost of raw pork meat for producing processed pork products was above 60%. It was very different for the pork processors in quality management of raw materials as there was no grading system for hogs. By eliminating the input variance, the statistical process control techniques become much more efficient because it is possible to concentrate on the factors which can be controlled internally, such as the performance of both the machinery and the employees (Forza and Filippini, 1998). (3) Our empirical results fail to find the significant moderating effect of the prospector strategy on the relationships between in-company quality management, employee involvement on firm performance for both the upstream and the downstream model.

- Our research findings reveal that the financial and technological support of the government authorities has a significant impact on firm performance of the pork processors. According to Van der Meulen and Van der Velde (2004), government authorities are quite dominant with a strong power position and clear interests in food safety and quality management. They influence food quality via rules and procedures, and inspection. Another aspect of great importance is the government effort in promoting R&D capabilities of the pork processing companies. The financial and technological support to the pork processing sector is indicated in Section 6.2.3. However, our study failed to find a moderating effect of the prospector strategy in the relationship between government support in finance and technology and firm performance.

7.1.5 Summary of testing the proposed hypotheses

Based on the findings of empirical studies and the discussions on this chapter, we summarise the results of the major propositions in Appendix F.

7.2 Managerial implications

The business landscape for pork sector has been subject to many changes in the last decade in China. Consolidation and food safety are perhaps the prevailing issues in the sector. Pork processors are increasingly challenged by the development of value-added and branded products, more strict requirements on environmental outcomes, and the need for traceability in the pork production system. These changes pose great challenges for chain integration and quality upgrading. This part aims at answering the central research question of this study:

*What are the key factors in supply chain management and quality management practices
that affect the performance of the pork processing firms in China and how do governance
mechanisms align with quality management of pork processing firms?*

By answering this question, we achieve the objective to provide important recommendations
for managers of pork processing firms in China and also in countries with a similar transitional
business setting as China.

7.2.1 Firms should invest in quality management to achieve higher performance

Our empirical study reveals that the attention to quality management turns out to be critical
to generating sales growth, improving customer satisfaction and providing profits for Chinese
pork processing firms. The findings provide impetus to managers on various levels in the pork
processing industry to continue adopting quality management practices in their organizations.
As many companies put it: 'Quality is the life of the enterprise'. Firms that wish to improve
their performance should therefore invest in quality management. When linking the specific
quality management practices to firm performance, we found that especially the following
practices contribute to higher firm performance: in-company quality management, supplier
quality management, employee involvement in quality management and process management.
Therefore, firms should pay special attention to these practices.

7.2.2 Firms should strive for integrated quality management at chain level to improve firm performance

The rapid economic development has fuelled up pork consumption in China in the past two
decades. However, the Chinese pork processors are greatly challenged by the recent economic
crisis and food safety scandals. The competition is becoming fiercer for the firms. Thus they
have to integrate their processes with suppliers and customers more tightly to deal with
complex quality management pressures. If consumers lose confidence in the safety and quality
of food, this affects all the stakeholders in the supply chain. Therefore, pork processing firms
in China should forge quality management practices and combine these with strategic supply
chain partnerships so as to develop closer relationships with their suppliers.

Equally important for the firms to take into consideration is the indirect link of supply chain
integration through quality management with firm performance. To improve the quality of
the products and reduce uncertainty in hog supply chains, companies should therefore develop
more integrated chains with their suppliers. In the survey, we found (especially large) pork
processors paying more attention to building strategic relationships with their most important
suppliers and customers in order to provide high-quality pork products to consumers.

7.2.3 In the long run, the use of integrated information technology and logistics management is critical to achieve higher firm performance.

Though we did not find significant positive relationships between either integrated IT or integrated logistics management and firm performance, managers indicated the great importance of modern information technology and logistics management in our in-depth case studies. With more intense competition, consolidation and professionalism in pork supply chains, more integration in information technology and logistics management can be foreseen in the future. It will therefore be increasingly important for managers in the information systems and logistics fields to strengthen their working relationships and, more importantly, with their upstream suppliers and downstream customers. It is widely acknowledged that information technology serves as a key enabler of supply chain integration through the capture and sharing of vital information regarding key business processes, both within and outside the firm. It contributes to firm profits by improving quality, and reducing coordination and transaction costs (Frohlich and Westbrook, 2001; Vickery *et al.*, 2003). In pork supply chains the implementation of information technology can facilitate inventory management, logistics planning, production scheduling, demand forecasting and human resource management. These activities will enable processors and their upstream suppliers and downstream customers to increase accuracy, improve agility and cut costs, eventually leading to better firm performance.

7.2.4 It is important for managers to opt for appropriate governance arrangements to ensure quality management in the pork chain

Quality control is of a specific nature in the case of pork products, since pork processing firms regularly face problems in monitoring the quality and safety of raw materials. Drug residues and disease aspects are difficult to detect but influence business relationships. Equally true is that for the retailers it is also difficult to detect the processes of pork production. Furthermore, processed pork products consist of heterogeneous ingredients. In order to guarantee reliable supply of quality pork products, the managers of pork processing firms in China should not only develop more integrated governance regimes, such as contractual governance, but also develop sustainable partnerships with suppliers and customers that reduce information and screening costs and reinforce mutual trust amongst chain members (Hueth *et al.*, 1999; Ruben *et al.*, 2007).

7.2.5 A prospector strategy is clearly a successful strategy to strengthen the relationship between quality management practices and firm performance

Managers should change their mind-set in managing their pork supply chain. Traditional quality programs focus on total quality management to reach (international) quality standards. However, modern business management must be transferred to the simultaneous use of supply chain partnerships and quality management practices as they are both essential to customer satisfaction (Robinson and Malhorta, 2005). In Section 6.4, we found a negative relationship between customer quality management and firm performance. Our further investigation into firms applying the prospector strategy revealed different and useful findings for managers. For firms that focused more on new products and markets and less on low cost-driven activities, the prospector strategy strengthened the link between firms' customer quality management and firm performance. In a transitional economy like China, one would expect that it is better to make an effort in exploring new markets than developing new products. It is more risky to invest in new product development and new technologies (Wheelwright and Clark, 1992). However, our research finding indicates that a prospector strategy might be an appropriate orientation for pork processors in China's highly complex and dynamic market.

This finding is of particular significance to pork processing firms in the current economic situation. The global economic crisis is having a major impact on pork consumption. The competition among the pork processing firms is becoming increasingly fierce. With a large population and a great income disparity, the mass market and niche market will co-exist for a long time. Firms will need to become more innovative and entrepreneurial if they want to be successful in the niche market. Among many good practices, focusing on the production of differentiated pork products to meet the needs of increasingly demanding consumers is one of them.

7.3 Theoretical and methodological contributions

7.3.1 Theoretical contributions

This thesis is among the first to study the impact of supply chain governance and quality management on firm performance in the Chinese pork processing industry. It has made six main contributions to literature.

First, this thesis combined a number of theoretical perspectives to develop and test theoretical arguments for the use of supply chain governance and quality-enhancing practices at the pork chain level. Specifically, we use transaction cost economics (TCE) and relational exchange theory (RET) to study the interrelationships among transaction attributes (transaction specific investments and uncertainty), governance structure and quality management practices. Supply chain management (SCM) and total quality management (TQM) were applied to study the joint impact of supply chain integration and quality management practices on firm performance. In addition, contingency theory was used to examine how pork processors link their strategic decisions to their internal capabilities in quality management and the external environment (government support in finance and technology). These theories have their own focus, assumptions and framework for studying buyer-supplier relationships. Nevertheless, they provided complementary explanations for pork processors to manage their upstream and downstream relationships. For example, TCE is important to explain that a higher degree of governance coordination (formal contractual governance versus spot market transaction) contributes to better quality management practices. However, our research not only confirms the significant impact of relational governance on firm performance, but also supports the complementary role of relational governance to formal contractual governance mechanisms in managing buyer-supplier relationship in pork supply chains. Therefore, our findings raise new insights into how an integrated theoretical approach can be used in the application of appropriate governance mechanisms to manage pork quality chain and achieve higher firm performance.

Second, the present study has contributed to the development of Supply Chain Quality Management (SCQM), which is regarded by Robinson and Malhotra (2005) as a new stage in the evolution of quality management (see Chapter 3). Up to now, supply chain management and quality management have been investigated extensively, but few studies examined these topics jointly. Van Plaggenhoef's (2007) study validated the usefulness of the SCQM paradigm across multiple supply chains, investigating meat supply chains, potted flower chains and vegetable chains. This study has operationalised SCQM and offers a statistically validated and reliable basis for SCQM.

Third, the measurement and operationalization of supply chain integration contribute to the supply chain management discipline. This study, through literature review and repeated refinement, has arrived at constructs and operational measures for supply chain integration. The quantitative analyses strongly supported their measurement properties (i.e. reliable, valid and unidimensional). The scientific development of a coherent supply chain management discipline requires that advances be made in the development of measurement instruments, as well as in theoretical models to improve our understanding of supply chain phenomena (Croom et al., 2000). While research on various supply chain relationships has been growing, there has not been a comprehensive approach to construct development and measurement, so far (Chen and Paulraj, 2004).

Fourth, this study confirmed the complementary relationships between relational governance mechanisms and formal contractual governance mechanisms. Guthrie (2001) concluded that many Chinese firms are currently less likely to use informal and network-based practices. Economic strategies and practices that resemble those of foreign firms are more likely to be adopted by these firms. However, Zhou et al. (2003) from their survey of 620 firms in 1999/2000 showed that social relations play a critical role in interfirm relationships in addition to the use of contracts. Styles and Ambler (2003) also argue that there is a coexistence of transaction and relational marketing in the Chinese business context. To our knowledge, no study has been conducted with regard to the complementary effect of relational governance to formal contractual mechanisms in Chinese pork supply chains. A similar study has only been carried out in China's vegetable supply chains (Lu, 2007). The findings of the present study contribute to the important debate on the relationship between relational governance and contractual governance mechanisms.

Fifth, past studies in transaction cost economics have focused on the relationship between transaction attributes and the selection of different organizational arrangements (Hobbs,

1996; Reimer, 2006). Relatively little research has been done with regard to the influence of different organizational arrangements on the implementation of quality management practices. Furthermore, in seeking solution for governance problems, transaction cost economics only focuses on formal mechanisms, neglecting the important role of informal (or social) mechanisms in reducing transaction costs. Our study confirmed the strong positive effects of both contracts and relational governance on quality management.

Sixth, the significant positive effect of the prospector strategy on the relationships between both supplier and customer quality management and firm performance contributes to the strategic management literature. China is the largest and fastest growing emerging economy in the world, with a substantially different market setting compared to Western countries (Luo and Park, 2001). The specific configuration of business strategy and environment in this highly uncertain and dynamic market needs special attention of the business firms to match their competencies and capabilities to their strategic decisions. The findings of this study are in line with the strategic management propositions in Western countries and thus enrich the theory.

7.3.2 Methodological contributions

The present study made two methodological contributions. First of all, iterations were proved to be useful in designing good quality questionnaires. Before the questionnaire was designed, we visited 10 pork processors to get an insight into the practical situation of quality management and how pork processors cooperated with their upstream suppliers and downstream customers. This was very important, since no validated constructs of supply chain integration and quality management practices in China's pork chains were available. A multiple-item questionnaire was designed on the basis of the literature review, the research objectives and the initial company visits. The measurements of the constructs were improved according to feedback from pre-tests among academics and practitioners. Our study indicated that supply chain integration and quality management form second-order constructs. They have been validated by our empirical study and thus can help our understanding of supply chain phenomena and quality management in future studies of agri-food supply chains in China.

Second, two different analytical tools were proved to be successful in examining the proposed relationships among the major constructs of our study. Firstly, AMOS was applied to study the joint impact of supply chain integration and quality management practices on firm performance as well as the impact of supply chain management on quality management practices. AMOS, an acronym for 'Analysis of Moment Structures' or in other words, the analysis of mean and covariance structures, has a dual approach: confirmatory factor analysis and full structural equation modelling. Secondly, a component-based structural model called Partial Lease Squares (PLS) was applied to analyse the relationship among integrated information technology, integrated logistics management, quality management practices and firm performance and among transaction attributes, governance structures and quality management practices. Unlike the covariance methodology developed by Jöreskog (1969), which is based on maximum likelihood estimation and has special restrictions attached to it (sample size and scale, parametric assumptions of normality and independency of observations, and use of reflective variables), the requirements of PLS with respect to sample size, scale of variables and their distribution are minimal (Chin, 1998; Fornell and Bookstein, 1982). Compared with the more popular structural equation modelling approach Lisrel (Steenkamp and Baumgartner, 1998), the PLS also has the merit of incorporating both formative and reflective constructs in one model. The application of AMOS and PLS enriched the statistical analysis of the empirical studies of pork supply chains in China. In this way we contributed to their adoption in social science research.

7.4 Limitations of the study and directions for further research

The findings of this study should be evaluated by taking the following limitations into account. Directions for further research are also given in this last section.

First, previous research suggests that buyer-supplier relationships in supply chains might be affected by the characteristics of the firms, for example the size of the firm. Kim (2006) found that the degree of supply chain integration (SCI) might influence the performance of firms of different sizes in different ways. Though SCI had a significant effect on firm performance in both large and small firms, the direct effect of SCI in small firms was stronger while the indirect effect of SCI on firm performance was more dominant in large firms. Large firms have already achieved considerable levels of SCI. Based on such high level of SCI, SCM practice and competition capability have more significant direct effects on firm performance. Therefore, there is an opportunity to further investigate whether there are differences for large and small pork processors in implementing SCI and whether the degree of SCI contributes differently to firm performance. Furthermore, differences may exist in the application of specific supply chain integration strategies in firms of different size. For example, larger firms are able to commit more resources to IT and integrated logistics management and thus may achieve better performance.

Second, although our approach to getting data from the most knowledgeable informant is consistent with prior research on vertical relationships (e.g. Heide and John, 1990; Poppo and Zenger, 2002), the dependence on a single respondent for data on buyer-seller relationships suggests the possibility of common method bias (the divergence between observed and true relationships among constructs, mostly due to bias from measurement method). Further studies could use multiple data sources of buyer-supplier relationships to improve the reliability of the measures and increase the confidence in the results.

Third, the generalisability of our results must be carefully considered. The sample of China's pork processors may reflect some unique characteristics. It is imperative to replicate the present study in other research settings to see whether the findings are robust. Furthermore, the analysis is cross sectional in nature and provides only static snapshots of SCI and quality management and their impact on firm performance. Research needs to extend from this static analysis of SCI and QM practices towards a more dynamic analysis by taking into account firms' involvement into SCI and QM in different periods of time. This will provide a worthwhile undertaking for further study.

Fourth, the operationalization of the competitive strategy is limited in scope. In addition to the prospector strategy, there are three other strategies: Analyser, Defender and Reactor. A large number of studies that examine the relationship between strategic types and performance suggest that organizational performance will be (a) equal in Defender, Prospector, and Analyser organizations; and (b) lower in reactor organizations (Conant *et al.*, 1990). Previous research has indicated that the company's strategy should be aligned properly with the different development stages of the company (e.g. Sharif, 1994). Empirical findings also show that firms having low cost Defender strategy have the least benefits from using advanced manufacturing technology and quality management systems (e.g. Dean and Snell, 1996). Some studies also found significant positive relationships between a combination of the above mentioned strategies and firm performance. As the largest developing country in transition, there is a coexistence of different markets in China. Future research could be directed to the moderating relationship between different types of business strategy and firm performance.

References

Ahire, S.L. and P. Dreyfus, 2000. The impact of design management process management on quality: an empirical examination. Journal of Operations Management 18: 549-575.

Ahire, S.L. and K.C. O'Shaughnessy, 1998. The role of top management commitment in quality management: an empirical analysis of the auto parts industry. International Journal of Quality Science 3(1): 5-37.

Ahire, S.L., D.Y. Golhar and M.A. Walter, 1996. Development and validation of TQM implementation constructs, Decision Sciences 27: 23-56.

Alchian, A.A. and H. Demsetz, 1972. Production, information costs and economic organization. American Economic Review 62(5): 777-795.

Allen, R.S. and M.M. Helms, 2006. Linking strategic practices and organizational performance to Porter's generic strategies. Business Process Management Journal, 12(4): 433-454.

Al-Mashari, M. and A. Al-Mudimigh, 2003. ERP implementation: lessons from a case study. Information Technology & People 16(1): 21-33.

Anderson, E. and D.C. Schmittlein, 1984. Integration of the sales force: An empirical examination. Rand Journal of Economics 15: 3-19.

Anderson, J.C., 1987. An approach for confirmatory measurement and structural equation modeling of organizational properties. Management Science 33(4): 525-541.

Anderson, J.C. and D.W. Gerbing, 1984. The effect of sampling error on convergence, improper solution, and goodness-of-fit indices for maximum likelihood confirmatory factor analysis. Psychometrika 49(2): 155-173.

Anderson, J.C. and D.W. Gerbing, 1988. Structural equation modeling in practice: a review and recommended two-step approach. Psychological Bulletin, 103(3): 411-423.

Anderson, J.C. and J.A. Narus, 1990. A model of distributor firm and manufacturer firm working partnerships. Journal of Marketing 54: 42-58.

Antia, K.D. and G.L. Frazier, 2001. The severity of contract enforcement in interfirm channel relationships. Journal of Marketing 65(October): 67-81.

Arbuckle, J.L., 1997. Amos Users' Guide Version 3.6. SmallWaters Corporation, Chicago, IL.

Armistead, C.G. and J. Mapes, 1993. The impact of supply chain integration on operating performance, Logistics Information Management. 6(4): 9-14.

Armstrong, J.S. and T.S. Overton, 1977. Estimating non-response bias in mail surveys. Journal of Marketing Research 14(3): 396-402.

Bagozzi, R.P., Y. Yi and L.W. Phillips, 1991. Assessing construct validity in organizational research, Administrative Science Quarterly 36: 421-458.

Bagozzi, R.P., 1981. Evaluating structural equation models with unobservable variables and measurement error: a comment. Journal of Marketing Research, 18(3): 375-381.

Baker, G., R. Gibbons and K.J. Murphy, 1994. Subjective performance measures in optimal inventive contracts. Quarterly Journal of Economics 109: 1125-1156.

Balakrishnan, S. and B. Wernerfelt, 1986. Technical change, competition and vertical integration, Strategic Management Journal. 7 (July-August): 347-359.

References

Ballou, R.H., S.M. Gilbert and A. Mukherjee, 2000. New managerial challenges from supply chain opportunities. Industrial Marketing Management, 29(1): 7-18.

Bamford, J., 1994. Driving America to tiers. Financial World 163: 24-27.

Bardi, E.J., T.S. Raghunathan and P.K. Bagchi, 1994. Logistics information systems: the strategic role of top management. Journal of Business Logistics, 15(1): 71-85.

Barney, J.B. and M.H. Hansen, 1994. Trustworthiness as a source of competitive advantage. Strategic Management Journal 15: 175-190.

Barney, J.B. and W. Hesterly, 1999. Organizational economics: understanding the relationship between organizations and economic analysis. In: R.C. Steward and C. Hardy (eds.), Studying Organization. Sage Publications, 109-141.

Barzel, Y., 1982. Measurement costs and the organization of markets. Journal of Law and Economics XXV: 27-48.

Bean, R., 2003. People's Republic of China, retail food sector. Annual, USDA FAS GAIN report nr CH3825, November 12.

Bean, C. and J. Zhang, 2007. China, People's Republic of China, Livestock and Products Semi-Annual Report, USDA Foreign Agricultural Service GAIN Report Number: CH7014, March 1.

Bensaou, M. and E. Anderson, 1999. Buyer-supplier relations in industrial markets: when do buyers risk making idiosyncratic investment? Organization Science, 10(4): 460-481.

Bharadwaj, A.S., 2000. A resource-based perspective on information technology capability and firm performance: an empirical investigation. MIS Quarterly 24(1): 169-196.

Boal, F., 2006. Competition from eastern Europe and beyond – new players in the global pork industry. Advances in Pork Production, 17: 49-64.

Boger, S., 2001a. Agricultural Markets in Transition, an empirical study on contracts and transaction costs in the Polish hog sector. PhD thesis, Shaker Verlag, Aachen, Germany.

Boger, S., 2001b. Quality and contractual choice: a transaction cost approach to the Polish pork market. European Review of Agricultural Economics 28(3): 241-261.

Bollen, K.A., 1989. Structural equations with latent variables. Wiley, New York, NY.

Bolwijn, P.T. and T. Kumpe, 1990. Manufacturing in the 1990's – Productivity, flexibility and innovativeness. Long Range Planning 23: 44-57.

Bowersox, D.J. and P.J. Daugherty, 1995. Logistics paradigms: the impact of information technology. Journal of Business Logistics, 16(1): 65-80.

Boyd, B.K. and J. Fulk, 1996. Executive scanning and perceived uncertainty: A multidimensional model. Journal of Management 22(1): 1-21.

Boyer, K.K., P.T. Ward and G.K. Leong, 1996. Approaches to the factory of the future. An empirical taxonomy. Journal of Operations Manage 14(4): 297-314.

Brown, J.R., C.S. Dev and D.J. Lee, 2000. Managing marketing channel opportunism: the efficacy of alternative governance mechanism. Journal of Marketing 64(April): 51-65

Brown, S.P. and W.W. Chin, 2004. Satisfying and retaining customers through independent service representatives. Decision Sciences 35(3): 527-550.

Bunduchi, R., 2008. Trust, power and transaction costs in B2B exchanges – A socio-economic approach. Industrial Marketing Management 37: 610-622.

Burchell, B. and F. Wilkinson, 1997. Trust, business relationships and contractual environment. Cambridge Journal of Economics 21(2): 217-237.

Burgelman, R.A., 1983. Corporate entrepreneurship and strategic management: insights from a process study. Management Science 29(12): 1349-1364.

Butler, M., P. Herlihy and P.B. Keenan, 2005. Integrating information technology and operational research in the management of milk collection. Journal of Food Engineering 70: 341-349.

Buvik, A., 2002. Hybrid governance and governance performance in industrial purchasing relationships. Scandinavian Journal of Management 18: 567-587.

Buvik, A. and T. Reve, 2001. Asymmetrical deployment of specific assets and contractual safeguarding in industrial purchasing relationships. Journal of Business Research 51(2): 101-113.

Byrne, B.M., 2001. Structural equation modeling with AMOS: basic concepts, applications and programming. Lawrence Erlbaum Associates, New Jersey.

Cannon, J.P. and W.D. Perreault Jr., 1999. Buyer-seller relationships in business markets. Journal of Marketing Research 36(November): 439-460.

Capon, N., J.U. Farley and S. Hoenig, 1990. Determinants of financial performance: a meta-analysis. Management Science 36(10): 1143-1159.

Carr, A.S. and J.N. Pearson, 1999. Strategically managed buyer-seller relationships and performance outcomes. Journal of Operations Management 17(5): 497-519.

Chen, C. and Y.Z. Luo, 2003. Establishment of supply chain model of the processed meat products in China. Journal of Nanjing Agricultural University, No. 1: 89-92.

Chen, I.J. and A. Paulraj, 2004. Towards a theory of supply chain management: the constructs and measurements. Journal of Operations Management 22: 119-150.

Child, J., L. Chung and H. Davies, 2003. The performance of cross-border units in China: a test of natural selection, strategy choice and contingency theories. Journal of International Business Studies 34(3) 242-254.

Chin, W.W., 1998. The partial least square approach to structural equation modeling, In: Marcoulides, G.A. (ed.), Modern Methods for Business Research. London, Lawrence Erlbaum Associates Publisher, 295-336.

Chin, W.W., 1998. Commentary: Issues and Opinion on Structural Equation Modeling. MIS Quarterly 22(1): vii-xvi.

China Statistical Yearbook of Animal Husbandry, 2005. China Agricultural Publishing House, China.

China Meat Association, 2006. Result of the Brand Impact Assessment of China's Meat Industry. Meat Industry, September, 46-47.

China Meat Association, 2008. Top companies in China's meat food industry in 2008, China International Meat Seminar, China Meat Association Membership Conference, May 28, Beijing.

China statistical Yearbook, various issues. National Bureau of Statistics Press, China.

Chiu, H.N., 1995. The integrated logistics management system: a framework and case study. International Journal of Physical Distribution & Logistics Management 25(6): 4-22.

Choi, T. Y. and K. Eboch, 1998. The TQM paradox: relations among TQM practices, plant performance and customer satisfaction. Journal of Operations Management 17: 59-75.

Christiansen, T., W.L. Berry, P. Bruun and P. Word, 2003. A mapping of competitive priorities, manufacturing practices, and operational performance in groups of Danish manufacturing companies. International Journal of Operations & Production Management 23(10): 1163-1183.

Christopher, M., 2000. Managing the global supply chain in an uncertain world. Available at: http://www.rockfordconsulint.com, February 23.

Churchill, G.A., 1979. A paradigm for developing better measures of marketing constructs. Journal of Marketing Research 16(1): 64-73.

Churchill, G.A., 1999. Marketing research: Methodological foundations. Dryden Press, Orlando, Florida, United States of America, 1017p.

Clark, K.B., 1989. Project scope and project performance, the effect of parts strategy and supplier involvement on product development. Management Sciences 35(10): 1247-1263.

Clark, T., P.R. Varadarajan and W.M. Pride, 1994. Environmental management: The construct and research propositions. Journal of Business Research 29: 22-38.

Clark, M.A., 2006. Mastering the innovation challenge, Booz-Allen and Hamilton, Tysons Corner, Virginia.

Claro, D.P., G. Hagelaar and O. Omta, 2003. The determinants of relational governance and performance: How to manage business relationships. Industrial Marketing Management 32(8): 703-716.

Claro, D.P., 2004. Managing business networks and buyer-supplier relationships. PhD thesis, Wageningen University and Research Center, the Netherlands.

Cohen, J. and P. Cohen, 1983. Applied multiple regression/correlation analysis for the Sciences. 2nd ed., Lawrence Erlbaum Associates, London.

Cole, R.E., 1981. The Japanese lesson in quality. Technology Review 83: 29-40.

Conant, J.S., M.P. Mokwa and P.R. Varadarajan, 1990. Strategic types, distinctive marketing competencies and organizational performance: a multiple measures-based study. Strategic Management Journal 11(5): 365-383.

Cook, K.S. and R.M. Emerson, 1978. Power, equity and commitment in exchange network. American Sociological Review 43: 721-739.

Cramer, J., 2004. Chains and networks in sustainable business practices, In: Camps, T., P. Diederen, G.J. Hofstede and B. Vos (ed.), The emerging world of chains and networks, Bridging theory and practice, Reed Business Information, The Hague, The Netherlands, 73-86.

Croom, S., P. Romano and M. Giannakis, 2000. Supply chain management: an analytical framework for critical literature review. European Journal of Purchasing & Supply Management 6: 67-83.

Crosby, P.C., 1979. Quality is free, Hodder and Stoughton, Sevenoaks.

Dai, Y.C., J. Han and Y.R. Ying, 2006. An exploratory research on vertical coordination of innovative pork supply chain. Journal of Nanjing Agricultural University 29(3): 122-126.

Daly, S.P. and L.X. Cui, 2003. E-logistics in China: basic problems, manageable concerns and intractable solutions. Industrial Marketing Management 32: 235-242.

Das, A., R.B. Handfield, R.J. Calantone and S. Ghosh, 2000. A contingent view of quality management – the impact of international competition on quality. Decision Sciences 31(3): 649-690.

Daskin, M.S., 1985. Logistics: an overview of the state of the art and perspectives on future research. Transportation Research 19(5/6): 383-398.

Daugherty, P.J., A. Ellinger and C.M. Gustin, 1996. Integrated logistics: achieving logistics performance improvement. Supply Chain Management 1(3): 25-33.

Davenport, T.H. and J.D. Brooks, 2004. Enterprise systems and the supply chain. Journal of Enterprise Information Management 17(1): 8-19.

Delgado, C.M., W. Rosegrant, H. Steinfeld, S. Ehui, and C. Courbois, 1999. Livestock to 2020: the Next Food Revolution, Food, Agriculture, and the Environment Discussion Paper 28, International Food Policy Research Institute, Washington, DC.

Dean, Jr., J.W. and S.A. Snell, 1996. The strategic use of integrated manufacturing: an empirical examination. Strategic Management Journal 17(6): 459-480.

Deming, W.E., 1996. Out of crisis. Center for Advanced Engineering Study, MIT, Cambridge, MA.

Den Ouden, M., A.A. Dijkhuizen, R.B.M. Huirne and P.J.P. Zuurbien, 1996. Vertical cooperation in agricultural production-marketing chains, with special reference to production differentiation in pork. Agribusiness 12: 277-290.

Deng, F. J., 2005. Big industry, big market and big trade. Sino-Foreign Food: 26-28.

Deng, F. J., 2007. Several problems that the Chinese meat industry faces. Meat Research 5: 50.

Deng, F.J. 2007a. The current situation and future development of the meat industry in China. Paper read at The Fourth IMS World Pork Conference, 14th-17th September, 2007, at Nanjing, Jiangsu, China.

Diamantopoulos, A. and H.M. Winklhofer, 2001. Index construction with formative indicators: an alternative to scale development. Journal of Marketing Research 38: 269-277.

Dobson, W. and A.E. Safarian, 2008. The transition from imitation to innovation: an enquiry into China's evolving institutions and firm capabilities, Journal of Asian Economics 19: 301-311.

Dong, Y.G., and J.Q. Hou, 2005. The impact of SPS measures on China's pork trade. Agro-Technical Economy 2: 47-51.

Dooyoung, S., J.G. Kalinowski, and G. El-Enein, 1998. Critical implementation issues in total quality management. SAM Advanced Management Journal 63(1): 10-14.

Dow, D., D. Samson and S. Ford, 1999. Exploding the myth: do all quality management practices contribute to superior quality performance? Production and Operations Management 8(1): 1-27.

Dunn, S.C., R.F. Seaker and M.A. Waller, 1994. Latent variables in business logistics research: scale development and validation. Journal of Business Logistics 15(2): 145-172.

Dwyer, F.R. and S. Oh, 1987. Output sector munificence effects on the internal political economy of marketing channels. Journal of Marketing Research 24: 347-358.

Dyer, J.H. and H. Singh, 1998. The relational view: cooperative strategy and sources of interorganizational competitive advantage. The Academy of Management View 23(4): 660-679.

Dyer, J.H., 1996. Does governance matter? Keiretsu alliances and asset specificity as sources of Japanese competitive advantage. Organization Science 7(6): 649-666.

Efron, B. and G. Gong, 1983. A leisurely look at the bootstrap, then jackknife, and cross-validation. The American Statistician 37(1) 36-48.

Ellram, L.M., 1991. Supply chain management: the industrial organization perspective. International Journal of Physical Distribution and Logistics Management 21(1): 13-22.

Euromonitor International, 2006. Packaged food in China, Country Report. 17 March.

Evans, J.R., and J.W. Dean Jr., 2000. Total Quality: Management, Organization and Strategy second ed. South-Western College Publishing, Cincinnati, OH.

Fabiosa, J.F., D. Hu and C. Fang, 2005. A case study of China's commercial pork value chain, MATRIC Research Paper 05-MRP 11, Iowa State University, August.

FAO/WHO, 2002. Pan European conference on food safety and quality, Budapest, Hungary, available at: www.fap.org/docrep/fao/meeting/004/y3696e00.pdf, final report, accessed on October 11, 2008.

FAO, 2007. Livestock report. Available at: http://www.fao.org/statiscits.

Fawcett, S.E. and G.M. Magnan, 2002. The Rhetoric and Reality of Supply Chain Integration. International Journal of Physical Distribution and Logistics Management 32(5): 339-361.

Fearne, A., 1998. The evolution of partnerships in the meat supply chain: insights from the British Beef Industry. Supply Chain Management 3: 214-231.

Fearne, A., 1999. Building partnerships in the meat supply chain, the case of the UK beef industry. Agricultural Economics Research Institute (LEI), the Hague, the Netherlands.

Fearne, A., 2000. Building effective partnerships in the meat supply chain: lesson from the UK. Canadian Journal of Agricultural Economics 46(4): 491-518.

Feng, Y.H., 2009. China's hog market: analysis and forecasting. Available at: http://www.caaa.cn/show/article. Accessed on Jan. 12, 2009.

Ferguson, R.J., M. Paulin and J. Bergeron, 2005. Contractual governance, relational governance and the performance of interfirm service exchanges: the influence of boundary spanner closeness. Journal of the Academy of Marketing Science 33(2): 217-234.

Field, A., 2005. Discovering statistics using SPSS. Second Edition, Sage Publications, London, United Kingdom.

Field, A., 2003. Discovering Statistics using SPSS for windows. Sage Publications, London, United Kingdom, 496p.

Flynn, B.B., R.G. Schroeder and S. Sakakibara, 1994. A framework for quality management research and an associated measurement instrument. Journal of Operations Management 11: 339-366.

Flynn, B.B., R.G. Schroeder and S. Sakakibara, 1995. The impact of quality management practices on performance and competitive advantage. Decision Sciences 26: 659-691.

Forker, L.B., S.K. Vickery and C.L.M. Droge, 1996. The contribution of quality to business performance. International Journal of Operations & Production Management 16(8): 44-62.

Forker, L.B., D. Mendez and J.C. Hershauer, 1997. Total quality management in the supply chain: what is its impact on performance? International Journal of Production Research 35: 1681-1701.

Fornell, C. and D. Larcker, 1981. Evaluating structural equation modeling with unobservable variables and measurement error. Journal of Marketing Research 18: 39-50.

Fornell, C. and F. Bookstein, 1982. Two structural equation models: LISREL and PLS applied to consumer exit-voice theory. Journal of Marketing Research 19(4): 440-52.

Forza, C., 1995. Quality information systems and quality management: a reference model and associated measures for empirical research. Industrial Management and Data Systems 95(2): 6-14.

Forza, C. and R. Filippini, 1998. TQM impact on quality conformance and customer satisfaction: a causal model. International Journal of Production Economics 55: 1-20.

Foster, Jr., S.T., 2008. Towards an understanding of supply chain quality management. Journal of Operations Management 26(4): 461-556.

Frazier, G.L., 1983. On the measurement of interfirm power. Journal of Marketing Research 20: 158-166.

Frohlich, M.T. and R. Westbrook, 2001. Arcs of integration: an international study of supply chain strategies. Journal of Operations Management 19: 185-200.

Fusfeld, A.R., 1989. Formulating technology strategies to meet the global challenges of the 1990s. International Journal of Technology Management 4: 601-612.

Gale, F. and K. Huang, 2007. Demand for food quantity and quality in China. US Department of agriculture, ERR-32, January, http://www.ers.usda.gov/pbulications/er32/.

Ganesan, S., 1994. Determinants of long-term orientation in buyer-seller relationships. Journal of Marketing 58(2): 1-19.

Garvin, D.A., 1984. What does 'product quality' really mean? Sloan Management Review, Fall: 25-43

Garvin, D., 1986. Quality problems, policies, and attitudes in the US and Japan – An exploratory study. Academy of management Journal 29: 653-673.

Gattorna, J.L. and D.W. Walters, 1996. Managing the supply chain, a strategic perspective. MacMillan Press Ltd, Chippenham, Wiltshire, London, UK.

Gattorna, J., 1998. Strategic supply chain alignment: Best practice in supply chain management. Gower Publishing Limited, UK.

Gerbing, D. W. and J. C. Anderson, 1988. An updated paradigm for scale development incorporating unidimensionality and its assessment. Journal of Marketing Research 25: 186-192.

Ghoshal, S. and P. Moran, 1996. Bad for practice: a critique of the transaction cost theory. Academy of Management 21: 13-47.

Goldhar, J.D. and Lei, D., 1991. The shape of twenty-first century global manufacturing. The Journal of Business Strategy 12(2): 37-41.

Granovetter, M., 1985. Economic action and social structure: the problem of embeddedness. American Journal of Sociology 91: 481-510.

Greis, N.P. and J.D. Kasarda, 1997. Enterprise logistics in the information age. California Management Review 39(3): 55-78.

Griffith, C.J., 2005. Are we making the most of food safety inspections? A glimpse into the future. British Food Journal 107(3): 132-139.

Gryna, F., 2001. Supply chain management, quality planning and analysis. (Chapter 15), The McGraw-Hill Companies, Inc., New York, NY, 403-432.

Gulati, R., 1995. Does familiarity breed trust? The implications of repeated ties for contractual choice in alliances. Academy of Management Journal 38: 85-112.

Gundlach, G.T. and R.S. Achrol, 1993. Governance in exchange: contract law and its alternatives. Journal of Public Policy & Marketing 12(2): 141-155.

Guthrie, D., 2001. Dragon in a three-piece suit: the emergence of capitalism in China. (ed.), Princeton, NJ: Princeton University Press.

Hair, J., R. Anderson, R. Tatham and W. Black, 1995. Multivariate Data Analysis with Readings. 4th ed. Prentice Hall, Englewood Cliffs, NJ.

Hair, J.F., R.E. Anderson, R.L. Tatham and W.C. Black, 1998. Multivariate Data Analysis. Prentice Hall International Inc, Upper Sadle River, New Jersey, United States of America, 730p.

Hakansson, H., 1982. (ed.)International marketing and purchasing of industrial goods: an interaction approach. IMP Project Group, John Wiley and Sons, 406pp.

Han, S.L., D.T. Wilson and S.P. Dant, 1993. Buyer-supplier relationships today. Industrial Marketing Management 22(4): 331-338.

Han, J., J. Trienekens, T. Tan and S.W.F. Omta, 2006. Quality management and governance in pork processing industries in China. In: Ruben, R., M. van Boekel, A. van Tilburg and J. Trienekens (eds.), Tropical Food Chains, governance regions for quality management. Wageningen Academic Publishers, the Netherlands.

Han, J., S.W.F. Omta and J. Trienekens, 2007. The joint impact of supply chain integration and quality management on the performance of pork processing firms in China. International Food and Agribusiness Management Review 10(2): 67-98.

Han, J. J.H. Trienekens and S.W.F. (Onno) Omta, 2009. Integrated information technology and logistics management, quality management and firm performance of pork processing industry in China. British Food Journal 111(1): 9-25.

Handfield, R.B. and E.L. Nichols, 1998. Introduction to Supply Chain Management. Prentice-Hall, Upper Saddle River, NJ.

Hayes, R.H., 1985. Strategic planning: forward in reverse. Harvard Business Review, November-December: 111-119.

Heide, J.B. and G. John, 1988. The role of dependence balancing in safeguarding transaction specific assets in conventional channel. Journal of Marketing 52: 20-35.

Heide, J.B. and G. John, 1990. Alliances in industrial purchasing: the determinants of joint action in buyer-supplier relationships. Journal of Marketing Research 27: 24-36.

Heide, J.B. and G. John, 1992. Do norms matter in marketing relationships? Journal of Marketing 56(2): 32-44.

Heide, J.B., 1994. Interorganizational governance in marketing channels. Journal of Marketing 58(January): 71-85.

Hendricks, K.B. and V.R. Singhal, 1997. Does implementing an effective TQM program actually improve operating performance? Empirical evidence from firms that have won quality awards, Management Science 43(9): 1258-1274.

Hesterley, W.S., J. Liebeskind and T.R. Zenger, 1990. Organizational economics: an impending revolution in organization theory. Academy of Management Review 15(3): 402-420.

Hill, C.A. and G.D. Scudder, 2002. The use of electronic data interchange for supply chain coordination in the food industry. Journal of Operations Management 20(4): 375-387.

Hobbs, J.E., 1995. Evolving marketing channels for beef and lamb in the United Kingdom – a transaction cost approach. Journal of International Food & Agribusiness Marketing 7(4): 15-39.

Hobbs, J.E., 1996. A transaction cost approach to supply chain management. Supply Chain Management 1(2): 15-27.

Hobbs, J. E., W. A. Kerr and K. K. Klein, 1998. Creating international competitiveness through supply chain management: Danish pork. Supply Chain Management 3(2): 68-78.

Hobbs, J.E. and L.M. Young, 2000. Closer vertical coordination in agrifood supply chains, a conceptual model and some preliminary evidence. Supply Chain Management 5(3): 131-142.

Hobbs, J.E. and L.M. Young, 2001. Vertical linkages in agri-food supply chains in Canada and the United States, Research and Analysis Directorate Strategic Policy Branch, Agriculture and Agri-Food Canada.

Holm, D.B., K. Eriksson and J. Johanson, 1996. Business networks and cooperation in international business relationships. Journal of International Business Studies 27(5): 1033-1053.

Hsu, C.C., V.R. Kannan, K.C. Tan and G.K., Leong, 2008. Information sharing, buyer-supplier relationships, and firm performance, a multi-region analysis. International Journal of Physical Distribution & Logistics Management 38(4): 296-310.

Hu, D., T. Reardon, S. Rozelle, P. Timmer and H. Wang, 2004. The emergence of supermarkets with Chinese characteristics: challenges and opportunities for China's agricultural development. Development Policy Review 22(5): 557-586.

Hu, K., X.Q. Gan and L.N. Gan, 2007. Status, Problem and Trend of the Pork Supply Chain in China, Journal of Anhui Agricultural Sciences 35(12): 3667-3668, 3676

Huajing Tianzhong ECC, 2006. Development Report of the Meat Sector of China. July, Beijing.

Hueth, B., E. Ligon, S. Wolf and S. Wu, 1999. Incentive instruments in fruit and vegetable contracts: input control, monitoring, measuring and price risk, Review of Agricultural Economics 21(2): 374-389.

Huggiss, J.W. and R. G. Schmitt, 1995. Electronic data interchange as a cornerstone to supply chain management. Annual Conference Proceedings of the 1995 Council of Logistics Management.

Jayaram, J. and S.K. Vickery, 1998. Supply-based strategies, human resource initiatives, procurement lead-time, and firm performance. International Journal of Purchasing and Materials Management, Winter: 12-23.

Johnson, D., 2002. Empirical study of second-tier automotive suppliers achieving QS-9000 reference no. 718. International Journal of Operations & Production Management 22: 909-928.

Johnson, G. and K. Scholes, 1999. Exploring corporate strategy, Prentice Hall Europe, Hertfordshire, United Kingdom, 560p.

Johnson, J.L., 1999. Strategic integration in industrial distribution channels: managing the interfirm relationship as a strategic asset. Journal of the Academy of Marketing Science 27(1): 4-18.

Jöreskog, K. G., 1969. A general approach to confirmatory maximum likelihood factor analysis. Psychometrika 34: 183-202.

Jöreskog, K.G. and D. Sörbom, 1989. LISREL 7 User's Reference Guide, Scientific Software, Chicago, IL.

Jöreskog, K.G. and D. Sörbom, 1996. LISREL 8 structural equation modelling with SIMPLIS command language. Lawrence Erlbaum Associates, Hillsdale, United States of America.

Kaynak, H., 2002. The relationship between just-in-time purchasing techniques and firm performance. IEEE Transactions on Engineering Management 49(3): 205.

Kaynak, H., 2003. The relationship between total quality management practices and their effects in firm performance. Journal of Operations Management 21: 405-435.

Kaynak, H. and J.L. Hartley, 2008. A replication and extension of quality management into supply chain. Journal of Operations Management 26(4): 468-489.

References

Kenderdine, J.M. and P.D. Larson, 1988. Quality and logistics: a framework for strategic integration. International Journal of Physical Distribution and Materials Management 18(7): 5-10.

Kim, S.W., 2006. Effects of supply chain management practices, integration and competition capability on performance. Supply Chain Management: An International Journal 11(3): 241-248.

Klein, B., R.A. Crawford and A. A. Alchian, 1978. Vertical integration, appropriable rents and the competitive contracting process. Journal of Law and Economics 21: 297-326.

Klein, K.K., M.D. Faminow, A.M. Walburger, B. Larue, R. Romain and K. Foster, 1996. An evaluation of supply chain performance in the Canadian pork sector. Supply Chain Management 1(3): 12-24.

Kleindorfer, P.R. and F.Y. Partovi, 1990. Integrating manufacturing strategy and Technology choice. European Journal of Operations Research 47: 214-224.

Kotha, S. and A. Nair, 1995. Strategy and environment as determinants of performance: evidence from the Japanese machine tool industry. Strategic Management Journal 16(7): 497-518.

Koufteros, X.A., 1999. Testing a model of pull production: a paradigm for manufacturing research using structural equation modeling. Journal of Operation Management 17: 467-488.

Kuei, C. and C.N. Madu, 2001. Identifying critical success factors for supply chain quality management. Asia Pacific Management Review 6(4): 409-423.

Kuei, C., C. Madu and C. Lin, 2001. The relationship between supply chain quality management practices and organizational performance. International Journal of Quality and Reliability Management 18(8): 864-872.

Laframboise, K., 2002. Business performance and enterprise resource planning, Proceedings of ECIS 2002 Conference, Gdansk, Poland.

Laframboise, K. and F. Reyes, 2005. Gaining competitive advantage from integrating enterprise resource planning and total quality management. The Journal of Supply Chain Management: A Global Review of Purchasing and Supply, August: 49-64.

Lai, K., T.C.E. Cheng and A.C.L. Yeung, 2005. Relationship stability and supplier commitment to quality. International Journal of Production Economics 96: 397-410.

Lambert, D.M. and M.C. Cooper, 2000. Issues in supply chain management. Industrial Marketing Management 29: 65-83.

Lamming, R., T. Johnsen, J.R. Zheng and C. Harland, 2000. An initial classification of supply networks. International Journal of Operations & Production Management 20(5-6): 675-691.

Lattin, J., D. Carroll and P.E. Green, 2003. Analyzing multivariate data. Brooks/Cole Thompson Learning, Pacific Grove, the United States of America, 279p.

Lawrence, J.D. and M.L. Hayenga, 2002. The U.S. pork and beef sectors: divergent organizational patterns, paradoxes and conflicts. In: Trienekens, J.H. and S.W.F. Omta (eds.), Paradoxes in Food Chains and Networks. Wageningen Academic Publishers, the Netherlands, 512-521.

Lawrence, P.R. and J.W. Lorsch, 1967. Organization and Environment: Managing differentiation and integration, Harvard University, Boston, United States of America, 556p.

Lee, H. L., V. Padmanabhan and S. Whang, 1997. Information distortion in a supply chain: the bullwhip effect, Management Science 43(4): 546-558.

Lee, T.N., S.E. Fawcett, and J. Briscoe, 2002. Benchmarking the challenge to quality program implementation. Benchmarking: An International Journal 9(4): 374-387.

Leiblein, M.J., 2003. The choice of organizational governance form and performance: predictions from transaction cost, resource-based and real options theories. Journal of Management 29(6): 937-961.

Li, D.X. and W. Willborn, 1990. Quality improvement in China. International Journal of Quality and Reliability Management 7(5): 27-33.

Li, S., B. Ragu-Nathan, T. S. Ragu-Nathan and S. S. Rao, 2006. The impact of supply chain management practices on competitive advantage and organizational performance. Omega (The International Journal of Management Science) 34: 107-124.

Li, H., 2008. Battle for hogs: Yurun ranks only after Shineway in hog slaughtering, China Times, Nov., www.chinatimes.cc/cns/cjxw/qyxw.2008-11-22/1457.shtml.

Liu, Y., J. Chen, X. Zhang and B. Kamphuis, 2004. The vegetable industry in China, developments in policies, production, marketing and international trade. Agricultural Economics Research Institute, the Hague, The Netherlands, Project code: 62834, September.

Liu, Z.Y., S.M. Sun and J.Y. Wang, 2008. Development and trend of agri-food supply chain management in China. Digest of Management Science, 284-286.

Livestock report, 2006. Rome: Food and Agriculture Organization of the United Nations.

Longworth, J.W., C.G. Brown and S.A. Walbdron, 2001. Beef in China: agribusiness opportunities and challenges. University of Queensland Press, Box 6042, St. Lucia, Queensland 4067 Australia.

Lu, H. 2007. The role of guanxi in buyer-seller relationships in China. Wageningen Academic Publishers, the Netherlands.

Lu, C.S., K.H. Lai and T.C.E. Cheng, 2007. Application of structural equation modeling to evaluate the intention of shippers to use Internet services in liner shipping. European Journal of Operational Research 180: 845-867.

Lu, H., J.H. Trienekens and S.W.F. (Onno) Omta, 2008. The value of guanxi for small vegetable farmers in China. British Food Journal 110(4-5): 412-429.

Luo, Y.D. and S.H. Park, 2001. Strategic alignment and performance of market-seeking MNCs in China. Strategic Management Journal 22(2): 141-155.

Lusch, R. F. and J. R. Brown, 1996. Interdependency, contracting, and relational behavior in marketing channels. Journal of Marketing 60(October): 19-38.

MacNeil, I.R., 1978. Contracts: adjustments of long-term economic relationships under classical, neoclassical and relational contract law. Northwestern University of Law Review 72(6): 854-905.

MacNeil, I.R., 1980. The new social contract, New Haven, CT, Yale University Press.

MacNeil, I.R., 2000. Relational contract theory, challenges and queries. Northwestern University Law Review 94(3): 877-907.

Madu, C. N., C. Kuei, and C. Lin, 1995. A comparative analysis of quality practice in manufacturing firms in the U. S. and Taiwan. Decision Sciences 26(5): 621-635.

Mainardi, C.A., M. Salva and M. Sanderson, 1999. Label of origin: Made on earth. Strategy Management Competition. 2nd Quarter: 20-28.

Makise, K., 2002. Creating special pork for the Japanese market. Advances in Pork Production 13: 233-237.

Mansfield, E., 1993. The diffusion of flexible manufacturing systems in Japan, Europe, and the United States. Management Science 39(2): 149-160.

References

Marsch, H.W. and D. Hocevar, 1985. An application of confirmatory factor analysis of the study of self-concept: first and higher order factor models and their invariance across groups. Psychological Bulletin 97(3): 562-582.

Martinez, S.W. and K. Zering, 2004. Pork quality and the role of market organization, Agricultural Economics Report number 835, www.ers.usda.gov.

Mason, C. and W.D. Perreault, 1991. Collinearity, power, and interpretation of multiple regression analysis. Journal of Marketing Research 28(3): 268-280.

Mathews, J. and P. Katel, 1992. The cost of quality. Newsweek 120(10): 48-49.

Matsuno, K. and J.T. Mentzer, 2000. The effects of strategy type on the market orientation-performance relationship. The Journal of Marketing 64(4): 1-16.

Mehra, S., J.M. Hoffman, and S. Danilo, 2001. TQM as a management strategy for the next millennia. International Journal of Operations & Production Management 21: 855-876.

Ménard, C., 2004. The economics of hybrid organizations. Journal of Institutional and Theoretical Economics 160: 1-32.

Miles, R.E. and C.C. Snow, 1978. Organizational strategy, structure, and process. McGraw-Hill, New York.

Miles, R.E. and C.C. Snow, 1994. Fit, failure and the hall of fame, Free Press, McGraw-Hill, New York.

Miller, D., 1988. Relating Porter's business strategies to environment and structure: analysis and performance implications. Academy of Management Journal 31(2) 280-308.

Mintzberg, H., 1973. Strategy making in three modes. California Management Review 16(2): 44-53.

Mohrman, S.A., R.V. Tenkasi, E.E. Lawler III and G.G. Ledford Jr., 1995. Total quality management: practice and outcomes in the largest US firms. Employee Relations 17(3): 26-41.

Motohashi, K., 2008. IT, enterprise reform, and productivity in Chinese manufacturing firms. Journal of Asian Economics 19: 325-333.

Muris, T.J., D.S. Scheffman and P.T. Spiller, 1992. Strategy and transaction costs: the organization of distribution in the carbonated soft drink industry. Journal of Economics and Management Strategy 1(1): 83-128.

Murphy, G.B., J.W. Trailer and R.C. Hill, 1996. Measuring performance in entrepreneurship research. Journal of Business Research 36: 15-23.

Nair, A., 2006. Meta-analysis of relationship between quality management practices and firm performance – implications of quality management theory development. Journal of Operations Management 24: 948-975.

Narasimhan, R. and J.R. Carter, 1998. Linking business unit and material sourcing strategies, Journal of Business Logistics 19(2): 155-171.

Narasimhan, R. and S.W. Kim, 2001. Information system utilization strategy for supply chain integration. Journal of Business Logistics 22(2): 51-75.

Narasimhan, R. and S.W.Kim, 2002. Effect of supply chain integration on the relationship between diversification and performance: Evidence from Japanese and Korean firms. Journal of Operations Management 20(3): 303-323.

Nelson, R.R. (ed.), 1993. National innovation system: A comparative analysis. Oxford: Oxford University Press.

Noordewier, T.G., G. John and J.R. Nevin, 1990. Performance outcomes of purchasing arrangements in industrial buyer-vendor relationships, Journal of Marketing 54(October): 80-93.

North, D.C, 1990. Institutions, institutional change, and economic performance, Cambridge: Cambridge University Press.

Nunnally, J.C., 1988. Psychometric theory. New York: McGraw-Hill.

OECD, 2006. Science, technology and industry outlook. http://www.oecd.org.

O'Leary-Kelly, S. and R. J. Vokurka, 1998. The empirical assessment of construct validity, Journal of Operations Management 16: 387-405.

Omta, S.W.F., J.H. Trienekens and G. Beers, 2002. A framework for the knowledge domain of chain and network science. In: Trienekens, J.H. and S.,W.F. Omta (eds.), Paradoxes in Food Chains and Networks. Wageningen Academic Publishers, the Netherlands, 13-20.

Pagell. M., 2004. Understanding the factors that enable and inhibit the integration of operations, purchasing and logistics. Journal of Operations Management 22: 459-487.

Palmer, M., 1996. Building effective alliances in the meat supply chain: lessons from the UK. Supply Chain Management 1(3): 9-11.

Pan, C. and J. Kinsey, 2002. The supply chain of pork: U.S. and China, Working paper 02-01, University of Minnesota, USA, March.

Pan, C., 2003. China's Meat Industry Overview, Food & Agribusiness Research. Rabobank International, May

Pan, C., 2004. Status-quo and implications of the quality and safety of livestock products in China. Agricultural Economics 9: 46-47.

Parthasarthy, R. and S.P. Sethi, 1992. The impact of flexible automation on business strategy and organizational structure. Academy of Management Review 17(1): 86-111.

Pearson, J.N., J.R. Carter and L. Peng, 1998. Alliances, logistics barriers, and strategic actions in the People's Republic of China, International Journal of Purchasing and Materials Management, August: 27-36.

Peng, M.W. and Y. Luo, 2000. Managerial ties and firm performance in a transition economy: the nature of a micro-macro link. Academy of Management Journal 43(3): 486-501.

Peng, M.W., Y. Lu, O. Shenkar, and D. Wang, 2001. Treasures in the China house: a review of management and organizational research in greater China. Journal of Business Research 52(2): 95-110.

Peng, M.W., 2003. Institutional transitions and strategic choices. Academy of Management Review 28(2): 275-296.

Petersen, B., S. Knura-Deszczka, E.Ponsgen-Schmidt and S. Gymnich, 2002. Computerized food safety monitoring in animal prodcution. Liverstock Production Science 76(3): 207-213.

Poon, C., 2006. An Overview of China's Pork Industry, Embassy of the Kingdom of the Netherlands, Department of Agriculture, Nature and Food Quality, Fall 2006

Poppo, L. and T. Zenger, 2002. Do formal contracts and relational governance function as substitutes or complements? Strategic Management Journal 23: 707-725.

Porter, M.E., 1980. Competitive strategy: techniques for analyzing industries and competitors. Free Press, New York, NY.

References

Porter, M.E., 1985. Competitive advantage: creating and sustaining superior performance, Free Press, New York, NY, 28-46.

Porter, M.E. and V.E. Miller, 1985. How Information Gives Your Competitive Advantage. Harvard Business Review, July-August: 149-160.

Powell, T.C., 1992. Organizational alignment as competitive advantage. Strategic Management Journal 13(2): 119-134.

Powell, T.C., 1995. Total quality management as competitive advantage: a review and empirical study. Strategic Management Journal 16(1): 15-37.

Power. D. J., A. Sohal and S. U. Rahman, 2001. Critical success factors in agile supply chain management: an empirical study. International Journal of Physical Distribution and Logistics Management 31(4): 247-265.

Prahald, C.K. and G. Hamel, 1990. The core competence of the corporation. Harvard Business Review 68(3): 71-91.

Purani, K. and S. Sahadev, 2008. The moderating role of industrial experience in the job satisfaction, intention to leave relationship: an empirical study among salesmen in India. Journal of Business & Industrial Marketing 23(7): 475-485.

Putzger, I., 1998. All the ducks in a row. World Trade 11(9): 54-56.

Rao, S.S., T.S. Raghunathan and L.E. Solis, 1999. The best commonly followed practices in human resources dimension of quality management in new industrializing countries: the case of China, India and Mexico. International Journal of Quality & Reliability Management 16(3): 215-226.

Raynaud, E., L. Sauvee and E. Valceschini, 2005. Alignment between quality enforcement devices and governance structures in the agro-food vertical chains. Journal of Management and Governance 9: 47-77.

Reardon, T., C. P. Timmer and J. A. Berdegue, 2003. The rise of supermarkets and private standards in developing countries: illustration from the produce sector and hypothesized implications for trade. paper presented at international conference, Capri, Italy, June 23-26.

Reddington, J.J., 2008. Global pork trade. 2008 Pork Management Conference, May 7-9, Destin, Florida,www.porkboard.org/documents/News/Global%20Trade%20-%20John%20Reddington. ppt.

Reed, R., D. Lemak and J. Montgomery, 1996. Beyond process: TQM content and firm performance. Academy of Management Review 21(1): 173-202.

Reimer, J.J., 2006. Vertical integration in the pork industry. American Journal of Agricultural Economics 88(1): 234-248.

Rindfleisch, A. and J.B. Heide, 1997. Transaction cost analysis, past, present and future applications. Journal of Marketing 61: 30-54.

Robinson, C.J. and M.K. Malhotra, 2005. Defining the concept of supply chain quality management and its relevance to academic and industrial practices. Int. J. Production Economics 96: 315-337.

Rosenzweg, E.D., A.V. Roth and J.W. Dean Jr., 2003. The influence of an integrated strategy on competitive capabilities and business performance, an exploratory study of consumer products and manufacturers. Journal of Operations Management 21(4): 437-456.

Ruben, R., A. van Tilburg, J. Trienekens and M. van Boekel, 2007. Linking market integration, supply chain governnance, quality and value added in tropical food chains. In: Ruben, R., A. van Tilburg, J. Trienekens and M. van Boekel (eds.), Tropical Food Chains, Wageningen Academic Publishers, the Netherlands, 13-46.

Ruben, R., D. Boselie and H. Lu, 2007a. Vegetable procurement by Asian supermarkets: a transaction cost approach. Supply Chain Management: An International Journal 12(1): 60-68.

Rungtusanatham, M., C. Forza, B.R. Koka, F. Salvador and W. Nie, 2005. TQM across multiple countries: Convergence Hypothesis versus National Specificity arguments. Journal of Operations Management 23: 43-63.

Ryu, S., S. Min and N. Zushi, 2008. The moderating role of trust in manufacturing-supplier relationships. Journal of Business & Industrial Marketing 23(1): 48-58.

Samson, D. and M. Terziovski, 1999. The relationship between total quality management practices and operational performance. Journal of Operations Management 17(4): 393-409.

Saraph, J.V., P.G. Benson and R.G. Schroeder, 1989. An instrument for measuring the critical factors of quality management. Decision Sciences 20(4): 810-829.

Saunders, M., 1997. Strategic Purchasing and Supply Chain Management. Pitman Publishing, London.

Saxton, T. 1997. The effect of partner and relationship characteristics on alliance outcomes. Academy of Management Journal 40: 443-461.

Scholten, V.E., 2006. The early growth of academic spin-offs, factors influencing the early growth of Dutch spin-offs in the life sciences, ICT and consulting. PhD thesis, Wageningen University, the Netherlands.

Schroeder, D.M., 1990. A dynamic perspective on the impact of process innovation upon competitive strategies. Strategic Management Journal 11: 25-41.

Schulze, B., A. Spiller and L. Theuvsen, 2007. A broader view on vertical coordination: lessons from German pork production, Journal on Chain and Network Science 7(1): 35-53.

Segars, A. 1997. Assessing the unidimensionality of measurement: a paradigm and illustration within the context of information systems research, Omega, Int. J. Mgmt. Sci. 25(1): 107-121.

Segars, A.H. and V. Grover, 1993. Re-examining perceived ease of use and usefulness: a confirmatory factor analysis. MIS Quarterly 17(4): 517-525.

Segev, E., 1987. Strategy, strategy making, and performance – an empirical investigation. Management Science 33(2): 258-269.

Sharif, N., 1994. Integrating business and technologies in developing countries. Technological Forecasting and Social Change 45: 151-167.

Sharma, S., R.M. Durand and O. Gur-Arie, 1981. Identification and analysis of moderator variables. Journal of Marketing Research 18: 291-300.

Shen, T. 2005. Linking supply chain practices to operational and financial performance. Supply Chain 2020 Project Working Paper. Lapide, L. and B. Schneck Allen (ed.), the MIT Center for Transportation and Logistics, USA, August.

Shin, H., D.A. Collier and D.D. Wilson, 2000. Supply management orientation and supplier/buyer performance. Journal of Operations Management 18(3): 317-333.

Sigurdson, J. 2004. China becoming a technological superpower – a narrow window of opportunity, Working paper, June, http://www.hhs.se/eijs, accessed on Oct. 16, 2008.

Sila, I., M. Ebrahimpour and C. Birkholz, 2006. Quality in supply chains: an empirical analysis. Supply Chain Management, An International Journal 11(6): 491-502.

Simatupang, T.M. and R. Sridharan, 2002. The collaborative supply chain. International Journal of Logistics Management 13(1): 15-30.

Simons, D., M. Francis, M. Boulakis and A. Fearne, 2003. Identifying the determinants of value in the UK red meat industry: a value chain analysis approach. Journal of Chain and Network Science 3(2): 109-121.

Slater, S.F. and E.M. Olson, 2000. Strategy type and performance: the influence of sales force management. Strategic Management Journal 21(8): 813-829.

Snow, C.C. and D.C. Hambrick, 1980. Measuring organizational strategies: some theoretical and methodological problems. Academy of Management Review 5(4): 527-538.

Soltani, E., 2005. Conflict between theory and practice: TQM and performance appraisal. International Journal of Quality & Reliability Management 22(8): 796-818.

Song, M., R.J. Calantone and C.A. Di Benedetto, 2002. Competitive forces and strategic choice decisions: an experimental investigation in the United States and Japan. Strategic Management Journal 23: 969-978.

Sousa, R. and C.A. Voss, 2001. Quality management: universal or context dependent? Production and Operations Management 10(4): 383-404.

Spiller, P.T. and A. Zellner, 1997. Product complementarities, capabilities and governance: a dynamic transaction cost perspective. Industrial and Corporate Changes 6(3): 561-594.

Stank, T., M. Crum and M. Arongo, 1999. Benefits of interfirm coordination in food industry supply chains. Journal of Business Logistics 20(2): 21-41.

Stank, T.P., S.B. Keller and P.J. Daugherty, 2001. Supply chain collaboration and logistical service performance. Journal of Business Logistics 22(1): 29-48.

Steenkamp, J.E.M. and H.C.M. van Trijp, 1991. The use of LISREL in validating marketing constructs. International Journal of Research in Marketing 8(4): 283-299.

Steenkamp, J. and H. Baumgartner, 1998. Assessing measurement invariance in cross-national consumer research. Journal of consumer research 25: 78-90.

Stevens, G., 1989. Integrating the supply chain. International Journal of Physical Distribution & Materials Management 19(8): 3-8.

Stock. G.N., N.P. Greis and J.D. Kasarda, 2000. Enterprise logistics and supply chain structure: the role of fit. Journal of Operations Management 18: 531-547.

Storey, J., C. Emberson, J. Godsell and A. Harrison, 2006. Supply chain management: theory, practice and future challenges. International Journal of Operations & Production Management 26(7): 754-774.

Strandholm, K., K. Kumar and R. Subramanian, 2004. Examining the interrelationship among perceived environmental change, strategic response, managerial characteristics, and organizational performance, Journal of Business Research 57: 58-68.

Styles, C. and T. Ambler, 2003. The coexistence of transaction and relational marketing: insights from the Chinese business context. Industrial Marketing Management 32: 633-642.

Su, Q., J.H. Shi and S.J. Lai, 2008. Study on supply chain management of Chinese firms from the institutional view. International Journal of Production Economics 115: 362-373.

Sun, S.M., 2006. Quality and safety of pork: managing the supply chain. Issues in Agricultural Economy, April: 7.

Tan, K.C., R.B. Handfield and D.R. Krause, 1998. Enhancing firm's performance through quality and supply base management: an empirical study. International Journal of Production Research 36(10): 2813-2837.

Tan, K.C., V.R. Kannan, R.B. Handfield and S. Ghosh, 1999. Supply chain management: an empirical study of its impact on performance. International Journal of Operations & Production Management 19(10): 1034-1052.

Tan, K.C., 2001. A framework of supply chain management literature. European Journal of Purchasing & Supply Management 7: 39-48.

Tan, K.C., S.B. Lyman, and J.D. Wisner, 2002. Supply chain management: a strategic perspective. International Journal of Operations & Production Management 22(6): 614-631.

Tan, X. and X. Xin, 2001. Market analysis for Chinese major agriproducts, Chinese Agricultural Press (in Chinese).

Taylor, D.H., 2006. Strategic considerations in the development of lean agri-food supply chains: a case study of the UK pork sector, Supply Chain Management: An International Journal 11(3): 271-280.

Taylor, W.A. and G.H. Wright, 2003. A longitudinal study of TQM implementation: factors influencing success and failure, Omega 31(2): 97-111.

Taylor, W.A. and G.H. Wright, 2003a. The impact of senior managers' commitment on the success of TQM programs, An Empirical Study, International Journal of Manpower 24(5): 535-550.

Terziovski, M., D. Power and A.S. Sohal, 2003. The longitudinal effects of the ISO 9000 certification process on business performance. European Journal of Operational Research 146: 580-595.

Tracey, M. and C.L. Tan, 2001. Empirical analysis of supplier selection and involvement, customer satisfaction, and firm performance. Supply Chain Management 6(3/4): 174-188.

Trent, R.J. and R.M. Monczka, 1998. Purchasing and supply management: trends and changes throughout the 1990s. International Journal of Purchasing and Materials Management, Fall: 2-11.

Trienekens, J.H. and A.J.M. Beulens, 2001. Views on inter-enterprise relationships. Production Planning and Control 12(5): 466-477.

Trienekens, J.H. and J.G.A.G., Van der Vorst, 2003. Quality, safety and traceability in food supply chains, lecture notes for course Supply Chain Management, Wageningen, the Netherlands, 36p

Trienekens, J.T. and P. Zuurbier, 2008. Quality and safety standards in the food industry, developments and challenges. Journal of Production Economics 13(1): 107-122.

Ulusoy, G., 2003. An assessment of supply chain and innovation management practices in the manufacturing industries in Turkey. Journal of Production Economics 88: 251-270.

Ulrich, K., and S. Pearson, 1998. Assessing the importance of design through product archaeology. Management Science 44(3): 352-369.

United Nations Development Programme, 2006. Human development report 2006. http://dhr.undp.org/hdr2006/statistics.

USDA FAS, 2006. Livestock and Poultry: World Markets and Trade, March

USDA-FAS, 2007. Attaché reports, official statistics, and results of office research. Population statistics from U.S. Census Bureau, Population Division, International Programs Center, http://www.fas.usda.gov/psdonline) and WASDE release of April 10, 2007.

References

Uzzi, B., 1997. Social structure and competition in interfirm networks: The paradox of embeddedness, Administrative Science Quarterly 42(1): 35-67.

Uzzi, B., 1999. Embeddedness in the marketing of financial capital: how social relations and networks benefits firms seeking financing, American Sociological Review 64(August): 481-505.

Van der Meulen, B. and M. Van der Velde, 2004. Food safety law in the European Union: An introduction, Wageningen Academic Publishers, the Netherlands.

Van der Vorst, J.G.A.G., 2000. Effective Food Supply Chains, creating, generating, modeling and evaluating supply chain scenarios, Wageningen University, Wageningen, The Netherlands, 305p.

Van der Vorst, J.G.A.G. and A.J.M. Beulens, 2002. Identifying sources of uncertainty to generate supply chain redesign strategies. International Journal of Physical Distribution & Logistics Management 32(6): 409-430.

Van der Zee, H., 2004. Chains, networks and the enabling role of IT. In: Camps, T., P. Diederen, G.J. Hofstede and B. Vos (ed.), The emerging world of chains and networks, Bridging theory and practice, Reed Business Information, The Hague, The Netherlands, 87-102

Van Plaggenhoef, W., 2007. Integration and self regulation of quality management in Dutch agri-food supply chains, PhD thesis, Wageningen Academic Publishers, The Netherlands.

Venkatraman, N., 1989. The concept of fit in strategic management: a methodological perspective, Journal of Management Studies 14(3): 423-444.

Verdú Jover, A.J., J.F. Lloréns Montes and V.J. García Morales, 2005. Flexibility, fit and innovative capacity: an empirical examination. International Journal of Technology Management 30(1-2): 131-146.

Vickery, S.K., R. Calantone and C. Droge, 1999. Supply Chain Flexibility: An Empirical Study. The Journal of Supply Chain Management 35(3): 16-24.

Vickery, S. K., J. Jayaram, C. Droge and R. Calantone, 2003. The effects of an integrative supply chain strategy on customer service and financial performance: an analysis of direct versus indirect relationships. Journal of Operational Management 21: 523-539.

Wang, Q., K. Zantow, F. Lai and X. Wang, 2006. Strategic postures of third-party logistics providers in mainland China. International Journal of Physical Distribution & Logistics Management 36(10): 793-819.

Wang, R, 2006. China: Pork powerhouse of the world, Jinnai Agribusiness Research Center. China Agricultural University, Beijing

Wheelwright, S.C. and K.B. Clark, 1992. Creating project plans to focus product development. Harvard Business Review 70(2): 70-82.

Williamson, O.E., 1975. Markets and hierarchies: analysis and antitrust implications, New York: Free press, 253-267.

Williamson, O.E., 1979. Transaction cost economics: the governance of contractual relations. The Journal of Law and Economics 22(2): 233-261.

Williamson, O.E. and W.G. Ouchi, 1981. The markets and hierarchies program of research: origins, implications, prospects. In: Van der Ven, A.H. and W.F. Joyce (eds.), Perspectives on Organization Design and Behavior. John Wiley & Sons, Inc., New Pork, USA, 347-70.

Williamson, O.E., 1985. The Economic Institutions of Capitalism: Firms, Markets, and Relational Contracting. The Free Press, New York, USA.

Williamson, O.E., 1989. Transaction cost economics. In: Schnalense, R. and R.D. Willig (eds.), Handbook of Industrial Organizations, New York: Elsevier Science, 136-182.

Williamson, O.E., 1991. Comparative economic organization: The analysis of discrete structural alternatives. Administrative Science Quarterly 36(June): 269-296.

Williamson, O.E., 1991a. Strategizing, economizing, and economic organization, Strategic Management Journal Winter Special Issue 12: 75-94.

Williamson, O.E., 1996. The mechanisms of governance, New York: Oxford University Press.

Wold, H., 1980. Soft modeling: intermediate between traditional model building and data analysis, Mathematical Statistics 6: 333-346.

Wold, H., 1981. The fix-point approach to independent system: review and outlook. In Wold, H. (editors), The fix-point approach to interdependent systems, Amsterdam: North-Holland, 1-35.

Wold, H., 1982. Systems under indirect observation using PLS. In: Fornell, C. (ed.), A Second Generation of Multivariate Analysis, Praeger, New York, 325-47.

Wong, A., D. Tjosvold, W.Y.L. Wong and C.K. Liu, 1999. Relationships for quality improvement in the Hong Kong-China supply chain. International Journal of Quality and Reliability Management 16(1): 24-41.

Wood, A., 1997. Extending the supply chain: strengthening links with IT, Chemical Week 159(25): 26.

World Bank (Ed.), 2005. The dynamics of vertical coordination in agrifood chains in eastern Europe and central Asia: implications for policy and World Bank operations, Washington DC: World Bank.

Wu, X. M., 2006. Studies on the pork quality and safety management systems in China, PhD thesis, Zhejiang University, April, China

Xu, B.Y. and F.S. Liu, 2003. The second employment opportunities for the agro-produce wholesale markets in mainland China and Taiwan under WTO. China Price Press, May. 256-290.

Yasai-Ardekani, M. and P.C. Nystrom, 1996. Designs for environmental scanning systems: Tests of contingency theory, Management Science 42(2): 187-204.

Yeung, A.C.L., T.S. Lee and L.Y. Chan, 2003. Senior management perspectives and ISO 9000 effectiveness: an Empirical Research. International Journal of Production Research 41(3): 545-569.

Yeung, H.W.C., 2006. Change and continuity in Southeast Asian ethnic Chinese business. Asian Pacific Journal of Management 23(3): 229-254.

Yeung, J.H.Y., W. Selen, C. Sum and B. Huo, 2006. Linking financial performance to strategic orientation and operational priorities. International Journal of Physical Distribution & Logistics Management 36(3): 210-230.

Yu, C.-M.J., T.-J. Liao and Z.-D. Lin, 2006. Formal governance mechanisms, relational governance mechanisms, and transaction specific investments in supplier-manufacturer relationships. Industrial Marketing Management 35: 128-139.

Zaheer, A. and N. Venkatraman, 1995. Relational governances as an interorganizational strategy: An empirical test of the role of trust in economic exchange. Strategic Management Journal 16(5): 373-392.

Zailani, S., and P. Rajagopal, 2005. Supply chain integration and performance: US versus East Asian companies. Supply Chain Management: An International Journal 10(5): 379-393.

References

Zhang, Z.H., A. Waszink and J. Wijnaard, 2000. An instrument for measuring TQM implementation for Chinese manufacturing companies. International Journal of Quality & Reliability Management 17(7): 730-755.

Zhang, L., M.K.O. Lee, Z. Zhang and P. Banerjee, 2003. Critical success factors of enterprise resource planning systems implementation success in China, in: 36th Annual Hawaii International Conference on System Sciences (HICSS'03), Big Island, Hawaii, January 6-9.

Zhou S.D. and Y.C. Dai, 2005. Selection of vertical coordination forms by the hog producers under the supply chain management context, China Rural Economy 6: 30-36.

Zhou, G., 2006. The changing dynamic in China: the development of meat industry and consumers, presentation at World Meat Congress, Brisban, Australia, April. http://www.2006worldmeatcongress.com.au/presentations/index.php.

Zhou, K.Z., L. Poppo and Z. Yang, 2008. Relational ties or customized contracts? An exanimation of alternative governance choice in China, Journal of International Business Studies 39: 526-534.

Zhou, X., X. Zhao, Q. Li and H. Cai, 2003. Embeddedness and contractual relationships in China's transitional economy, American Sociological Review 68(1): 75-102.

Zúñiga-Arias, G.E., 2007. Quality management and strategic alliances in the mango supply chain from Costa Rica, PhD thesis, Wageningen University, the Netherlands.

Appendices

Appendix A. Questionnaire for pork slaughterhouses and processors

The tracking number included here is for internal use only. ....

I. General profile

1. How many years have you been working in the pork processing business?
2. How long have you been working in this company?
   What is your main responsibility? _____
   ☐ general manager   ☐ deputy manager   ☐ production manager
   ☐ quality control manager   ☐ marketing manager
   ☐ financial and office administrator   ☐ others
3. Your company is:
   ☐ State-owned   ☐ Collectively-owned   ☐ Private   ☐ Joint venture
   ☐ Private and shareholding
4. Your company is:
   ☐ pork slaughtering firm   ☐ pork further processing firm
   ☐ pork slaughtering-processing integrated firm
5. Which markets do your products serve?
   ☐ Local market   ...%
   ☐ Other cities/areas in the province   ...%
   ☐ Other cities/areas in China   ...%
   ☐ International market   ...%
   ☐ Others, e.g.   ...%
   Total   100%
6. Who are your direct suppliers and the percentage (Note: only for slaughterhouses and integrated pork processors)?
   ☐ Agents (middlemen)   ....%
   ☐ Specialised hog producers   ....%   (more than 50 to less than 9, 999 hogs per year)

   ☐ Household farmers   ...%   (under 50 hogs per year)
   ☐ Commercial big farms   ...%   (more than 10,000 hogs per year)
   ☐ Own pig farm (invested by the company ...%, joint venture ...%)
   ☐ Others, e.g.   ...%
   Total   100%
7. Who are your direct suppliers and the percentage (Note: only for processors and integrated firms)?
   ☐ pork wholesale market   ☐ middlemen   ☐ slaughterhouses   ☐ Others, e.g.

8. Who are your buyers and the percentage of the purchase?
   ☐ Supermarkets   ...%
   ☐ Wet market   ...%
   ☐ Franchise shops   ...%
   ☐ Meat wholesale markets   ...%
   ☐ Own shops   ...%
   ☐ Grocery stores   ...%
   ☐ Others,   ...%
   Total   100%
9. Number of employees in your company
10. Total turnover of pork slaughtering and processing (10,000 Yuan)
11. Have you ever heard of supply chain management? ☐ Yes ☐ No
    If yes, please explain what is SCM?

2. Constructs

Please indicate the number that best reflects your judgment with regard to your company. On the Likert scale, '1'=not true at all or totally disagree; '4'=neutral and '7'=totally true or totally agree.

Part I: Upstream model (the relationship between the pork processing firms and their most important suppliers)

Construct 'Supply Chain Integration' (SCI)

Internal integration
Integ1: We have a team involving different departments to decide jointly about company objectives.
Integ2: We have a good team to discuss and solve operational problems jointly.
Integ3: We have a good information management system covering different departments.

External integration
Exintup1: Our company works with our most important suppliers to make production plans.
Exintup2: Our company participates in the sourcing decisions of our most important suppliers.
Exintup3: Our most important suppliers provide us with the inventory data of hogs (meat) they have.
Exintup4: We share risks with our most important suppliers (Deleted after exploratory factor analysis).

Supplier-buyer relationship coordination
Coordup1: Our most important suppliers are trustworthy.
Coordup2: Our most important suppliers and our company deal with problems that arise in the course of cooperation.

Coordup3: We have cooperated with our most important suppliers for a long time.
Coordup4: We frequently measure the performance of our most important suppliers (with 'once less than 6 months' ranking 7, 'once every year' 4) (Deleted)

Integrated information technology
Infoup: For most of the times, we share information with our most important suppliers by using e-mail/fax.

Integrated logistics management
Logis: We can organise production in an efficient way according to market information.
Logisup1: Our logistics activities are well integrated with those of our most important suppliers.
Logisup2: We work together with our most important suppliers to reduce logistics costs instead of the internal cost of the company.

Construct 'Quality Management Practices' (QMP)[30]

Management leadership
QMP1: The quality strategy of our company is based on long-term planning.
QMP2: Our managers actively participate in quality improvement processes (Deleted).
QMP3: Our mid-managers are trained frequently in quality management practices.
QMP4: Our employees are rewarded for quality improvement suggestions (Deleted).
QMP5: We train our employees how to implement quality practices frequently.
QMP6: Our company has very good quality assurance systems (HACCP, ISO 9000 series or ISO14000).
QMP7: We can trace and track products from field to table.
QMP8: We make an effort in making quality goals and policies understood in the departments of our company.

Supplier quality management
SQM1: Our most important suppliers are selected based more on quality than on price.
SQM2: We pay our most important suppliers a premium for good quality pigs.
SQM3: We provide our most important suppliers with feed and technology in order to get good quality hogs (Deleted).
SQM4: We check the quality of the pigs (meat) delivered by our most important suppliers frequently (with 'once every year' ranking 4).

---

[30] Exploratory factor analysis for construct 'quality management practices' turned out to be five sub-dimensions instead of the original four identified. We rename the sub-dimensions as 'in-company quality management' (measured by QMP1, QMP6 and QMP8), 'employee involvement in quality management' (measured by QMP3, QMP4, QMP5 and PM2), 'quality design' (measured by QMP2, QMP7, Design1, Design2), 'process management' (measured by PM1 and PM3), and 'supplier quality management' (measured by SQM1, SQM2, SQM3 and SQM4).

Quality design
Design1: We focus more on quality than on price in developing new products/services.
Design2: The employees of our company are well informed about the procedures and operation
standards.

Process Management
PM1: Our company has a well-developed cold chain (from production to distribution and
selling)
PM2: Our mid-level managers inspect the work floor on a regular basis to check all operational
processes.
PM3: We pay great attention to in-process inspection, review or checking in pork production.

Construct 'Asset Specificity'
Asset1: If we switch to other products, we would lose a lot of investment in facilities and
human resources (Deleted).
Asset2: If we switch to new suppliers, we would lose a lot of investment in time and effort in
establishing relationship with our former key suppliers.
Asset3: We invested a lot of time and effort in maintaining collaborative relationship with our
most important suppliers.

Construct 'Uncertainty'
Uncertainty1: The amount of hogs (meat) supplied by our most important suppliers is always
stable.
Uncertainty2: Quality of hogs (meat) supplied by our most important suppliers is always
stable.
Uncertainty3: The price of the hogs (meat) we arrange with our most important suppliers is
always stable.
Uncertainty4: If the supply is not stable, our production will be influenced greatly (Deleted).

Construct 'Governance Structure'

Spot market
Spot: Most of hogs (meat) are purchased through spot market transaction.

Contractual governance mechanism
Contract: We always trade with most important suppliers on the basis of contract (Please
judge the score according to the availability of following clauses in the contract:
price, quantity, quality, delivery time and place, rights and obligations, and way of
conflict settlement).

Relational governance mechanism

Relational1: We have an extremely collaborative relationship with our most important suppliers.

Relational2: We share long- and short-term goals and plans with our most important suppliers (Deleted).

Relational3: We expect our most important suppliers to work with us for a long time.

Relational4: We can rely on our most important suppliers to keep their promises.

Construct 'Government Support'

Support1: Government authorities provide financial support to our company (tax reduction, and other financial preferential treatment to company's business operation.)

Support2: Government authorities provide technological support (technical know-how, research programs, employee training, etc.) to improve our R&D capacity.

Construct 'Competitive Strategy'

Prospector1: Our company's strategy focuses on offering a wide range of products for different markets.

Prosepctor2: Consumers like our products because the brand(s) of our pork products is (are) more competitive than our main competitors.

Prospector3: Our company has a good reputation among both the customers and the consumers.

Dependent variable 'Firm Performance' (FP)

Sales growth

FP1: Total volume of our company has grown faster than that of our main competitors in the last three years.

Market share

FP2: Market share of our company has increased faster than that of our main competitors in the last three years.

Profitability

FP3: We achieved better profitability than that of our main competitors in the last three years.

Perceived customer Satisfaction

FP4: We achieved better customer satisfaction on product quality than our most important competitors in the last three years.

Control variables
Company ownership: Your company is:
☐ State-owned   ☐ Collectively-owned   ☐ Joint venture   ☐ Private and share holding
Size: Please give the number of employees of your company in 2004.

Part II: Downstream model (the relationship between the pork processing firms and their most important customers)

Construct 'Supply Chain Integration' (SCI)

Internal integration
Integ1: We have a team involving different departments to decide jointly about company objectives. (suppressed due to factor loadings below 0.4 in principal component analysis)
Integ2: We have a good team to discuss and solve operational problems jointly. (suppressed due to factor loadings below 0.4 in principal component analysis)
Integ3: We have a good information management system covering different departments.

External integration
Exintds1: Our company works with our most important customers to make production plans (Deleted).
Exintds2: Our most important customers provide us with sales forecast for the products our company sells to them.
Exintds3: Our company works together with most important customers to promote our products.
Exintds4: We share risks with our most important customers.

Supplier-buyer relationship coordination
Coordds1: Our most important customers are trustworthy.
Coordds2: Our most important customers and our company deal with problems that arise in the course of cooperation.
Coordds3: We have cooperated with our most important customers for a long time.
Coordds4: We frequently measure the performance of our most important customers (with 'once less than 6 months' ranking 7, 'once every year' 4) (Deleted)

Integrated information technology
Infods1: Our most important customers share sales information with us through information management systems.
Infods2: Most of the time, we share information with our most important customers by e-mail.
Infods3: We have an ERP system in communication with our most important customers.

Integrated logistics management

Logis: We can organise production in an efficient way according to market information.

Logisds1: Our logistics activities are well integrated with those of our most important customers.

Logisds2: We work together with our most important customers to reduce logistics costs instead of the internal cost of the company.

Construct 'Quality Management Practices' (QMP)[31]

Customer quality management

CQM1: We involve our most important customers in quality improvement process.

CQM2: Our most important customers pay more attention on quality than on price.

CQM3: Before commencing business with our most important customers, we make sure of the clean environment.

Construct 'Asset specificity'

Asset1: If we switch to other products, we would lose a lot of investment in facilities and human resources (Deleted).

Asset2: If we decided to stop working with our most important customers, we would be wasting a lot of knowledge regarding their method of operation.

Asset3: We invested a lot of time and effort in maintaining collaborative relationship with our most important customers.

Construct 'Uncertainty'

Uncertainty1: The demand of our most important customers is always stable.

Uncertainty2: The quality specification of the products demanded by our most important customers is always stable.

Uncertainty3: The price of the products we arrange with our most important customers is always stable.

Uncertainty4: The unstable demand from our most important customers greatly influences our planning.

---

[31] Exploratory factor analysis for construct 'quality management practices' turned out to be five sub-dimensions instead of the original four identified. We rename the sub-dimensions as 'in-company quality management' (measured by QMP1, QMP6 and QMP8), 'employee involvement in quality management' (measured by QMP3, QMP4, QMP5 and PM2), 'quality design' (measured by QMP2, QMP7, Design1, Design2), 'process management' (measured by PM1 and PM3), and 'customer quality management' (measured by CQM1, CQM2 and CQM3). Apart from 'customer quality management', the other sub-dimensions are all company specific scales. As they are the same with those in the upstream model, please refer the upstream model for detailed questions.

Construct 'Governance Structure'

Spot market
Spot: Most of our pork products are sold through spot market transaction.

Contractual governance mechanism
Contract: We always trade with most important customers on the basis of contract (Please judge the score according to the availability of following clauses in the contract: price, quantity, quality, delivery time and place, rights and obligations, and way of conflict settlement).

Relational governance mechanism
Relational1: Our most important customers have an extremely collaborative relationship with us.
Relational2: We share long- and short-term goals and plans with our most important customers (Deleted).
Relational3: We expect our most important customers to work with us for a long time.
Relational4: We can rely on our most important customers to keep promises.

Constructs 'Government Support' and 'Competitive Strategy', dependent variable 'Firm Performance' and control variables are the same as the upstream model. Please refer to them for more details.

Appendix B. Protocol for in-depth interviews

The major questions used in the interviews are:
1. Respondent information
   a. How long have you been working in this sector/company?
   b. What is your function in the company?
2. The company profile
   a. When was the company established?
   b. Is pork slaughtering/processing always the core business of the company?
   c. How many people are employed by the company?
   d. What was the turnover for pork products in 2002 and 2004 and what are your forecasts for the next 3 years?
3. Procurement channels and marketing channels of pork products and their percentages.
4. Governance structure
   a. What major governance mechanisms are used with the suppliers (upstream partners) and buyers (downstream partners) of your company? What is the impact of these mechanisms on the quality management?
   b. What changes have occurred in the governance structure in buyer-supplier relationships?
   c. What transactional specific investments your company has made in relation with your most important suppliers and customers?
   d. What is the impact of long-term relational governance mechanism on the buyer-supplier relationships? How does it affect the transaction characteristics, especially transaction specific investment and uncertainty?
   e. What is the relationship between the relational governance and the other two governance mechanisms, spot market and contractual governance?
   f. How does relational governance influence quality management?
5. Supply chain integration activities
   a. How does your company work together with your upstream suppliers and downstream customers in information and communication technology and logistics management?
   b. What information do you share with your exchange partners?
6. Quality management practices
   a. What quality management standards do you follow?
   b. What are the major practices in quality management? What is their impact on firm performance?
   c. What is the impact of buyer-supplier relationship on quality management?
   d. How does information technology and logistics management affect quality management in your company?
7. Competitive strategy
   a. Which is more important to your company in market expansion, cost leadership, differentiation and market leadership through innovation and brand construction?
   b. What is the impact of your strategic decision on the relationship between quality management and firm performance?

8. Quality management system and government support
   a. How does the quality management system of the government influence your quality management?
   b. What are the major financial and technological supports to pork sector? Can your company benefit from these supports?
9. Firm performance
   a. Are you satisfied with hog supply and hog quality? And are your customers satisfied with your products? Do you have a customer service department?
   b. What are the major indicators you use in measuring firm performance?
   c. Did you achieve the targeted profitability in the past three years?
   d. What are your expectations as regards pork processing in the next 3 years?

Appendix C1. Factor analysis for constructs SCI and QMP (Upstream model, n=229)

Item code	Corrected--item total correlation	Factor loading	Factor	Cronbach's alpha
Integ1	0.640	-0.788	Internal integration	0.787
Integ2	0.665	-0.871		
Integ3	0.610	-0.606		
Exintup1	0.536	0.819	External integration	0.773
Exintup2	0.632	0.869		
Exintup3	0.700	0.760		
Exintup4	0.519	**0.525**		
Coordup1	0.550	0.907	Buyer-supplier relationship	0.658
Coordup2	0.500	0.652	coordination	
Coordup3	0.503	0.750		
Coordup4	**0.263**	-		
Infoup	-	0.920	Integrated IT & logistics	0.855
Logis	0.700	0.815	management	
Logisup1	0.570	0.928		
Logisup2	0.703	0.686		
QMP1	0.629	0.713	In-company quality management	0.849
QMP6	0.780	0.904		
QMP8	0.752	0.800		
QMP3	0.634	0.813	Employee involvement	0.750
QMP4	**0.394**	-		
QMP5	0.577	0.747		
PM2	0.542	0.885		
SQM1	0.658	0.894	Supplier quality management	0.778
SQM2	0.569	0.769		
SQM3	**0.150**	-		
SQM4	0.629	0.689		
QMP2	**0.454**	-	Product/service design	0.714
QMP7	0.522	0.887		
Design1	0.591	0.753		
Design2	0.502	0.790		
PM1	0.644	0.861	Process management	0.783
PM3	0.644	0.808		

Note: Extraction Method for both SCI and QMP constructs: Principal Component Analysis. Rotation Method: Oblimin with Kaiser Normalization. Rotation converged in 8 iterations for SCI construct and 3 iterations for QMP construct.)

Appendix C2. Factor analysis for constructs SCI and QMP (Downstream model, n=229)

Item code	Corrected--item total correlation	Factor loading	Factor	Cronbach's alpha
Integ1	Suppressed in principal component		Internal integration	-
Integ2	analysis (factor loadings ≤0.4).			
Integ3	-	-		
Exintds1	**0.410**	-	External integration	0.760
Exintds2	0.659	0.779		
Exintds3	0.589	0.823		
Exintds4	0.532	0.702		
Coordds1	0.541	0.874	Buyer-supplier relationship	0.721
Coordds2	0.556	0.601	coordination	
Coordds3	0.564	0.833		
Coordds4	**0.120**	-		
Infods1	0.634	0.934	Integrated IT	0.819
Infods2	0.723	0.807		
Infods3	0.696	0.600		
Logis	0.670	0.843	Integrated logistics management	0.793
Logisds1	0.682	0.941		
Logisds2	0.568	0.685		
QMP1	0.629	0.695	In-company quality management	0.849
QMP6	0.780	0.924		
QMP8	0.752	0.882		
QMP3	0.634	0.843	Employee involvement	0.750
QMP4	**0.394**	-		
QMP5	0.577	0.774		
PM2	0.542	0.832		
CQM1	0.643	0.962	Customer quality management	0.839
CQM2	0.756	0.743		
CQM3	0.728	0.942		
QMP2	**0.454**	-	Product/service design	0.714
QMP7	0.522	0.887		
Design1	0.591	0.703		
Design2	0.502	0.760		
PM1	0.644	0.931	Process management	0.783
PM3	0.644	0.822		

Note: Extraction Method for both SCI and QMP constructs: Principal Component Analysis. Rotation Method: Oblimin with Kaiser Normalization. Rotation converged in 10 iterations for SCI construct and 4 iterations for QMP construct.)

Appendix D1. Loadings and cross loadings (upstream model, n=219)

To make the tables easy to read, we omitted the correlations below 0.5.

Construct	Scale	1	2	3	4	5	6
1. Asset specificity	Asset2	**0.922**					
	Asset3	**0.855**					
2. Uncertainty	Uncertainty1		**0.848**				
	Uncertainty2		**0.755**				
	Uncertainty3		**0.790**				
3. Spot market	Spot			**1.000**			-0.536
4. Contractual governance mechanism	Contract				**1.000**		
5. Relational governance mechanism	Relational1					**0.834**	
	Relational3					**0.779**	
	Relational4					**0.757**	
6. Quality management practices	In-company QM			-0.546			**0.916**
	Supplier QM						**0.870**
	Employee involvement						**0.535**
	Quality design						**0.639**
	Process management						**0.877**

Note: The bold numbers indicate the loadings of the items to the corresponding construct.

Appendix D2. Loadings and cross loadings (downstream model, n=219)

To make the tables easy to read, we omitted the correlations below 0.5.

Construct	Scale	1	2	3	4	5	6
1. Asset specificity	Asset2	0.875					
	Asset3	0.919					
2. Uncertainty	Uncertainty1		0.790				
	Uncertianty2		0.798				
	Uncertainty3		0.795				
	Uncertainty4		0.712				
3. Spot market	Spot	-0.515	1.000				-0.589
4. Contractual governance mechanism	Contract			-0.722	1.000		
5. Relational governance mechanism	Relational1					0.955	0.532
	Relational3					0.628	
	Relational4					0.672	
6. Quality management practices	In-company QM			-0.593	0.532		0.894
	Customer QM						0.569
	Employee involvement						0.587
	Quality design						0.675
	Process management						0.845

Note: The bold numbers indicate the loadings of the items to the corresponding construct.

Appendix E. Factor analysis for prospector strategy and government support

Variables	Indicator	CITC*	Factor loading	Cronbach's alpha
Prospector strategy	Prospector1	0.54	0.78	0.77
	Prospector2	0.64	0.86	
	Prospector3	0.66	0.87	
Government's financial and	Support1	0.68	0.93	0.81
technological support	Support2	0.68	0.90	
Control variables	Organisational status (ownership)*: Your company is:			
	☐ State-owned ☐ Collectively-owned ☐ Joint venture			
	☐ Private and share holding			
	Please give the number of employees of your company in 2004.			

* Dummy variables are used in the regression analysis. State-owned and collectively owned firms are coded as '1' (the base group); the foreign joint ventures are coded as '2'; and private and shareholding firms are coded as '3'.

Appendix F. Proposed hypotheses with the empirical results

Hypotheses	Upstream model (Relationship with suppliers)	Downstream model (Relationship with customers)
Joint impact of supply chain integration and QM practices		
H1a: Supply chain integration→firm performance	Not supported	Not supported
H1b: Quality management practices→firm performance	Supported	Supported
H1c: Supply chain integration→QM practices	Supported	Supported
Impact of integrated information technology, logistics management and QM practices		
H2a: Integrated IT → firm performance		Not supported
H2b: Integrated logistics management→firm performance		Not supported
H2c: Integrated IT→integrated logistics management		Supported
H2d: Integrated IT→QM practices		Supported
H2e: Integrated logistics management→QM practices		Supported
H2f: QM practices→firm performance		Supported
Impact of transaction attributes and governance structure		
H3a: Asset specificity→spot market	Supported	Supported
H3b: Asset specificity→Contractual governance	Supported	Supported
H3c: Asset specificity→Relational governance	Not supported	Supported
H3d: Uncertainty→spot market	Supported	Supported
H3e: Uncertainty→Contractual governance	Supported	Supported
H3f: Uncertainty→Relational governance	Supported	Not supported
H3g: Relational governance→Contractual governance	Supported	Supported
H3h: Spot market→QM practices	Supported	Supported
H3i: Contractual governance→QM practices	Supported	Supported
H3j: Relational governance→QM practices	Supported	Supported
Impact of QM practices and government support		
H4a: In-company QM→firm performance	Supported	Supported
H4b1: Supplier QM→firm performance (upstream model)	Supported	
H4b2: Customer QM→firm performance (downstream model)		Negative
H4c: Employee involvement in QM→firm performance	Supported	Supported
H4d: Quality design→firm performance	Not supported	Not supported
H4e: Process management→firm performance	Supported	Supported
H4f: Government support→firm performance	Supported	Supported

Appendix F. Continued.

Hypotheses	Upstream model (Relationship with suppliers)	Downstream model (Relationship with customers)
Moderating role of competitive strategy (Prospector strategy)		
H5a: Prospector strategy strengthens the link between in-company QM and firm performance	Rejected	Rejected
H5b1: Prospector strategy strengthens the link between supplier QM and firm performance (upstream model)	Supported	
H5b2: Prospector strategy strengthens the link between customer QM and firm performance (downstream model)		Supported
H5c: Prospector strategy strengthens the link between employee involvement in QM and firm performance	Not supported	Not supported
H5d: Prospector strategy strengthens the link between quality design→firm performance	Supported	Not supported
H5e: Prospector strategy strengthens the link between process management and firm performance	Supported	Not supported
H5f: Prospector strategy strengthens the link between government support and firm performance	Not supported	Not supported

Summary

Since 1990, China has grown into the largest pork production country in the world. With an output of more than 51 million tonnes in 2006, China was responsible for more than 50% of the world's total production. Yet even though government authorities have been promoting pork exports over the past two decades in order to raise farmers' income and enhance the competitiveness of the sector, the proportion of exports has only been around 1% of total pork production. One of the biggest stumbling blocks to higher exports has been the poor quality and safety of the products. Another bottleneck is the fragmentation of production, processing and distribution in the Chinese pork sector and the lack of coordination between the subsequent supply chain links, all of which negatively impacts (international) customer relationships as well as the quality and safety of products. Concerns about quality and safety among domestic consumers have also been increasing due to several sector-wide incidents related to pork products, such as the outbreak of *Streptococcus suis* in June 2005 and Clenbuterol contamination in November 2008. In a related food safety incident, a scandal in 2008 involving milk for infants adulterated with melamine brought disaster to the entire dairy industry in China.

To survive in this dynamic environment, firms increasingly look for ways to improve quality management in order to be competitive and improve firm performance. Supply chain analysis is of vital importance to reach this objective. Existing literature stresses the importance of supply chain quality management to firm performance; however, the factors that underlie the process of achieving good quality and supply chain management are largely unexplored, especially in developing countries. Therefore, our study aims to identify these factors and how they contribute to higher performance of pork processing firms in China.

Research questions

The challenge of this research is to study buyer-supplier relationships from both a supply chain management and quality management perspective. This study focuses on how combined supply chain and quality management can improve firm performance and investigates relationships between specific (total) quality management and supply chain management practices, in particular logistics and information management.

Since the pork supply chains in China include many buyers and suppliers, the complexity of business relationships makes the use of diversified governance mechanisms necessary for firms to manage transactions. Spot market transactions are the most commonly used governance mechanism in China. In addition, contracts and informal relational governance structures are also used in business relationships. It is therefore interesting to explore the impact of different governance mechanisms on quality management practices.

Firms are operating in an increasingly stringent environment. Both internal and external factors, such as firm strategy and pressure from the business network (e.g. government, buyers and suppliers) influence firm performance. Besides market forces, in China the government in particular plays an important role in structuring the pork industry. Thus, it is important for firms to find the right balance between the relevant contingencies in the business environment (external fit) and the firm's internal resources, competencies and capabilities (internal fit). For pork processing firms, good quality management practices are critical resources and competencies for gaining competitive advantage in the marketplace. Therefore, the firm's competitive strategy may have an important impact on the way it performs quality management and on its overall performance.

To address these issues, five research questions are formulated:
1. What is the joint impact of supply chain integration and quality management practices on firm performance in the pork processing industry in China?
2. How do information technology and logistics management interact with quality management practices and how do they influence the performance of pork processing firms in China?
3. What is the relationship between governance mechanisms and quality management practices in China's pork processing industry?
4. What is the influence of specific quality management practices on firm performance and what is the role of firm strategy to moderate this relationship?
5. What is the impact of government support on firm performance and what is the role of firm strategy to moderate this relationship?

Research model and methodology

This study integrates various theoretical perspectives, namely supply chain management, total quality management, transaction cost economics, and contingency theory. Supply Chain Management emphasises the fundamental role of integration of key activities in buyer-supplier relationships. High levels of internal and external integration, integrated information technology and integrated logistics management and relationship coordination are considered critical to higher firm performance. Total Quality Management emphasises the importance of quality management practices in improving firm performance, for example, applying quality management systems in business operations, managing supplier/customer quality management, and involving employees to improve quality design and process management. Using these five dimensions, quality management in a supply chain perspective can be analysed. Transaction Cost Economics points at the influence of transaction attributes (asset specificity and uncertainty) on the choice of governance mechanisms as well as the importance of governance mechanisms in relation to quality management practices. The effect of competitive strategy on the relationships between quality management practices and government support (external impact) and between quality management practices and firm performance is underlined by Contingency Theory. The key elements in these theories were

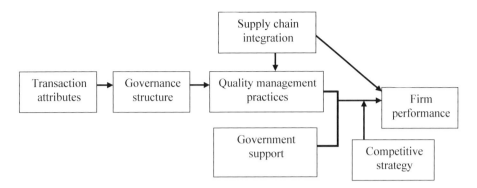

Figure 1. Research framework.

developed into an integrated research framework (see Figure 1) to analyse pork supply chain integration and quality management and their relationships with firm performance.

A mixed methodology was used, combining both semi-structured interviews and a large-scale survey carried out among Chinese pork slaughtering and processing firms. Three steps were followed in developing the measures and conducting empirical studies. The first step started with theory research followed by pilot studies in selected pork processing firms and academic institutions in 2004. The objective of this step was to get more theoretical and practical insight into Chinese pork supply chain integration and quality management practices and their links with firm performance. Due to limited number of empirical studies on supply chain integration and quality management in China, insight from practitioners and researchers was very important for the reliability and validity of the scales to be used in the survey. In the second step, a large-scale survey of the pork processing sector in two provinces in eastern China (Jiangsu and Shandong) and one municipality (Shanghai) was conducted in 2005. Data collection was conducted through personal interviews at more than 250 pork slaughterhouses and pork processors. In total, 229 valid questionnaires were used for the analysis. The third step was to verify the findings from the earlier quantitative part of the research through in-depth case studies carried out in 2007 among 5 pork processing firms in the survey area.

Data were analysed by applying structural equation modelling. We identified two relationships in our study. The relationships between the pork processing firms and their most important suppliers were reflected by the upstream model, while the downstream model reflected the relationships between the firms and their most important buyers. For the operationalization of the variables in the conceptual model, please refer to Section 3.3.1 and Section 5.4.2 for more details.

Results and conclusions

With regard to the first research question *'What is the joint impact of supply chain integration and quality management practices on firm performance in the pork processing industry in China'*, this study has shown that quality management practices are directly linked to firm performance, while supply chain integration is indirectly linked to firm performance through quality management practices in the two models. It was concluded that pork processing firms can expect to achieve higher performance through collaboration in quality management in buyer-supplier relationships.

Another important finding of this study was the significant positive relationship between supply chain integration and quality management practices. The firms integrate more with their customers than with their suppliers in most of the dimensions, especially in external integration and integrated information technology and logistics management.

This brings us to the second research question *'How do information technology and logistics management interact with quality management practices and how do they influence the performance of pork processing firms in China'*. Since the relationships between integrated information technology and firm performance and between integrated logistics management and firm performance are much stronger between the pork processing firms and their buyers than they are with their suppliers, we focused on the downstream model. Our findings indicated that neither integrated information technology nor integrated logistics management made significant contributions to firm performance. The explanation might be that application of modern information technologies (e.g. Enterprise resource planning, information automation) is still limited among China's pork processing firms. Moreover, poor infrastructure and inventory management hinder the efficiency and effectiveness of logistics. On the other hand, the application of integrated information technology did contribute significantly to the

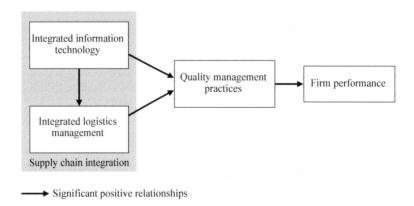

Figure 2. Path diagram for research question 2 for the downstream model.

logistics management of the pork processors and both integrated information technology and logistics management contributed significantly positively to quality management practices. The path diagram to achieve firm performance is shown in Figure 2.

Regarding the third research question *'What is the relationship between governance mechanisms and quality management practices in China's pork processing industry'*, this study provides empirical evidence that for both models, the degree of asset specificity and uncertainty does matter in the alignment of governance structures in pork supply chains. With increasing asset specificity and uncertainty, the pork processing firms applied more formal contractual and informal relational and less spot market governance mechanisms in order to safeguard investments and reduce risks of opportunistic behaviour on the part of their exchange partners. This finding is in line with the domain of transaction cost economics and relational marketing theory.

Interestingly, our study showed mixed findings with regards to the impact of asset specificity and uncertainty on the use of relational governance in the upstream and downstream models. In their relationships with customers, the pork processors appear more concerned about long-term cooperation and trust in the presence of asset specificity, which is in clear contrast to their relationships with hog or meat suppliers. The most likely explanation is that in order to secure and expand their market channels, firms had more specific investments in their relationships with their customers. For example, firms are confronted with more human asset specificity in dealing with business transactions in the downstream chain. On the other hand, we found a significant positive relationship only between the pork processors and their most important suppliers in the presence of uncertainty. This might be explained by the innate volatility of feed and hog supply in swine production. Therefore, long-term relationships are critical for pork processors to secure raw materials.

Our study supported the positive relationship between more integrated governance mechanisms (contract and relational governance mechanisms compared to spot market transactions) and the use of quality management practices in pork processing firms in China. As suggested by existing literature, our study indicates that contracts can reinforce monitoring, reduce opportunistic behaviour in buyer-supplier relationships and improve quality. In addition, relational governance mechanisms can help the pork processors to develop long-term cooperative relationships. The commitment developed in these trusted relationships facilitates quality management in both upstream and downstream relationships. Our empirical analyses also indicated complementary effects between formal contractual and relational governance mechanisms in buyer-supplier relationships. Because the legal system is under-developed in China, the combination of formal and informal governance mechanisms seems to be the best alternative toward achieving supply chain-wide quality management. The results of these analyses are indicated in Figure 3.

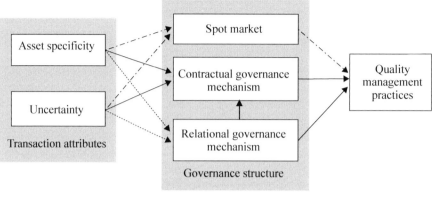

———▸ Significant positive relationships;
- - - -▸ Significant negative relationship;
..........▸ Significant in upstream or downstream model

Figure 3. Path diagram for research question 3.
Note: The significant impact of asset specificity on relational governance is only found in the downstream model. The significant impact of uncertainty on relational governance is only found in the upstream model.

The fourth research question was *'What is the influence of specific quality management practices on firm performance and what is the role of firm strategy to moderator this relationship'.* Our quantitative analysis revealed several important findings:

- In-company quality management, employee involvement in quality management and process management are positively related to firm performance in both models. This reaffirms the significant importance of quality goals, quality standards, quality systems and employee involvement in quality management to improve firm performance. The positive impact of process management on firm performance indicates that higher firm performance largely depends on quality conformance from the incoming raw material to production processes, including reducing input and process variation.
- Supplier quality management shows a positive association with firm performance. However, in contrast to our expectation, a positive relationship between customer quality management and performance in the downstream model has not been found. The increase in customer quality investments and low profit margins due to intense competition might explain the negative impact of customer quality management on firm performance. Pork processors have to make high specific investments in cold chain facilities and sanitation to guarantee high quality. Confronted with powerful retailers, pork processors are usually not in a position to negotiate a favourable profit margin. However, pork processors greatly value this business relationship as these retailers, in contrast to traditional wet markets, represent modern marketing channels and help to promote the image of the processors. The results of this part of the analysis are indicated in Figure 4.

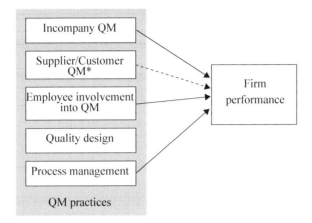

→ Significant positive relationships;
--→ Only significant in the relationship between supplier quality management and firm performance

Figure 4. Path diagram for the relationship between specific QM practices and firm performance.

- Our empirical findings indicate that an innovative prospector strategy of a company has a significant impact on performance. One of the most important results of this study is the significant positive effect of this strategy on strengthening the relationships between both supplier and customer quality management and firm performance. This again reaffirms the shift of the management mindset from product-oriented internally driven quality management to customer-oriented supply chain driven quality management.

Regarding the fifth research question *'What is the impact of government support on firm performance and what is the role of firm strategy to moderate this relationship'*, our research findings reveal that the financial and technological support of government authorities had a significant positive impact on pork processors' firm performance. Government authorities are quite powerful, showing clear interest in food safety and quality management and trying to improve food quality via rules, procedures and inspection. Another important aspect is the government effort to promote the R&D capabilities of pork processing companies. However, our study failed to find a moderating effect of the Prospector strategy in the relationship between government support in finance and technology and firm performance.

Managerial implications

This research has several important implications for managers in the pork processing industry.

First, firms are recommended to invest in quality management to achieve higher performance. Quality management turns out to be critical to generating sales growth, improving customer satisfaction and providing profits for Chinese pork processing firms. As many companies put it: *'Quality is the life of the enterprise'*. Firms that wish to improve their performance should therefore invest in quality management, especially in in-company quality management, supplier quality management, employee involvement in quality management and process management.

Second, firms are recommended to strive for integrated quality management systems at the supply chain level to improve firm performance. Firms have to tightly integrate their processes with suppliers and customers to cope with complex quality management pressures because if consumers lose confidence in the safety and quality of food, it affects all the stakeholders in the supply chain.

Third, pork processing companies in China are recommended to align their buyer-supplier relationships on the basis of appropriate governance regimes. Supplier quality control is of essential importance since pork processing firms regularly face problems in monitoring the quality and safety of raw materials. To guarantee a reliable supply of quality pork products, the managers of pork processing firms in China should not only develop more integrated governance regimes, such as contractual governance, but also use relational governance to collaborate with their suppliers and buyers in long-term relationships, thereby reducing information and screening costs and reinforcing trust amongst chain members.

Fourth, a prospector strategy may support positive effects of quality management practices on firm performance. Firms that focus more on new products and markets and less on (low) cost-driven activities showed a strong positive link between customer quality management and performance. Therefore, our research findings indicate that a prospector strategy can be an appropriate strategy for pork processors in China's highly complex and dynamic market.

About the author

Jiqin Han was born in Jiangsu province, China on June 23, 1965. In 1987, she obtained her Bachelor degree from Nanjing Normal University in English literature and linguistics. Since then she has been working as a coordinator for international cooperation and educational programs at Nanjing Agricultural University. She obtained an MSc in agricultural economics and management from Nanjing Agricultural University in 2000. Since the late 1990s, she has been researching agri-food supply chain and quality management. In 2003, she started working on her thesis in the Department of Business Administration at Wageningen University. She has published a number of scientific articles and presented her work at international conferences in the field. In the last several years, she has been involved in some international and national research projects related to agri-food supply chain management, for example, the EU – 6th Framework Plan project 'Q-Porkchains', EU – Asian Link project on agribusiness management in Mekong River and EU Asian Facility program on education and promotion of agrifood quality and safety in China after joining the WTO.

Recent publications

Dai, Y. C., **J. Han** and R. Y. Ying, 2006. On the vertical coordination of innovative pork supply chain. Journal of Nanjing Agricultural University (Social Science Edition), No. 3, 122-126.

Han, J., J.H. Trienekens, S.W.F. Omta and T. Tan, 2007. Quality management and governance in pork processing industries in China, in: R. Ruben, M. van Boekel, A. van Tilburg and J. Trienekens (eds.), Tropical Food Chains, Wageningen Academic Publishers, the Netherlands, 133-151.

Han, J., S.W.F. (Onno) Omta and J. H. Trienekens, 2007. The joint impact of supply chain integration and quality management on the performance of pork processing firms in China. International Food and Agribusiness Management Review Vol. 10 Issue 2, 2007, 67-98.

Han, J. and K. Wang, 2008. An empirical study of the quality management and vertical coordination in the pork supply chain in China. China Rural Economy, No. 5, 33-43.

Han, J., J.H. Trienekens and S.W.F. (Onno) Omta, 2009. Integrated information and logistics management, quality management and firm performance of pork processing industry in China. British Food Journal, Vol. 111 No. 1, 9-25.

Han, J., 2009. The Chinese pork sector, in: J. Trienekens, B. Petersen, N. Wognum and D. Brinkmann (eds.), European Pork Chains, Wageningen Academic Publishers, the Netherlands, 213-231.

Han, J., J.H. Trienekens and S.W.F. (Onno) Omta, 2009. Relationships and quality management in the Chinese pork chain. International Journal of Production Economics. In press.

International chains and networks series

Agri-food chains and networks are swiftly moving toward globally interconnected systems with a large variety of complex relationships. This is changing the way food is brought to the market. Currently, even fresh produce can be shipped from halfway around the world at competitive prices. Unfortunately, accompanying diseases and pollution can spread equally rapidly. This requires constant monitoring and immediate responsiveness. In recent years tracking and tracing has therefore become vital in international agri-food chains and networks. This means that integrated production, logistics, information- and innovation systems are needed. To achieve these integrated global supply chains, strategic and cultural alignment, trust and compliance to national and international regulations have become key issues. In this series the following questions are answered: How should chains and networks be designed to effectively respond to the fast globalization of the business environment? And more specificly, How should firms in fast changing transition economies (such as Eastern European and developing countries) be integrated into international food chains and networks?

About the editor

Onno Omta is chaired professor in Business Administration at Wageningen University and Research Centre, the Netherlands. He received an MSc in Biochemistry and a PhD in innovation management, both from the University of Groningen. He is the Editor-in-Chief of The Journal on Chain and Network Science, and he has published numerous articles in leading scientific journals in the field of chains and networks and innovation. He has worked as a consultant and researcher for a large variety of (multinational) technology-based prospector companies within the agri-food industry (e.g. Unilever, VION, Bonduelle, Campina, Friesland Foods, FloraHolland) and in other industries (e.g. SKF, Airbus, Erickson, Exxon, Hilti and Philips).

Guest editor

Jacques H. Trienekens is associate professor at Management Studies Group of Wageningen University. His research interests include (international) food chain and network management and business operations management. He is co-founder of the biannual International Conference on Management of Agri-food Chains and Networks and of Journal on Chain and Network Science. Jacques Trienekens has been visiting professor at University of Bonn in Germany and University of Pretoria in South Africa and is also member of the board of directors of International Food and Agribusiness Management Association (IAMA). He is editor and associate editor of Journal on Chain and Network Science and International Food and Agribusiness Management Review respectively, and has published in a variety of peer reviewed international journals such as International Journal for Production Economics, British Food Journal, Production Planning and Control, Computers in Industry and International Food and Agribusiness Management Review.